JN045498

速単の英文で学ぶ

英語長文問題70

CONTENTS

本書の構成と利用法

1. 構成

本書は『速読英単語 必修編 改訂第 7 版増補版』の英文を題材にした全 70 題の長文問題集です。

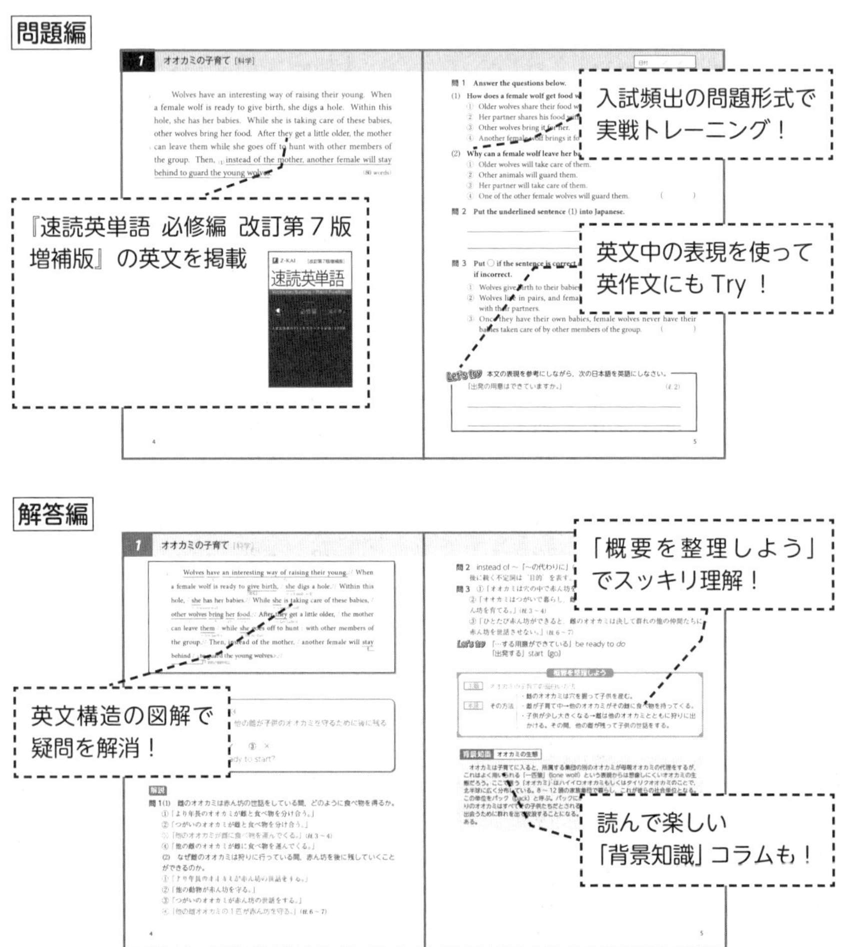

2. 利用法

本書の効果的な使い方は以下の 3 Step です。

Step1 問題を解く → **Step2** 解説を読む → **Step3** 映像を見る

Step1 問題を解く

入試頻出の問題形式を多く扱っています。トレーニングを重ねて「設問に正しく答える力」を身につけましょう。

<本書で扱っている入試頻出問題形式の例>
★下線部説明（選択式）
★空所補充（選択式）
★内容一致（選択式）※複数解答も含む
★正誤問題（True or False）
★要約（選択式）
★下線部和訳（記述式）※指示語説明も含む

Step2 解説を読む

読んだときに意味がつかめなかった英文を中心に，英文図解をチェックします。

◆英文図解の凡例
═══：同一のものを結ぶ　⟶：矢印の先のものに係る　⟷：対比
色の網かけ：トピックセンテンスやポイント箇所　**グレーの網かけ**：ディスコースマーカー
/：節や意味の区切り　//：文の区切り　＝：同義　≒：類義語（句）
S：主語　V：述語動詞　O：目的語　C：補語　∧：省略
[　]…関係詞節・名詞節　<　>…動詞句（不定詞など）

最後に，「概要を整理しよう」で内容を正しくおさえているか確認しましょう。

Step3 映像を見る

各英文には，英文の理解を助ける解説講義映像が付属しています。特に注意すべき文構造をピックアップして解説しています。映像は右の二次元コード，または下記の URL からご覧いただけます。
https://www.zkai.co.jp/books/sokutanhisshu7-revised/movies/

1 オオカミの子育て［科学］

Wolves have an interesting way of raising their young. When a female wolf is ready to give birth, she digs a hole. Within this hole, she has her babies. While she is taking care of these babies, other wolves bring her food. After they get a little older, the mother can leave them while she goes off to hunt with other members of the group. Then, (1) <u>instead of the mother, another female will stay behind to guard the young wolves.</u> (80 words)

日付　／　／

問 1　**Answer the questions below.**

(1)　**How does a female wolf get food while taking care of her babies?**

① Older wolves share their food with her.
② Her partner shares his food with her.
③ Other wolves bring it for her.
④ Another female wolf brings it for her.　(　　　)

(2)　**Why can a female wolf leave her babies while she goes hunting?**

① Older wolves will take care of them.
② Other animals will guard them.
③ Her partner will take care of them.
④ One of the other female wolves will guard them.　(　　　)

問 2　**Put the underlined sentence (1) into Japanese.**

____

____

問 3　**Put ○ if the sentence is correct according to the passage, and put × if incorrect.**

① Wolves give birth to their babies in a hole.　(　　　)
② Wolves live in pairs, and female wolves raise their babies together with their partners.　(　　　)
③ Once they have their own babies, female wolves never have their babies taken care of by other members of the group.　(　　　)

Let's try　本文の表現を参考にしながら，次の日本語を英語にしなさい。

「出発の用意はできていますか。」　(ℓ. 2)

____

____

2 お茶の種類［文化］

Green tea has a long history in Japan and (1) strong ties with Japanese culture. (2) Because of this, one might think that green tea comes from a plant unique to Japan. However, all tea, no matter what its color or taste, comes from the same plant. Then what causes the differences in taste and color? They are, in fact, the result of different ways of growing the tea and treating it after it is picked. (74 words)

問 1　Answer the questions below.

(1) **Which of the following has a meaning closest to (1) strong ties?**

① long-lasting relationships
② close relationships
③ powerful binds
④ unbreakable bondage

(2) **Which of the following causes the differences in taste and color of green tea? You may choose more than one options.**

① growing the tea in different ways
② growing a plant unique to Japan
③ treating the tea in different ways after it is picked
④ growing different kinds of plants

問 2　下線部 (2) を，**this** が指す内容を明確にして和訳しなさい。

____

____

問 3　Put ◯ if the sentence is correct according to the passage, and put × if incorrect.

① Japanese people have enjoyed green tea since olden times.(　　　　)
② Green tea and other types of tea come from different kinds of plants. (　　　　)
③ Different ways of processing tea leaves produce different tastes and colors. (　　　　)

Let's try　本文の表現を参考にしながら，次の日本語を英語にしなさい。

「それがどんなものであろうと，私たちは計画を遂行しなければならない。」　(ℓ.3)

____

____

3 ジェスチャーの違い [言語]

Physical gestures may have different meanings in different cultures, and misunderstanding these signals can sometimes be embarrassing. I once had an experience which I have never forgotten. Some years ago, I took a small group of foreign students to Kyoto. (1) I counted them with the index finger, which is common in Japan. But one of them became quiet and looked puzzled. When I asked him what was the matter, he replied, "In my country, we count people with our eyes. We use our fingers to count pigs."

(87 words)

日付　／　／

問 1　Answer the questions below.

(1) **Which of the following best fits to fill in the blank below?**
Physical gestures may have different meanings because (　　　　　).

① people in different cultures never use the same physical gestures
② some people understand physical gestures in different ways
③ some people are not used to making physical gestures
④ using physical gestures is quite different from using words

(2) **Choose the most suitable word below to fill in the blanks (ア)—(ウ).**
Write the number ① to ⑤ that corresponds to your answer.

One of the foreign students looked (　ア　) when the author counted them with the index finger. According to him, people in his country use their (　イ　) to count people because they use their (　ウ　) to count pigs.

① puzzling　② puzzled　③ eyes　④ heads　⑤ fingers

問 2　下線部 (1) を，**them** が何を指すかを明確にして和訳しなさい。

____

____

問 3　Put ○ if the sentence is correct according to the passage, and put × if incorrect.

① Physical gestures mean the same thing in every culture.　(　　　)
② It is usual for people in Japan to use their fingers to count people.　(　　　)
③ One of the students said that people in his country use the same physical gesture as the Japanese use when they count people.　(　　　)

Let's try　本文の表現を参考にしながら，次の日本語を英語にしなさい。

「そんな間違いをすると，ばつが悪いかもしれない。」　(ll. 2 ～ 3)

____

____

4 ビタミンCの働き［医療］

(1) Vitamin C plays an important role in keeping us healthy. Most mammals produce it in their livers, so they never suffer from a lack of it. Curiously, however, some mammals, such as humans and apes, cannot do so. What happens when you lack this important vitamin? You might see black-and-blue marks on your skin. Your teeth could suffer, too: the pink area around them might become soft and bleed easily. These are just a couple of good reasons to eat plenty of fresh fruit.

(84 words)

日付　／　／

問 1　Answer the questions below.

(1)　Why do most mammals never suffer from a lack of Vitamin C?

① They can store it in their livers.
② They can produce it in their livers.
③ They eat plenty of fresh fruit.
④ They can turn something else into Vitamin C.

(2)　Which of the following is NOT the result of a lack of Vitamin C?

① The pink area around your teeth might become soft.
② The pink area around your teeth might bleed easily.
③ You might see black-and-blue marks on your skin.
④ You might have a pain in the pink area around your teeth.

問 2　Put the underlined sentence (1) into Japanese.

____

____

問 3　Put ○ if the sentence is correct according to the passage, and put × if incorrect.

① Humans cannot stay healthy without vitamin C. (　　　)
② Humans and apes can produce vitamin C in their livers. (　　　)
③ Eating plenty of fresh fruit may prevent the pink area around your teeth from bleeding. (　　　)

Let's try　本文の表現を参考にしながら，次の日本語を英語にしなさい。

「新鮮なフルーツは私たちを健康な状態に保つことにおいて効果的である。」 (ℓ. 1)

____

____

5 drug の定義 [言語]

The word "drug" means anything that, even in small amounts, produces changes in the body, the mind, or both. (1) This definition, however, does not clearly separate drugs from what we usually think of as food. The difference between a drug and a poison is also unclear. All drugs become poisons in large amounts, and many poisons are useful drugs in carefully controlled amounts. Is alcohol, for instance, a food, a drug, or a poison? It can be any of the three, depending on how we use it. (87 words)

問 1　**Answer the questions below.**

(1)　**Why is the difference between a drug and food unclear?**

① Both are thought to be dangerous in large amounts.
② Both do us only good in small amounts.
③ Both can produce changes in the body and the mind.
④ Both can do you harm even in carefully controlled amounts.

(2)　**Why is the difference between a drug and a poison unclear?**

① Neither can do you good in small amounts.
② Neither can be taken in large amounts.
③ A certain amount of either can do you harm.
④ Both consist of various compounds.

問 2　**Put the underlined sentence (1) into Japanese.**

____

____

問 3　**Put ○ if the sentence is correct according to the passage, and put × if incorrect.**

① There is a clear difference between drugs and foods. (　　　)
② Drugs do us good, while poisons do us only harm. (　　　)
③ If you take too much of a drug, its effect is similar to that of a poison. (　　　)
④ Alcohol can be categorized only as a drug. (　　　)

Let's try　本文の表現を参考にしながら，次の日本語を英語にしなさい。

「プロジェクトの成功はいつ始めるべきかにかかっている。」　(ℓ.8)

____

____

6 皮膚の役割［医療］

Have you ever thought about what skin does for us? Most of us are aware that skin protects us from liquid, heat, cold, dirt, and bacteria. But that is not its only job. For instance, the skin is where our bodies make the vitamin D that we need. Another function has to do with the sense of touch. (1)<u>Without that sense, we could not feel any difference between rough and smooth surfaces.</u> Skin can even help us determine if someone is sick. The wrong color — slightly gray or very pale — may be a sign of disease. Skin may reflect a person's mental state, too. Unusual sweating, for example, may be a sign that a person is nervous or under stress. (120 words)

日付　／　／

問 1　**Answer the questions below.**

(1)　**Which of the following is NOT true for the skin?**

① It protects us from many unfavorable conditions.
② It helps us determine when to make vitamin D.
③ It tells us the difference in the condition of different surfaces.
④ It sends a sign that may show a person's mental state.

(2)　**Which of the following best fits in the blank below?**

We may be able to determine if someone is sick when (　　　　　).

① he or she shows unpleasant facial expressions
② the surface of his or her skin is not smooth
③ he or she looks slightly gray or very pale
④ he or she is sweating unusually

問 2　下線部 (1) を，**that** が何を指すかを明確にして和訳しなさい。

____

____

問 3　**Put ○ if the sentence is correct according to the passage, and put × if incorrect.**

① We can make vitamin D in our bones.　(　　　)
② We can infer whether someone is sick by looking at the color of their skin.　(　　　)
③ Unusual sweating may mean that a person is comfortable or happy.　(　　　)

Let's try　本文の表現を参考にしながら，次の日本語を英語にしなさい。

「私はその時，リサが疲れているのかどうか判断できなかった。」　(ℓ.7)

____

____

7 紳士服と婦人服でボタンが違う理由［社会］

Western clothes have buttons on the right for men. This is convenient because the majority of men are *right-handed. (1) It is easier for them to use the right hand when buttoning up. Why, then, do women's clothes have buttons on the left, even though most women are also right-handed? Is this a kind of discrimination? In fact, there is a reason why women's buttons are on that side. In the past, buttons were quite expensive and only very rich people could (2) afford them. Women in such wealthy families had servants who dressed them. Therefore, to make it easier for the servants, buttons were put on the left.

(107 words)

*right-handed「右利きの」

日付　／　／

問 1　Answer the question below.

(1) **Which of the following sets of words best fit the blanks（A）and（B）?**

The reason why women's clothes have buttons on the（　A　）is that very rich women in the past were dressed by servants who were（　B　）-handed.

① A: right　B: right　② A: right　B: left
③ A: left　B: right　④ A: left　B: left

(2) **Which of the following has a meaning closest to** (2) **afford them?**

① get expensive clothes　② buy expensive buttons
③ hire servants　④ keep expensive buttons

問 2　下線部 (1) を，**them** が何を指すかを明確にして和訳しなさい。

問 3　Put ○ if the sentence is correct according to the passage, and put × if incorrect.

① It is easy for the majority of men to button up when the buttons are on the right side of their clothes.（　　）
② Women's clothes have buttons on the left because most women were left-handed in the past.（　　）
③ It was easier for the servants to help button up women's clothes when the buttons were on the left.（　　）

Let's try　本文の表現を参考にしながら，次の日本語を英語にしなさい。

「トムはその問題をさらに解決しにくくした。」（ℓ. 9）

8 紫色のもと［文化］

The color purple has often been regarded as a symbol of wealth and power, but the dye used to produce it did not have an elegant beginning. (1) An ancient people living along the coast of the Mediterranean Sea first discovered how to make the dye from *Murex snails, small sea animals with hard shells. Unlike other snails, Murex snails give off a strong-smelling liquid that changes color when it comes into contact with air and light. From this liquid the people produced the purple dye. If we visit the places where the dye was produced, we might still be able to see the shells of Murex snails. Let us hope we cannot smell them. (114 words)

*Murex snail「アクキガイ」

日付　／　／

問 1　**Answer the questions below.**

(1)　**How did an ancient people make the dye for the color purple?**

① by using the hard shells of Murex snails
② by using a liquid that changes color when it is exposed to the air and light
③ by using the rocks along the coast of the Mediterranean Sea
④ by using the skin of snails that give off a strong-smelling liquid

(2)　**Why can't we say the dye for the color purple had an elegant beginning?**

① The dye was made from a bad-smelling liquid produced by small sea animals.
② It was very difficult to break the shell of the snails to make the dye.
③ The liquid used to make the dye changed color easily.
④ The small sea animals used to make the dye liked dark areas.

問 2　**Put the underlined sentence (1) into Japanese.**

＿＿＿＿＿＿＿＿＿＿＿＿＿＿＿＿＿＿＿＿＿＿＿＿

＿＿＿＿＿＿＿＿＿＿＿＿＿＿＿＿＿＿＿＿＿＿＿＿

問 3　**Put ○ if the sentence is correct according to the passage, and put × if incorrect.**

① People have often regarded the color purple to be a symbol of wisdom.　(　　　)
② The dye for the color purple was made from a certain kind of snail.　(　　　)
③ An ancient people living along the coast of the Mediterranean Sea first discovered Murex snails.　(　　　)

Let's try　本文の表現を参考にしながら，次の日本語を英語にしなさい。

「北海道は私がずっと住みたいと思っている場所です。」　(ℓ. 8)

＿＿＿＿＿＿＿＿＿＿＿＿＿＿＿＿＿＿＿＿＿＿＿＿

＿＿＿＿＿＿＿＿＿＿＿＿＿＿＿＿＿＿＿＿＿＿＿＿

9 本当のほほえみと偽りのほほえみ [人間]

The smile may no longer be an effective way to (1) <u>mask one's true feelings</u>. Some psychologists have claimed that true smiles and false smiles use different muscles. For example, in the true smile, the muscles surrounding the eyes tighten, while the cheek muscles pull the corners of the lips upward. On the other hand, in the false smile, the muscles between the eyebrows move slightly, while the muscles around the mouth pull the corners of the lips downward. If the psychologists' claim is proven to be true, perhaps (2) <u>people will worry less about what they say and more about which muscles to use when they smile</u>. (106 words)

日付　／　／

問 1　**Answer the questions below.**

(1) **Which of the following is the closest to the meaning of (1) mask one's true feelings?**

① overlook how one is truly feeling
② hide how one is truly feeling
③ show how one is truly feeling
④ point out how one is truly feeling

(2) **Which of the following best fits to fill in the blank below?**

Some psychologists have claimed that you can tell some smiles are true smiles by checking (　　　　　).

① the muscles between the eyes, and the corners of the lips
② the muscles between the eyebrows and those around the mouth
③ the muscles surrounding the eyes, and the corner of the lips
④ the muscles surrounding the eyebrows and those around the mouth

問 2　**Put the underlined sentence (2) into Japanese.**

____

____

問 3　**Put ○ if the sentence is correct according to the passage, and put × if incorrect.**

① The muscles we use when we smile truly are different from those we use when we smile falsely.　(　　　)
② In the false smile, the corners of your lips are pulled upward.　(　　　)
③ You won't be able to mask your true feelings by smiling if people know how muscles move when you smile.　(　　　)

Let's try　本文の表現を参考にしながら，次の日本語を英語にしなさい。

「トムは過去を気にするが，一方ジャックは未来のことを考える。」（ℓ. 4）

____

____

10 「熱い」か「辛い」か [言語]

When English-speaking people talk about "hot" food, are they saying the food is spicy like curry, or are they talking about its temperature, as in "hot" coffee? (1) These two different meanings of "hot" may seem confusing to Japanese students, but as a matter of fact, the word is the right one for describing the way the body responds to spice and heat. A simple explanation would go something like this: when we eat or drink, the same nerves in the mouth react both to spicy chemicals in the food and to a rise in temperature. The English expression, therefore, reflects this fact about the human body. (106 words)

問 1　Answer the questions below.

(1)　Why is the English word "hot" confusing to Japanese students?

① "Hot" means both "spicy" and "at a high temperature".
② They use "spicy" when they describe so-called "hot" food like curry.
③ They use the word "hot" only when they talk about the temperature.
④ They don't use "hot" to describe the way the body responds to spice.

(2)　Which of the following best fits to fill in the blank below?

When English-speaking people say curry is "hot" food, the word "hot" is being used to describe the way (　　　　　　).

① the human body senses the changes in body temperature
② the human body reacts to the curry at a high temperature
③ the nerves in the mouth react to spicy chemicals
④ the nerves in the mouth react to the curry at a high temperature

問 2　Put the underlined sentence (1) into Japanese.

____

____

問 3　Put ○ if the sentence is correct according to the passage, and put × if incorrect.

① The word "hot" has two different meanings.　(　　　)
② Our body reacts in totally different ways to spicy chemicals and a rise in temperature.　(　　　)
③ The word "hot" is used both for spicy foods and for a rise in temperature because the same nerves react in both cases.　(　　　)

Let's try　本文の表現を参考にしながら，次の日本語を英語にしなさい。

「率直な話し合いが，問題の解決につながるでしょうに。」　(ℓ.6)

____

____

People today are worried about food safety. As a result, the popularity of "organic" farming of fruits and vegetables is increasing. But what exactly does organic farming mean?

(1) <u>It is probably easier to explain what organic farming is not.</u> Organic farming does not use *pesticides or fertilizers. Instead, this style of farming uses natural methods to protect plants and help them grow. So, organic agricultural products are thought to be generally safer than non-organic ones.

In the United States, about two percent of all food is grown using organic methods. The U.S. government officially licenses farms as "organic" if they pass an examination. Presently, there are about 10,000 licensed farmers in the U.S., and this number is growing by about 20% a year. (123 words)

*pesticide「農薬」

問 1　Answer the questions below.

(1) Which of the following best fits to fill in the blank below?

In organic farming, farmers in the U.S. (　　　　　　).

① grow plants using as small an amount of pesticide as possible
② have to pass an examination before using organic methods
③ have to use licensed pesticides or fertilizers
④ grow about two percent of all food using natural methods

(2) How many licensed organic farmers will there be in the U.S. two years from now?

① about 12,000　　② about 14,000
③ about 16,000　　④ about 20,000

問 2　Put the underlined sentence (1) into Japanese.

____

____

問 3　Put ○ if the sentence is correct according to the passage, and put × if incorrect.

① Organic farming is becoming popular because people are concerned about the safety of food.　(　　　)
② Organic products are thought to be safer because they are protected by pesticides.　(　　　)
③ About 20% of American farmers are using an organic method of farming.　(　　　)

Let's try 本文の表現を参考にしながら，次の日本語を英語にしなさい。

「電気自動車はガソリン車より環境にやさしいと考えられている。」（ℓ.7）

____

____

12 食の安全と有機農業（2）［環境］

(1) In addition to food safety, another reason for the popularity of organic fruits and vegetables is that they taste better. This is why many restaurants only buy organic products.

A lot of people think organic farming is not competitive compared to other methods because it cannot grow the same quantity of food. However, new research has shown that organic farming only grows, on average, about five percent less than non-organic methods. Still, organic food today is more expensive than non-organic food. But when the environmental and health costs of non-organic farming are considered, such as the pollution of water by pesticides, most people would agree that the higher price of organic farming is in fact a small price to pay for our health and safety. (125 words)

問 1　Answer the questions below.

(1)　Why do many people think organic farming is not competitive?

① Organic fruits and vegetables, for example, are often smaller in size.
② Non-organic methods are also used taking food safety into consideration.
③ Organic farming grows a smaller quantity of food than non-organic.
④ Organic fruits and vegetables are popular with many restaurants.

(2)　Why would people agree to the higher price of organic food?

① Organic farming consumes natural resources in large quantities.
② Organic food is more and more popular with expensive restaurants.
③ Organic farming methods produce much less than non-organic food approaches.
④ Organic food is produced with consideration for both health and environment.

問 2　Put the underlined sentence (1) into Japanese.

____

____

問 3　Put ○ if the sentence is correct according to the passage, and put × if incorrect.

① There are restaurants that buy only organic products because they taste better than non-organic products.　(　　　)
② Organic food is expensive because organic farming produces much less food than non-organic methods.　(　　　)
③ The author thinks most people would complain about the higher price of organic farming despite its benefits.　(　　　)

Let's try　本文の表現を参考にしながら，次の日本語を英語にしなさい。

「僕が彼女に電話するのを忘れたんだ。こういうわけで，彼女は今も僕に怒っているんだよ。」　(ℓ. 2)

____

____

13 数学の歴史（1）[歴史]

The knowledge of mathematics developed rapidly in Europe and North America after the industrial revolution. But the study of mathematics was carried out many centuries before in other countries, like China.

Over two thousand years ago, the Chinese began their study of numbers, mostly related to astronomy and the perfection of a calendar. Already as early as 200 B.C. they had written a textbook on mathematics that was called *The Nine Chapters on the Mathematical Art*. (1) Interestingly, the ideas in this book seem to have been developed in China without any influence from Europe or other regions.

(97 words)

日付　／　／

問１　**Answer the questions below.**

(1)　**Why did the Chinese begin their study of numbers over two thousand years ago?**

① to better understand the stars and their movements
② to make mathematics a part of art
③ to spread their first calendar all over the world
④ to write a textbook on mathematics

(2)　**What regions had an influence on the ideas in a textbook on mathematics written by the Chinese as early as 200 B.C.?**

① some regions in Europe　② some regions in North America
③ some regions in Asia　④ no other regions

問２　**Put the underlined sentence (1) into Japanese.**

____

____

問３　**Put ○ if the sentence is correct according to the passage, and put × if incorrect.**

① China is the only country that studied mathematics before the industrial revolution.　(　　　)
② Chinese people were interested in perfecting a calendar over two thousand years ago.　(　　　)
③ We can't find any influence from Europe on the ideas in the textbook on mathematics written in 200 B.C.　(　　　)

Let's try　本文の表現を参考にしながら，次の日本語を英語にしなさい。

「アキラは早くも締め切りの２週間前には，その論文を書き上げていた。」(ℓ.7)

____

____

Various other books on mathematics appeared in the following centuries. But, (1) by the 5th century, it seems that the Chinese already had the concept of negative numbers and perhaps also had the concept of "zero". Around the 13th century, Chinese mathematicians were solving equations using methods that Europeans would not discover until 500 years later!

Unfortunately, near the end of the 14th century, the leaders of China began to be critical of math and science. Because of this change in attitude, people turned away from the study of math to study plants and medicine instead. It wasn't until the 19th century that the Chinese would become interested in math again, but this time under the influence of European mathematical knowledge. (120 words)

日付　／　／

問 1　Answer the questions below.

(1)　Choose the most suitable word or words to fill in the blanks（　ア　）—（　ウ　）. Write the number ① to ⑥ that corresponds to your answer.

It wasn't（　ア　）500 years later that Europeans discovered how to solve equations. Later in the（　イ　）, Chinese became interested in math again（　ウ　）European mathematical knowledge.

① until　　② before　　③ 14th century
④ 19th century　　⑤ influencing　　⑥ influenced by

(2)　Why did people in China once turn away from the study of math?

① People were interested only in plants and medicine.
② The leaders of China didn't allow them to study math any longer.
③ The leaders of China told them to study only plants and medicine.
④ The leaders of China changed their attitude to the study of math.

問 2　Put the underlined sentence (1) into Japanese.

____

____

問 3　Put ○ if the sentence is correct according to the passage, and put × if incorrect.

① The methods the Chinese used around the 13th century were discovered by Europeans in the 14th century.　（　　）
② China began to lose interest in math around the end of the 14th century.　（　　）
③ In the 19th century, there were not a few Chinese that learned from European mathematical knowledge.　（　　）

Let's try　本文の表現を参考にしながら，次の日本語を英語にしなさい。

「金曜日になって初めて，月曜日に試験があることに気づいた。」（ℓ. 10）

____

____

15 遺伝子と行動［科学］

(1) Genes, the basic parts of cells which are passed down from parents to children, may have something to do with human behavior. In an experiment, scientists put flies into a glass tube and placed a light at the end of it. Some of the flies began flying toward the light, some began walking, and some did not move at all. On the basis of the flies' actions, they were separated into different groups: flies that love light, flies that like light, and flies that like the dark. The researchers found that these three groups of flies had variations in a particular set of genes. This suggested to the researchers that the variations in these genes might explain the differences in the flies' behaviors. If genes influence behaviors in flies, (2) why not in humans too? (134 words)

問 1　Answer the questions below.

(1)　Which of the following best fits to fill in the blank below?

(　　　　　) the behaviors of the flies.

① The distance to the light might have caused the differences in
② The type of light might have had a strong influence on
③ The variations in their genes might have caused the differences in
④ Lack of specific genes might have caused the differences in

(2)　Which of the following has a meaning closest to the underlined part (2)?

① genes won't influence behaviors in humans.
② genes may also influence what humans do.
③ we should study the influence of genes in humans.
④ we can't explain the influence of genes in our behaviors.

問 2　Put the underlined sentence (1) into Japanese.

____

____

問 3　Put ○ if the sentence is correct according to the passage, and put × if incorrect.

① After an experiment the scientists divided the flies into three groups according to their size and weight. (　　　)
② The study of the flies' genes showed that there were differences in a particular set of genes. (　　　)
③ The scientists thought that a particular set of genes might explain the flies' different behaviors. (　　　)

Let's try　本文の表現を参考にしながら，次の日本語を英語にしなさい。

「紙の本が好きな学生もいれば，電子書籍の方が好きな学生もいる。」

(ll. 4 ～ 5)

____

____

16 風邪に関する常識 ［医療］

Ben Hemmens is the father of three children, including four-year-old Sophie. According to medical experts, it is normal for kids around this age to catch colds four to five times a year. In adults, the ratio is about two to three times a year, for reasons that are not completely clear. However, says Dr. Ranit Mishori of Georgetown University Hospital, (1) <u>many people believe that it is possible to become immune to the common cold so that one gets fewer and fewer colds as he ages.</u> "There are about 200 types of virus that cause the common cold, yet people think that once you get infected one time, you develop immunity for the rest of your life. This is entirely wrong," she claims. There are simply too many different viruses, many of which change in slight ways as they pass from person to person. (144 words)

問 1　Answer the questions below.

(1)　Which of the following is the fact not many people know?

① Adults are less likely to catch colds than children.
② Viruses that cause the common cold are spread from one person to another.
③ There are about 200 different types of virus that cause the common cold.
④ We become immune once we catch a common cold.

(2)　Which of the following is true according to Dr. Ranit Mishori?

① We cannot become immune to any common cold.
② The types of virus causing the common cold are too many to count.
③ Many of the different viruses may change in small ways.
④ One is less likely to catch colds as he becomes immune to some colds.

問 2　Put the underlined sentence (1) into Japanese.

____

____

問 3　Put ○ if the sentence is correct according to the passage, and put × if incorrect.

① Generally speaking, children at the age of about four catch colds two or three times a year.　(　　　)
② No one knows for sure why adults get fewer colds than children.　(　　　)
③ According to Dr. Ranit Mishori, there are so many types of virus that it is impossible to become immune to the common cold.　(　　　)

Let's try　本文の表現を参考にしながら，次の日本語を英語にしなさい。

「いったん怠け癖がつくと，やめるのは難しい。」　(ℓ.9)

____

____

17 英単語はいくつあるか（1）［言語］

English is a language with an enormous number of words, but how many English words are there? Most dictionaries used by college students have about 200,000 words, while most full-length dictionaries have about 300,000 to 600,000. Meanwhile, an organization called the Global Language Monitor positively claims that there are exactly 1,019,729 English words.

But counting the number of words in English is not an easy task. First of all, many words that we use in English today were originally words in other languages. (1) <u>Should the words *sushi* or *tsunami* be considered English words now that they are frequently used?</u> Then there is the question of words that were used centuries ago but are no longer used today. Should they be counted too? What about words that are only used in certain regions of a country? (135 words)

Let's try 本文の英語を参考にしながら，次の日本語を英語にしなさい。

「私の近所に，もはや使われていない大きなプールがある。」（*ll.* 11 ～ 12）

____

____

問 1　Answer the questions below.

(1) **Choose the most suitable word below to fill in the blanks（ア）―（エ）. Write the number ① to ⑧ that corresponds to your answer.**

Most English dictionaries for college students have almost 200,000 words, while most full-length dictionaries have about（　ア　）to（　イ　）as many, and an organization claims that the exact number of words is about（　ウ　）as（　エ　）.

① one-third　　② two-thirds　　③ one and a half times
④ twice　　⑤ three times　　⑥ five times
⑦ much　　⑧ large

(2) **Which of the following makes it more difficult to count the number of English words? You may choose more than one options.**

① The English language has borrowed many words from other languages.
② There is an organization to count English words.
③ Some words used centuries ago are no longer used today.
④ Some words are only spoken by people in certain regions of a country.

問 2　Put the underlined sentence (1) into Japanese.

____

____

問 3　Put ○ if the sentence is correct according to the passage, and put × if incorrect.

① Most English dictionaries for college students have about twenty thousand words.　（　　　）
② There is an organization that claims to have counted the exact number of English words.　（　　　）
③ Many words used in English today have origins other than English.　（　　　）

18 英単語はいくつあるか（2）［言語］

And the list of questions goes on. Should we count the verb, the adjective, the noun, and other forms of a word as separate words? In other words, would *drive, driving*, and *driver* be counted as separate words? Should a compound word be counted as one word or should each of the words in it be counted separately? How about the huge number of technical and scientific terms? Finally, (1) to add to the difficulties of counting words, we need to consider new words that are being created all the time.

The constantly changing nature of language is frustrating for anyone trying to count words. But this is also what makes language so interesting. English, like other languages, always offers something new to learn!

(123 words)

日付　／　／

問 1　**Answer the questions below.**

(1)　**Choose the most suitable word below to fill in the blanks（ア）―（ウ）. Write the number ① to ④ that corresponds to your answer.**

What makes it difficult to count words is that there are many forms of a word. For example, the word 'attend' is a（　ア　）, which has two（　イ　）forms, 'attendance' and 'attention'. In addition, its（　ウ　）form 'attendant' can also be used as a noun meaning a person who takes care of other people.

①　noun　　②　verb　　③　adverb　　④　adjective

(2)　**Which of the following is NOT a frustrating factor in counting words?**

①　There is a huge number of technical and scientific terms.
②　Compound words are difficult to count as one word or two.
③　Language will change constantly in itself.
④　Language will always offer something new to learn.

問 2　**Put the underlined sentence (1) into Japanese.**

____

____

問 3　**Put ○ if the sentence is correct according to the passage, and put × if incorrect.**

①　We can ignore the new words that are being created all the time.　（　　　）
②　People trying to count words may be frustrated because languages never stop changing.　（　　　）
③　We can always learn something new about a language.　（　　　）

Let's try　本文の表現を参考にしながら，次の日本語を英語にしなさい。

「山田先生は私達に学ぶ興味がわくものを提供してくれる。」（*ll*. 11 ～ 12）

____

____

19 結婚式の慣習（1）［文化］

Traditions and customs based on superstitions and religion have been an important aspect of weddings in all cultures. They vary greatly from one country to another and sometimes even between different ethnic groups in a particular country.

Though many traditions and customs have been forgotten through the years, many of today's wedding ceremonies have their beginnings in ancient beliefs and customs that originated in medieval times. In a Christian wedding, the *bride usually wears a white wedding *gown to show that she is pure. White was a color that was once believed to keep evil spirits away. On the other hand, in *Hinduism, white signifies the color of death. A Hindu bride usually wears a red dress with gold *stitching. (1) <u>In China, both the bride and *groom are dressed in red, which is a color associated with celebration and good fortune.</u>

(141 words)

*bride「新婦」 *gown「ロングドレス」 *Hinduism「ヒンドゥー教」 *stitching「縫い目」 *groom「新郎」

問 1　Answer the questions below.

(1) Which of the following is NOT true about today's wedding ceremonies?

① They are connected with ancient beliefs and customs.
② Traditions and customs in a wedding are different from country to country.
③ The customs of wedding ceremonies have greatly changed through the years.
④ People follow some of the old wedding traditions and customs.

(2) Which of the following is true about the color of a wedding dress?

① A bride in China doesn't wear a red dress because it signifies blood.
② A bride in China doesn't wear a white dress because it signifies death.
③ A Christian bride wears a white dress to show she is pure.
④ A Hindu bride wears a red dress to show she is a celebrity.

問 2　Put the underlined sentence (1) into Japanese.

____

____

問 3　Put ○ if the sentence is correct according to the passage, and put × if incorrect.

① In every culture, traditions and customs are a significant part of weddings.　(　　　)
② Christians like white for weddings because they think it symbolizes purity.　(　　　)
③ In Hinduism, red doesn't have a good meaning, but in China it does.　(　　　)

Let's try　本文の表現を参考にしながら，次の日本語を英語にしなさい。

「7という数字は幸運な数字だと信じられている。」　(*ll*. 9 ~ 10)

____

____

20 結婚式の慣習（2）[文化]

In many cultures, after the wedding it is traditional for the groom to carry the bride over the *threshold of their new home. This custom originated from the belief that bad luck may fall on the bride if she enters a new home with her left foot first. The custom of throwing rice or flowers at the newly married couple to wish them fertility and prosperity originated in Asia and later became popular in America. At a traditional Japanese wedding, it is considered unlucky to use words like "cut", "separate", or "leave".

Though weddings in many parts of the world still continue to be rituals that reflect ethnic, cultural, and social backgrounds, (1) <u>contemporary weddings incorporate more meaningful customs better suited to today's values.</u> (123 words)

*threshold「敷居」

日付　／　／

問 1　**Answer the questions below.**

(1) **In many countries, why does the groom carry the bride when they enter their new home?**

① Something unlucky might happen to her if he does not do so.
② He believes that he should take the lead in entering their new home.
③ He doesn't want her to walk ahead of him.
④ She is too tired to enter their new house by herself.

(2) **Which of the following is true about contemporary weddings?**

① They need not reflect ethnic, cultural, and social backgrounds.
② They take in new customs that correspond to recent values.
③ People always try to change some parts of the wedding.
④ People always try to firmly keep their own traditions and customs.

問 2　**Put the underlined sentence (1) into Japanese.**

____

____

問 3　**Put ○ if the sentence is correct according to the passage, and put × if incorrect.**

① It is considered unlucky for a bride to enter her new home left foot first. (　　　)
② American people were the first to throw rice or flowers at the newly married couple. (　　　)
③ Today's weddings combine traditional aspects and new customs. (　　　)

Let's try　本文の表現を参考にしながら，次の日本語を英語にしなさい。

「日本人にはお正月休みの間に餅を食べる習慣があります。」　(ℓ. 4)

____

____

21 遊びを通して学ぶこと（1）[教育]

When we watch *kittens and *puppies playing, we realize that through play they are learning how to live. They learn various physical skills, such as how to jump over barriers without getting hurt. They also learn social interaction. For example, if a kitten bites his sister too hard, she will get angry and bite him back. These physical and social skills form part of the training that young animals need in order to grow up.

(1) Just as kittens and puppies learn about how to live through play, so do children. But in present-day Japan, especially in cities, there is not much space for children to play in. Children need to release their energy for their mental and physical health. They need space, especially outdoors, so that they can run, jump, and yell. (132 words)

*kitten「子猫」 *puppy「子犬」

日付　／　／

問 1　**Answer the questions below.**

(1) **Which of the following is NOT the lesson kittens and puppies learn through play?**

① how to interact with other kittens and puppies
② how to jump over barriers without getting hurt
③ how to grow up to be adult cats and dogs with various skills
④ how to avoid biting their brothers or sisters

(2) **According to the author, why do children need enough outdoor space to learn how to live?**

① in order to learn to run, jump, and yell
② in order to learn to protect themselves from danger
③ in order to stay healthy by releasing their energy
④ in order to level up their various physical skills

問 2　**Put the underlined sentence (1) into Japanese.**

____

____

問 3　**Put ○ if the sentence is correct according to the passage, and put × if incorrect.**

① Kittens and puppies learn how to fight enemies through play. (　　　)
② Children in Japanese cities don't have much space to play in. (　　　)
③ Children need space, especially outdoors, in order to learn how to live. (　　　)

Let's try 本文の表現を参考にしながら，次の日本語を英語にしなさい。

「私は交通渋滞に巻き込まれないように，朝早く家を出た。」　(ℓ. 12)

____

____

22 遊びを通して学ぶこと (2) [教育]

Another point to consider is how much time children have to play. Some people say that four to five hours a day of playing outdoors with others is necessary, even for twelve-year-olds. (1) It is very doubtful, however, whether any Japanese children get that much free time. Concerned about their future in an increasingly competitive society, parents generally tell their children to study more; very few would tell them to go out and play.

What do these children do at home when they are not studying? They tend to spend time by themselves. They play video games or watch TV, for instance. These activities do not teach them how to get along with others. This can only be learned through playing with other children. They need to play without being told what to do by adults in order to learn about leadership and group harmony on their own. Outdoor space is particularly suitable for this purpose. Children need a proper outdoor environment where they can freely spend their time playing with friends. (171 words)

日付　／　／

問 1　**Answer the questions below.**

(1) **Why are parents today concerned about the future of their children?**

① Their children won't learn about leadership and group harmony.
② Their children might not go out and play with others any more.
③ Society is becoming too dependent on technology.
④ Society is becoming increasingly competitive.

(2) **How can children learn how to get along with others?**

① by playing video games or watching TV together at home
② by freely spending their time playing outdoors with others
③ by studying with others in a more competitive way
④ by freely talking about various topics with others

問 2　**Put the underlined sentence (1) into Japanese.**

____

____

問 3　**Put ◯ if the sentence is correct according to the passage, and put × if incorrect.**

① Average Japanese twelve-year-olds play four to five hours a day. (　　　)
② Playing video games and watching TV can teach children how to get along with others. (　　　)
③ In order to learn about leadership and group harmony, children need to play with friends. (　　　)

Let's try　本文の表現を参考にしながら，次の日本語を英語にしなさい。

「スミス夫妻は子供たちに邪魔されることなくディナーを楽しんだ。」
(ℓ. 12)

____

____

23 サッカーの起源（1）［歴史］

There is much debate on the origin of the game of football. The Japanese and Chinese claim to have invented a sport similar to modern soccer many centuries ago.

In comparison to modern soccer, the Japanese game of *kemari* was a game that used a large ball stuffed with *sawdust. This version used a field which was set up by choosing four trees. These trees were usually cherry, maple, pine and willow. Many large houses in Japan would grow these trees to make a field for *kemari*. *Kemari* was normally played with two to twelve players.

China's version, **tsu chu*, involved players hitting a leather, fur-stuffed ball into a small hole. As in soccer, no player could use his hands during play. (1) <u>It was considered an honor to be part of a team.</u> The first international soccer or *tsu chu* match is believed to have been held in China around 50 B.C. (152 words)

*sawdust「おがくず」 **tsu chu*「（中国版の）蹴鞠」

問 1　Answer the questions below.

(1) What was or were NOT usually needed in the Japanese game of *kemari*?

① four trees, usually cherry, maple, pine and willow
② two to twelve players
③ a small hole in a field
④ a large ball stuffed with sawdust

(2) What was considered an honor in China around 50 B.C.?

① holding an international *tsu chu* match in China
② playing as a member of a team in *tsu chu*
③ putting a leather, fur stuffed ball into a small hole
④ playing *tsu chu* without using hands

問 2　Put the underlined sentence (1) into Japanese.

____

____

問 3　Put ◯ if the sentence is correct according to the passage, and put × if incorrect.

① There is no doubt that *kemari* was established earlier than *tsu chu*. (　　　)
② The number of players in a *kemari* game is flexible. (　　　)
③ In *tsu chu*, players should hit a large sawdust-stuffed ball into a small hole. (　　　)

Let's try　本文の表現を参考にしながら，次の日本語を英語にしなさい。

「ミカは昨日，カナとけんかしたようだ。」　(ℓ.2)

____

____

24 サッカーの起源（2）[歴史]

The Emperor of the *Han Dynasty was an *avid, early player and fan of *tsu chu*. This spread the popularity of *tsu chu* all over China. Some people in China claim that it is even possible *tsu chu* could go back to 5000 B.C.

The British claim that soccer was created in the 8th century in Britain. It was not a recreational sport at the time, but a war game. It was a violent game and serious injury and even death were not uncommon. (1) It was not until 1815 when Eton College set up a series of rules for the game that it became a less violent sport. At that time, colleges began to play using similar rules. In 1848, the rules were set by Cambridge University. In the Cambridge rules, shin-kicking and carrying the ball were forbidden. This is where rugby and soccer developed into two different sports. (149 words)

*Han Dynasty「（中国の）漢」 *avid「熱烈な」

日付　／　／

問 1　**Answer the questions below.**

(1)　**Which of the following is NOT true about *tsu chu*?**

① The history of *tsu chu* could be more than 7,000 years old.
② The Emperor of the Han Dynasty spread *tsu chu* as a war game.
③ The Emperor in China was once a *tsu chu* player himself.
④ *Tsu chu* spread all over China because the Emperor loved the game.

(2)　**When soccer was created in the 8th century in Britain, what kind of sport was it?**

① It was the only sport that people were allowed to play for fun.
② Few players got seriously hurt during the game.
③ The players could not shin-kick or carry the ball.
④ It was a war game in which some players even died.

問 2　**Put the underlined sentence (1) into Japanese.**

____

____

問 3　**Put ○ if the sentence is correct according to the passage, and put × if incorrect.**

① The Emperor of the Han Dynasty was not only a great fan but also a player of *tsu chu*.　(　　)
② Some people in Britain claim that the origin of soccer could go back to 5000 B.C.　(　　)
③ In the early 19th century Cambridge University set rules which allowed the ball to be carried during the game.　(　　)

Let's try　本文の表現を参考にしながら，次の日本語を英語にしなさい。

「ここは多くの日本人が満開の桜を見物に訪れるところです。」　(ℓ. 12)

____

____

25 ハエの超能力（1）[科学]

A fly can do one thing extremely well: fly. Recently a team of British scientists declared that the common *housefly is the most talented *aerodynamicist on the planet, superior to any bird, bat, or bee. A housefly can make six turns a second; *hover; fly straight up, down, or backward; land on the ceiling; and perform various other *show-off maneuvers. And it has a brain smaller than a *sesame seed.

Michael Dickinson, who studies fly flight in his lab at the California Institute of Technology, says the housefly isn't actually the best flier. "*Hoverflies are *the be-all and end-all," he says. They can hover in one spot, dash to another location, and then race back to their original hovering point — precisely.

(1) Scientists, engineers, and military researchers want to know how creatures with such small brains can do that. Maybe they could *reverse-engineer a fly to make a robotic device that could *reconnoiter dangerous places, such as earthquake zones or collapsed mines.

(161 words)

*housefly「イエバエ」 *aerodynamicist「空気力学者」 *hover「空中でとどまる」
*show-off maneuver「見せびらかしの飛行」 *sesame「ゴマ」 *hoverfly「ハナアブ」
*the be-all and end-all「究極のもの」 *reverse-engineer「を解析して模倣する」
*reconnoiter「を偵察する」

問 1　Answer the questions below.

(1) **Which of the following is NOT true about the common housefly?**

① They can make six turns a second.
② They can hover, fly forward, and fly back to their original hovering point.
③ They can fly in a vertical direction.
④ They can land even on a ceiling.

(2) **Why do scientists, engineers, and military researchers want to study fly flight?**

① They want to apply fly flight's techniques to a robotic device.
② They want to know whether hoverflies have the best flight ability.
③ They want to develop an extremely small military device like a fly.
④ They want to find a new species which is superior to a fly.

問 2　Put the underlined sentence (1) into Japanese.

____

____

問 3　Put ○ if the sentence is correct according to the passage, and put × if incorrect.

① British scientists found out that common houseflies can be trained to perform in a kind of show.　(　　　)
② Michael Dickinson believes that hoverflies can fly better than common houseflies.　(　　　)
③ Some scientists and engineers are studying the possibilities of making flies fly in dangerous places.　(　　　)

Let's try 本文の表現を参考にしながら，次の日本語を英語にしなさい。

「コウタは私の親友で，コンピューターにとても詳しい。」　(ℓ.7)

____

____

26 ハエの超能力（2）［科学］

Dickinson's laboratory works with fruit flies. Researchers put them in *chambers and manipulate the visual field, filming the flies in super-slow motion, 6,000 frames a second. Dickinson is interested in knowing how flies avoid collisions. He has found that certain patterns, such as 90-degree turns, are triggered by visual cues and two *equilibrium organs on their backs that function like a *gyroscope.

Flies have only a dozen muscles for maneuvering, but they're loaded with sensors. (1) In addition to their compound eyes, which permit *panoramic *imagery and are excellent at detecting motion, they have wind-sensitive hairs and *antennae. They also have three light sensors on the tops of their heads, which tell them which way is up. Roughly two-thirds of a fly's entire nervous system is devoted to processing visual images. They take all this sensory data and boil it down to a few basic commands, such as "go left" and "go right."

(152 words)

*chamber「小室」 *equilibrium「平衡」 *gyroscope「ジャイロスコープ〔姿勢制御装置〕」
*panoramic「全景が見渡せる」 *imagery「画像」 *antennae「触角（antenna の複数形）」

問 1　Answer the questions below.

(1) **What do the researchers at Dickinson's laboratory do to see how fruit flies use their body sensors?**

① They let the flies fly very slowly and film them.
② They put up barriers and check how the flies avoid collisions.
③ They control the visual field and check how the flies react.
④ They let the flies use their gyroscope-like organs on the tops of their heads.

(2) **Which of the following is true about fruit flies?**

① They see which way is up by using their compound eyes.
② They use two-thirds of their nervous system to process visual images.
③ They have twelve muscles on the tops of their heads to detect motion.
④ They take all the sensory data in by using their light sensors.

問 2　Put the underlined sentence (1) into Japanese.

____

____

問 3　Put ○ if the sentence is correct according to the passage, and put × if incorrect.

① Dickinson uses super-slow motion filming to analyze the mechanism by which flies avoid collisions. (　　　)
② The muscle mass of flies is so little that they use sensitive hairs and antennae instead when flying. (　　　)
③ Flies have three light sensors on their backs along with other muscles. (　　　)

Let's try　本文の表現を参考にし，分詞構文を用いて次の日本語を英語にしなさい。

「学生たちはその大きな虹を指差しながら窓に駆け寄った。」　(ℓ. 2)

____

____

27 アレルギーが増加する背景（1）［医療］

The past thirty to forty years have seen a huge increase in the number of children who suffer from allergies, and scientists are still looking for the explanation. Some have blamed increased air pollution, but it has also been found that allergies are common not only among children in the city but also among children in the countryside, where pollution is typically much lower.

A currently popular explanation for the rise in allergies is the so-called "*hygiene hypothesis." The basic idea is that young children brought up in an environment which is too clean are more at risk of developing allergies. Nowadays, people bathe and wash their clothes more frequently than in the past, and thanks to vacuum cleaners homes are less dusty, too. One result of all these changes is that in their early lives children are exposed to fewer *allergens — substances that can cause allergies — and this means that their bodies cannot build up natural immunity to them. (1) <u>Simply put, exposure to allergy-causing substances is necessary for natural protection against them to develop.</u>

(175 words)

*hygiene「衛生」 *allergen「アレルゲン（アレルギーの原因となる物質）」

Let's try 本文の表現を参考にしながら，次の日本語を英語にしなさい。

「スマートフォンを使用する人たちは，睡眠障害（sleep disorder）を発症する危険性が高いことがわかっている。」 (ll. 3 ～ 4)

問 1　Answer the questions below.

(1) **Concerning the recent increase in the number of children suffering from allergies, which of the following is NOT an idea put forward by scientists?**

① This increase is partly due to worsening air pollution.
② The environment where children are brought up is often too clean.
③ Children in the city are more likely to develop allergies than those in the countryside.
④ Children's bodies cannot build up natural immunity to allergens unless they are exposed to them.

(2) **Why cannot children nowadays build up natural immunity to allergens? You may choose more than one options.**

① They keep their body clean because they take regular baths.
② They change their clothes too often.
③ People use house cleaning services frequently in order to keep their rooms clean.
④ People try to keep their children away from various allergens.

問 2　Put the underlined sentence (1) into Japanese.

____

____

問 3　Put ○ if the sentence is correct according to the passage, and put × if incorrect.

① The number of children who have allergies has increased during the past three to four decades. (　　　)
② Allergies are common only among children in the city. (　　　)
③ Exposure to allergy-causing substances is unnecessary for young children. (　　　)

28 アレルギーが増加する背景（2）［医療］

The trend towards smaller families also means that young children encounter fewer allergens in the home. In fact, it is known that children who have older brothers and sisters are more resistant to allergies. The same is true of children who share their home with a pet. (1) Such children are much less likely to develop the very common allergy to cat or dog hair, for example.

Scientists agree that being exposed to a wider range of allergens early in life helps children to develop greater immunity. There is, however, also some data suggesting that genetics, family income, and even the parents' level of education may play a part in how likely a child is to suffer from allergies. Thus, although the hygiene hypothesis is an important area for research, we cannot yet be sure that too much attention to cleanliness is the only explanation for the enormous rise in the number of allergy victims. (154 words)

Let's try 本文の表現を参考にしながら，次の日本語を英語にしなさい。

「睡眠不足は健康によくない。寝すぎることについても同じことが当てはまる。」 (ℓ.4)

日付　／　／

問 1　Answer the questions below.

(1) **Choose the most suitable word below to fill in the blanks（ア）—（ウ）. Write the number ① to ⑥ that corresponds to your answer.**

Another cause of the huge increase in allergies may be that, because of the trend towards（　ア　）families, young children with no（　イ　）brothers and sisters encounter（　ウ　）allergens in the home.

① more　　② fewer　　③ less
④ younger　　⑤ older　　⑥ smaller

(2) **Which of the following best fits in the blank below?**

With regard to the huge increase in allergies, scientists agree that（　　）.

① attention to cleanliness is the only explanation
② some people suffer from allergies because of their genetics
③ family income doesn't influence the likelihood of a child developing allergies
④ the parents' level of education is not relevant

問 2　下線部 (1) を，**Such** が示す内容を明確にして和訳しなさい。

____

____

問 3　Put ○ if the sentence is correct according to the passage, and put × if incorrect.

① The trend towards smaller families has resulted in young children encountering fewer allergens in the home.　（　　）
② If you want your children to be more resistant to allergies, you should have an only child.　（　　）
③ Children can develop greater immunity by being exposed to fewer allergens early in life.　（　　）

29 外国語を学ぶ際に必要なもの（1）[言語]

People may decide to study foreign languages for various reasons. (1) They may do so for the immediate purpose of satisfying the requirements of some public examination or of getting greater fun and enjoyment out of a holiday abroad. Business people may have to deal directly or indirectly with various kinds of information from abroad. Research workers may realize the importance of being able to read the latest reports of advances made in their studies as soon as they are published in foreign journals, without waiting for a translator, who may or may not have the ability to make an exact translation with one hundred percent accuracy. People may be keenly interested in the activities of a foreign nation for political reasons. They may need information about current affairs that foreign newspapers and journals alone can deliver. Students of literature must surely be able to read great works first hand.

(149 words)

Let's try 本文の表現を参考にしながら，次の日本語を英語にしなさい。

「大勢の人がその歌手を待っていたが，その歌手はコンサート会場に１時間遅れた。」

(ℓ. 8)

日付　／　／

問 1　**Answer the questions below.**

(1) **Which of the following is NOT one of the reasons mentioned regarding why people decide to study foreign languages?**

① They may have to take examinations in a foreign language.
② It will be enjoyable if they can speak a local language when they are traveling.
③ The ability to speak the language is necessary for promotion at work.
④ They can get various kinds of information directly from abroad.

(2) **What kind of trouble are people likely to have if they do not study a foreign language?**

① They cannot find translators to deal with information from abroad.
② They cannot find the latest information when it is made public.
③ They may lose interest in the activities of a foreign nation.
④ They may not be able to get information about the current affairs of a foreign country.

問 2　下線部 (1) を，**do so** の内容を明確にして和訳しなさい。

____

____

問 3　**Put ○ if the sentence is correct according to the passage, and put × if incorrect.**

① There are various reasons for people to study foreign languages. (　　　)
② Research workers think it better to wait for an exact translation of a report published in a foreign journal to come out. (　　　)
③ Students of literature have to be able to read a great work in the language it was first written in. (　　　)

30 外国語を学ぶ際に必要なもの（2）［言語］

Learning a new language implies entering a new world, and it inevitably leads to a widening of intellectual experience. Learning a new language well enough to be able to understand it when heard, to speak it, read it, and write it, is such hard training that we certainly need some strong urge to drive us on. The four distinct and separable activities just mentioned — listening, speaking, reading, and writing — call for constant, preferably daily, exercise. (1) <u>These activities are concerned in varying degrees with four aspects of language study</u> — pronunciation, grammar, vocabulary, and *idiom. It is useful to keep these four activities and four aspects clearly in mind.

Learning a new language calls for no great originality of mind or critical talent, but it does demand an eager intellectual curiosity and a constant and lively interest in the endless ways in which human ideas may be expressed. It demands quick observation first of all, reasonable ability to *mimic and imitate, good powers of association and *generalization, and a good memory. (169 words)

*idiom「熟語」 *mimic「をまねる」 *generalization「一般化」

問 1　Answer the questions below.

(1)　Which of the following is true about learning a new language?

① A strong desire to master it is not always necessary.
② All you need is four activities — listening, speaking, reading, and writing.
③ It is better to listen, speak, read and write a new language every day.
④ Few of us will continue to make efforts to learn it.

(2)　Which of the following is NOT needed in learning a new language?

① the ability to generalize separate items of knowledge
② quick observation and the ability to mimic and imitate
③ special talent to be always critical of the new human ideas
④ an eager intellectual curiosity and a constant and lively interest

問 2　下線部 (1) を，**These activities** の具体的な内容を明確にして和訳しなさい。

____

____

問 3　Put ○ if the sentence is correct according to the passage, and put × if incorrect.

① Constant exercise in listening, speaking, reading, and writing are needed in order to learn a new language.　(　　　)
② The "four aspects of language study" mentioned in the passage include grammar and idiom.　(　　　)
③ Learning a new language requires great originality and critical talent.　(　　　)

Let's try　本文の表現を参考にしながら，次の日本語を英語にしなさい。

「そこはとてもうるさい部屋だったので，私たちはお互いに話していることが聞こえなかった。」　(ℓ.4)

____

____

31 ディズニーの大きな決断 (1) [社会]

On April 4, 2003, (1) Glen Keane, one of Walt Disney's most respected animators, called for a meeting to discuss the war breaking out at the studio. Disney's animators had settled into two opposing camps: those who were skilled in computer animation and those who refused to give up their pencils.

Keane, a 31-year *veteran who created the beast for "Beauty and the Beast" and Ariel for "The Little Mermaid," was a Disney *traditionalist. But after a series of experiments to see whether he could create a computer-animated *ballerina, (2) his opposition softened. So he invited the 50 animators to discuss the *pros and cons of both art forms, calling his seminar "The Best of Both Worlds." (115 words)

*veteran「ベテラン」 *traditionalist「伝統主義者」 *ballerina「バレリーナ」
*pros and cons「賛否；良し悪し」

問 1　Answer the questions below.

(1)　Which of the following is NOT true about Glen Keane?

① He was the most talented animator in the world.
② He created the beast for "Beauty and the Beast."
③ He called his seminar "The Best of Both Worlds."
④ He didn't want to give up his pencils at first.

(2)　What does (2) his opposition softened imply?

① He started to oppose computer animation softly.
② He opposed computer animation in fewer words.
③ He gradually came to admit the advantages of computer animation.
④ He was not consistent in his opposition any longer.

問 2　Put the underlined sentence (1) into Japanese.

____

____

問 3　Put ○ if the sentence is correct according to the passage, and put × if incorrect.

① There were two groups at Walt Disney's studio who were opposed to each other. (　　　)
② Glen Keane was an animator who was skilled in computer animation. (　　　)
③ Keane called for a meeting to evaluate two different art forms. (　　　)

Let's try　本文の表現を参考にしながら，次の日本語を英語にしなさい。

「弟が塾に通うのかどうかはわからない。」　(ℓ. 8)

____

____

32 ディズニーの大きな決断（2）［社会］

For an hour, Keane listed the pluses and minuses of each technique while the other animators listened quietly. After a few questions, the crowd burst into chatter as animators shouted over one another, some arguing that computers should not replace people and others expressing fears that they would be forced to draw by hand.

In a recent interview, Keane recalled that Kevin Geiger, a computer animation *supervisor, then stood up and demanded of him, "(1) If you can do all this cool stuff that you're talking about — that you want to see in animation — but you have to give up the pencil to do it, are you in?" Keane hesitated before answering, "I'm in."

Three weeks later, the company's animators were told that Disney would concentrate on making computer-animated movies, abandoning a 70-year-old hand-drawn tradition in favor of a style popularized by newer and more successful rivals like Pixar Animation Studios and DreamWorks Animation. (153 words)

*supervisor「監督」

日付　／　／

問 1　**Answer the questions below.**

(1)　**What happened during the discussion among the animators?**

① Animators all admitted that they loved to draw by hand.
② Most of the animators listened quietly to the speakers all the time.
③ Some animators were afraid of being forced to draw by hand.
④ All the animators thought computers should not replace people.

(2)　**Which of the following is NOT true about the result of the discussion?**

① Disney decided to concentrate on computer animation.
② Animators were told to abandon a 70-year-old hand-drawn tradition.
③ Keane agreed to join in the making of a computer-animated film.
④ Disney let some animators maintain its hand-drawn tradition.

問 2　**Put the underlined sentence (1) into Japanese.**

____

____

問 3　**Put ○ if the sentence is correct according to the passage, and put × if incorrect.**

① The discussion went very peacefully until they came to a conclusion. (　　　)
② The technology of computer animations was so impressive that animators made up their minds immediately. (　　　)
③ Keane was 70 years old when Disney decided to give up the traditional style of making animations. (　　　)

Let's try　本文の表現を参考にしながら，次の日本語を英語にしなさい。

「私は左利きだが，右手で字を書くことを強いられるのではないかという不安を感じていた。」　(ℓ.5)

____

____

33 ディズニーの大きな決断 (3) [社会]

The results were nothing short of a cultural revolution at the studio, which is famous for the hand-drawn classics championed by its founder, Walt Disney, like "Snow White and the Seven Dwarfs" and "Peter Pan."

Two years and a half after that decision, Disney released "Chicken Little," the first of four computer-animated films developed at the newly *reorganized studio. The company hoped that this movie, along with others like "Meet the Robinsons," "American Dog," and Keane's "Rapunzel Unbraided," would return Disney to its past glory.

(1) <u>There was a lot more than pride, however, riding on its success.</u> Animation was once Disney's heart, a profitable *lifeline that fed the company's theme park, book, and home video divisions. And restoring profit was as essential to Disney in those days as *regaining its reputation. (131 words)

*reorganize「を再編成する」 *lifeline「生命線」 *regain「を取り戻す」

日付　／　／

問 1　Answer the questions below.

(1)　Which of the following is NOT true about Disney's "Chicken Little"?

① It was nothing less than a cultural revolution at the Disney studio.
② It was a film championed by animators like Walt Disney.
③ It was Disney's first computer-animated film.
④ It was a film intended to return Disney to its past glory.

(2)　What was Disney aiming at with its decision to give up hand-drawn animation?

① The reorganization of the studio
② The development of a new style using computers
③ The feeding of Disney's lifeline, including its theme park
④ The restoration of profit and recovery of its reputation

問 2　Put the underlined sentence (1) into Japanese.

____

____

問 3　Put ○ if the sentence is correct according to the passage, and put × if incorrect.

① "Peter Pan" is a famous hand-drawn Disney animation. (　　　)
② It took Disney two and a half years to release their first computer-animated film. (　　　)
③ Regaining its reputation was not so important for Disney as regaining profit. (　　　)

Let's try　本文の表現を参考にしながら，次の日本語を英語にしなさい。

「規則正しい食事をすることは，適度な運動をすることと同様に大切だ。」
(ℓ. 13)

____

____

34 ネコの習性［科学］

Although cats appear to perform most actions instinctively, they also seem to react to human behavior and adapt themselves to it. (1) For instance, some cats behave as if they understood their owners' feelings. One cat owner told of the time when she lay crying and exhausted on her bed, and her cat put its front legs around her head and comforted her. Cats also sometimes appear to be able to understand the function of many of the things human beings use. For example, some cats, when they bring a captured bird or mouse into the house, put it on a plate or in a dish. There are also cats who know how to open a door by turning the handle. Furthermore, a lot of cats seem to understand what their owners say. A writer tells a story of her cat who used to sleep on top of her word processor. At first, when the cat's tail *got in the way of the screen, the owner would push its tail away and say, "Move your tail, please." Eventually, she didn't have to push the tail but only had to tell the cat to move it. (194 words)

*get in the way「邪魔をする」

日付　／　／

問 1　**Answer the questions below.**

(1) **Which of the following is NOT true about how cats react to human behavior and adapt themselves to it?**

① Some cats bring a captured bird or mouse to feed their owner.
② Some cats seem to know that a plate is for putting food on.
③ One cat owner felt her cat tried to console her.
④ Some cats can turn the handle of a door to open it.

(2) **How did a writer know that her cat could understand what she said?**

① When she told her cat a story, it used to sleep on her word processor.
② When she told her cat to move its tail, it pushed its tail on the screen.
③ When she told her cat to move its tail, the cat did as she told it to.
④ When she said she'd use her word processor, the cat moved away from it.

問 2　**Put the underlined sentence (1) into Japanese.**

____

____

問 3　**Put ○ if the sentence is correct according to the passage, and put × if incorrect.**

① Cats seem incapable of understanding their owners' feelings.　(　　　)
② A cat put a captured bird on a plate. This suggests that it understood the function of a plate.　(　　　)
③ A writer's cat moved its tail away from the screen when it was told to do so.　(　　　)

Let's try　本文の表現を参考にしながら，次の日本語を英語にしなさい。

「先生は私たちに靴をはいたままこの部屋に入らないよう言った。」(ℓ. 15)

____

____

35 「触れること」の作用（1）［人間］

Touching is the language of physical intimacy. Because of this, touch can be the most powerful of all the communication channels. In May 1985, Brigitte Gerney was trapped for six hours beneath a collapsed construction crane in New York City. Throughout her *ordeal, she held the hand of a rescue worker, who stayed by her side as heavy machinery removed the tons of twisted steel from her crushed legs. A stranger's touch gave her hope and the will to live.

Touch appears to affect the sexes differently. Women sometimes react much more favorably to touch than men. In an interesting study, psychologists asked a group of nurses to lightly touch a patient once or twice shortly before the patient underwent surgery. The touching produced a strongly positive reaction — but only among women. It appeared to lower their blood pressure and anxiety levels both before and after surgery.

(1) For men, however, the touching proved to be very upsetting. Their blood pressure and anxiety levels both rose. The psychologists suspect that because men are taught to be more *stoic, that is, to hide their feelings and to ignore their fears, the touching *rattled them by reminding them that life is *fragile. (199 words)

*ordeal「つらい経験」 *stoic「冷静な」 *rattle「を混乱させる」 *fragile「もろい」

問 1　Answer the questions below.

(1) What happened to Brigitte Gerney?

① She was saved by a construction crane.
② She was trapped in a construction accident.
③ She helped the rescue workers during a disaster.
④ She refused to stay with the rescue workers.

(2) What were the results of the study on touching?

① Both women and men reacted positively to being touched.
② Most men became stoic when they were touched.
③ Most women felt uneasy when they were touched.
④ Women responded more positively to being touched than men.

問 2　Put the underlined sentence (1) into Japanese.

____

____

問 3　Put ○ if the sentence is correct according to the passage, and put × if incorrect.

① It is possible that touch is the most powerful way of all to communicate. (　　　)
② There seems to be no difference between the sexes in the way that they react to touch. (　　　)
③ Softly touching a female patient before the surgery lowered her blood pressure and anxiety levels. (　　　)

Let's try 本文の表現を参考にしながら，次の日本語を英語にしなさい。

「ユウコが私に教室で待っているように頼んだの。」　(ℓ. 10)

____

____

36 「触れること」の作用（2）［人間］

How do you feel about touching and being touched? Salespeople think they know — research shows that it is harder to say "no" to someone who touches you when making a request — but not everyone is happy about being touched by a stranger. Think about your own comfort level when you find yourself in a crowd. Are you relaxed and loose, or does physical contact make you feel *awkward and tense?

In some situations, we can't help touching each other. Take a crowded elevator, for instance. Normally, people stand shoulder to shoulder and arm to arm, accepting such close contact without complaint. The rule seems to be "Touch only from shoulder to elbow, but nowhere else." (1) Even though the Japanese are regarded as a nontouching society, their crowded cities force them to be jammed into subways and trains. Edward T. Hall, an anthropologist, says the Japanese handle their *uneasiness about being packed into public places by avoiding eye contact and drawing within themselves emotionally, thus "(2) touching without feeling." (167 words)

*awkward「居心地が悪い」 *uneasiness「落ち着かない気持ち；不快さ」

問 1　**Answer the questions below.**

(1) **Which statement about the way people feel about being touched is true?**

① People feel it easier to refuse a request when being touched.
② People feel relaxed and loose when physical contact is made.
③ People feel awkward and tense only when being touched in a crowd.
④ Not all people like being touched by a stranger.

(2) **Which of the following has a meaning closest to (2) touching without feeling?**

① touching without feeling they are touched
② touching without feeling they are forced to touch
③ touching while drawing within themselves emotionally
④ touching while avoiding looking at each other

問 2　**Put the underlined sentence (1) into Japanese.**

____

____

問 3　**Put ○ if the sentence is correct according to the passage, and put × if incorrect.**

① Salespeople believe that it is harder to say "no" to a request if they are touched by the person making a request.　(　　　)
② People seem to accept shoulder to shoulder contact in the crowded elevator.　(　　　)
③ When they have to accept close contact with strangers, the Japanese try to make eye contact with people around them.　(　　　)

Let's try　本文の表現を参考にしながら，次の日本語を英語にしなさい。

「ミカは，母親からの手紙を読んで泣かずにはいられなかった。」　(ℓ.8)

____

____

37 インターネット時代の印刷物の役割（1）［社会］

The Internet is very much like television in that it takes time away from other pursuits, provides entertainment and information, but in no way can compare with the warm, personal experience of reading a good book. This is not the only reason why the Internet will never replace books, for books provide the sufficient knowledge of a subject that sitting in front of a computer monitor cannot provide. We can transfer text from an Internet source, but the artistic quality of sheets of transferred text leaves much to be desired. A well-designed book makes the reading experience important.

The book is still the most *compact and economical means of conveying a lot of knowledge in a convenient package, and (1) this is what makes it popular. The idea that one can carry in one's pocket a play by Shakespeare, a novel by *Charles Dickens or the Bible in a small book with a *stiff, paper cover is incredible. We take such uncommon convenience for granted, not realizing that the book itself has undergone quite an evolution since the production of the Gutenberg Bible in 1455 and Shakespeare's book of plays in 1623.

(191 words)

*compact「小型の」 *Charles Dickens「（小説家）チャールズ・ディケンズ」 *stiff「硬い」

問 1　Answer the questions below.

(1) **How is the Internet very much like television?**

① We cannot spend enough time on other work while using it.
② We can have a personal experience by watching it.
③ We can get sufficient knowledge just by sitting in front of it.
④ We can get information directly from the source.

(2) **Why does the author think a book is still better than the Internet even now?**

① The book provides more entertainment and information.
② The book has a stiff, paper cover that makes it convenient.
③ The book is economical for the huge amount of knowledge it contains.
④ The book is compact because it has undergone an evolution over time.

問 2　下線部 (1) を，**this** と **it** の内容を明確にして和訳しなさい。

____

____

問 3　Put ○ if the sentence is correct according to the passage, and put × if incorrect.

① The author thinks television gives a much better experience than the Internet does.　(　　)
② The author thinks the text transferred from an Internet source is quite desirable.　(　　)
③ One of the reasons the author likes books is that they're very compact for the amount of information they carry.　(　　)

Let's try　本文の表現を参考にしながら，次の日本語を英語にしなさい。

「人は言語を話せるという点で，他の動物とはまったく異なる。」　(ℓ. 1)

____

____

38 インターネット時代の印刷物の役割（2）[社会]

Not only has the art and craft of printing and making books been greatly improved over the centuries, but the great variety of subject matter now available in books is surprising, *to say the least. In fact, the Internet requires the constant entry of authors and their books to obtain the information that makes it a useful tool for research and learning.

Another important reason why the Internet will never replace books is because those who wish to become writers want to see their works permanently published as books — something you can hold, see, feel, look through, and read at your leisure without the need for an electric current apart from a lamp. The writer may use a computer instead of a pen and pad, but (1) <u>the finished product must eventually end up as a book if it is to have value to the reading public</u>. The writer may use the Internet in the course of researching a subject just as he may use a library for that purpose, but the end product will still be a book.

(178 words)

*to say the least「控えめに言っても」

日付　／　／

問 1　**Answer the questions below.**

(1)　**According to the author, what makes books so surprising?**

① Writers can make books a very useful tool for research and learning.
② The art and craft of printing and making books is excellent.
③ A great variety of subject matter is available in books.
④ Books don't require the constant entry of authors and their books.

(2)　**Why does the author think the Internet will never replace books?**

① The Internet consumes an electric current which costs a lot.
② People want something they can hold, feel, and read at leisure.
③ You can write in books with a pen whenever you like.
④ Writers usually depend on books in a library to research a subject.

問 2　**Put the underlined sentence (1) into Japanese.**

____

____

問 3　**Put ○ if the sentence is correct according to the passage, and put × if incorrect.**

① There are all kinds of books on a great many subjects available now. (　　　)
② The good thing about a book, according to the author, is that you can hold and feel it. (　　　)
③ The writer uses a library to research books for the Internet users. (　　　)

Let's try　本文の表現を参考にしながら，次の日本語を英語にしなさい。

「私のボーイフレンドは，私の誕生日を忘れただけでなく，忘れたことを謝りもしなかった。」 (ℓℓ. 1 ～ 2)

____

____

39 つらい経験について書くことの効用（1）［人間］

Why is it that many people who have suffered a major shock, such as divorce or the death of a family member, seem to be weaker against a variety of major and minor illnesses? One common idea among psychologists has been that (1) people could deal with suffering more effectively if they were able to understand and accept it. Indeed, many experts emphasize the value of expressing thoughts and feelings associated with upsetting events.

Recently, a team of medical researchers investigated the links between describing psychologically painful events and long-term health. In one experiment healthy college students were asked to write about either personally disturbing experiences or ordinary topics over a period of four days. In the months afterwards, students who had chosen to reveal their inner thoughts and feelings in their writing visited the health center for illness much less often than those who had written about everyday topics. (149 words)

Let's try 本文の表現を参考にしながら，次の日本語を英語にしなさい。

「トムが，今日は授業に遅れてきたのはいったいなぜだろう。」 (ℓ. 1)

問 1　**Answer the questions below.**

(1) **Why is expressing thoughts and feelings associated with upsetting events important?**

① It might make upsetting events less painful.
② It might prevent people from being more prone to become ill.
③ It might help people conceal their true feelings about such events.
④ It might help people understand the cause of such events.

(2) **Choose the most suitable word below to fill in the blanks（ア）―（ウ）. Write the number ① to ⑤ that corresponds to your answer.**

In one experiment healthy college students wrote about（　ア　）personally disturbing experiences or everyday topics. Some months later, it turned out that those who revealed their（　イ　）thoughts and feelings visited the health center for illness much（　ウ　）often than those who had written about ordinary topics.

① inner　② both　③ either　④ more　⑤ less

問 2　**Put the underlined sentence (1) into Japanese.**

問 3　**Put ○ if the sentence is correct according to the passage, and put × if incorrect.**

① People can deal with suffering more effectively if they don't understand it.　（　　）
② Medical researchers investigated how psychologically painful events would influence long-term health.　（　　）
③ Some psychologically troubled students were chosen for a research experiment.　（　　）

40 つらい経験について書くことの効用（2）［人間］

In an experiment that followed, another group of healthy students were given the four-day writing exercise. Some chose to write about highly personal and upsetting experiences (including loneliness, problems with family and friends, and death). When questioned immediately afterwards, they stated that they did not feel any better. However, their blood samples taken before and after the experiment showed evidence of an improved resistance to illness. The white cells that fight off bacteria and viruses had increased their reaction and sensitivity to these "invaders." This trend continued over the following six weeks, when another blood sample was taken. Individuals who showed the best results were those who wrote about topics that they had actively refrained from telling others about.

The researchers propose that failure to face up to painful experience can be a form of stress itself, and can increase the possibility of illness. (1) It follows, then, that actively dealing with a major shock makes possible its understanding and acceptance. The answer is not to suffer in silence. It may not always be possible to talk about personal problems, but writing them down will help the body to fight disease in the long run.

(194 words)

Let's try 本文の表現を参考にしながら，次の日本語を英語にしなさい。

「私が７時にお風呂に入っていると，突然明かりが消えた。」　（ℓ. 10）

日付　　／　／

問 1　**Answer the questions below.**

(1) **Which of the following is NOT true about the students who wrote about personal and upsetting experiences?**

① They realized their physical condition had become better.
② Their blood samples showed they had become more resistant to illness.
③ They didn't feel any better right after the writing exercise.
④ The reaction and sensitivity of their white cells had improved.

(2) **Which of the following is the suggestion from the researchers?**

① If you understand and accept your painful experience, you will deal with it actively.
② Unless you deal actively with a major shock, you will suffer in silence.
③ If you do not face up to painful experience, it may cause stress and make you more susceptible to illness.
④ Writing about your personal problems will help your body fight disease more effectively than talking about them.

問 2　**Put the underlined sentence (1) into Japanese.**

____

____

問 3　**Put ○ if the sentence is correct according to the passage, and put × if incorrect.**

① The students who had written about upsetting experiences said they felt much better.　(　　　)
② If you fail to face up to painful experience, you may face a greater possibility of illness.　(　　　)
③ If you talk or write about personal problems, it will help the body to fight disease.　(　　　)

41 テレビゲームの影響力（1）［社会］

"The impact of exposure to violent video games has not been studied as extensively as the impact of exposure to TV or movie violence," the researchers write in **Psychological Science in the Public Interest*. "However, on the whole, the results reported for video games to date are very similar to those obtained in the investigations of TV and movie violence." (1) <u>Among the effects of violent game playing are increases in *physiological arousal and physically aggressive behavior</u>, such as hitting, kicking, and pulling clothes or hair. Studies also have found a reduction in helpful behavior among youths exposed to violent video games.

Males tend to prefer action-oriented video games involving shooting, fighting, sports, action adventure, fantasy role-playing, and strategy, according to the Michigan State survey. Females prefer classic board games, trivia quizzes, puzzles, and arcade games. Electronic game playing gets young people involved with technologies and opens up opportunities in high-paying tech careers, notes communications professor Bradley Greenberg of Michigan State.

(160 words)

**Psychological Science in the Public Interest*：Association for Psychological Science（科学的心理学会：アメリカの学会）の解説論文誌

*physiological arousal「生理的な覚醒〔興奮〕」

問 1　Answer the questions below.

(1) **Which of the following is true about the impact of exposure to violent video games?**

① It has widely been studied but the results have not been reported yet.
② It is not so serious as the researchers are worried it is.
③ It shows about the same impact as exposure to TV or movie violence.
④ Youths exposed to violent video games showed more helpful behaviors than others.

(2) **Which of the following is true about video games boys or girls prefer?**

① Boys prefer adventure games to fantasy games.
② Boys prefer games associated with physical movement.
③ Girls prefer fantasy games to classical games.
④ Girls prefer games that need some knowledge or strategy.

問 2　Put the underlined sentence (1) into Japanese.

____

____

問 3　Put ○ if the sentence is correct according to the passage, and put × if incorrect.

① The impact of exposure to violent video games has long been studied. (　　　)
② Violent game playing increases physiological arousal and physically aggressive behavior. (　　　)
③ Professor Greenberg says that electronic game playing opens up opportunities in high-paying tech careers. (　　　)

Let's try　本文の表現を参考にしながら，次の日本語を英語にしなさい。

「彼の熱い思いが多くの人々をそのプロジェクトに関わらせた。」 (ℓ. 15)

____

____

"It is believed that these opportunities *accrue to boys because they spend more time working with electronic games and computers," says Greenberg. "If girls become more involved with technology at an early age, it is likely that the interest in technology will continue into the work world." (1) <u>If females do become more involved in technology fields, including game development, they may create less-violent games</u> that promote cooperation rather than aggression.

Video games are in 80% of U.S. homes with children; they generated $6 billion in 2000 and $11 billion by 2003. "All indications are that the industry will continue to grow at a healthy *clip," says Greenberg. "The emerging market is for games designed more with girls in mind that engage them for longer periods of time and force them to investigate more the technology behind the games. The next frontier involves transferring video game technology to educational settings and using the young people's fascination with the games to involve them more with innovative teaching technologies." Until that day comes, however, more awareness is needed of the impact of violent games on young people's behavior, *Anderson and his colleagues conclude.

(190 words)

*accrue「生じる；増加する」 *clip「速度」

*Anderson: アイオワ州立大学の心理学教授である Craig A. Anderson のこと

日付　／　／

問 1　**Answer the questions below.**

(1)　**According to Greenberg, which of the following is true?**

① Girls became more involved with technology at an early age.
② Boys will be less aggressive because of the new video games.
③ Girls may in the future create games that promote cooperation.
④ Both boys and girls will spend more time playing electronic games.

(2)　**Which of the following is NOT true about video games?**

① Video games generated almost double the amount of profit in 2003 than in 2000.
② Greenberg supposes the game industry will continue to grow.
③ Games in the future will be designed more for boys than for girls.
④ Video game technology will be used in the field of education.

問 2　**Put the underlined sentence (1) into Japanese.**

____

____

問 3　**Put ○ if the sentence is correct according to the passage, and put × if incorrect.**

① If females become more involved in game development, they may find a more efficient way of creating new games.　(　　　)
② Everything indicates that the video game industry will decline before long.　(　　　)
③ Anderson concludes that we should watch the impact of violent games on young people's behavior more carefully.　(　　　)

Let's try　本文の表現を参考にしながら，次の日本語を英語にしなさい。

「とてもテレビゲームに没頭していたので，時間が過ぎるのを忘れてたよ。」　(ℓ. 12)

____

____

43 真実を使ったうそ（1）［人間］

*Beware of those who deliberately use aspects of the truth to deceive you and others. When someone tells you something that is true, but intentionally leaves out important information that should be included for full *comprehension on your part to take place, they can create a false impression.

For example, an acquaintance might tell you, "I just won a hundred dollars in the state *lottery and it was fantastic when I took that one dollar ticket back to the store and turned it in for one hundred *bucks!" This woman's a winner, right? Maybe, maybe not. In fact, you later learn that she had purchased not one ticket but instead two hundred for this specific lottery — and only one of these a winner! Eventually, you realize this woman, who you thought was 'lucky' or 'fortunate' is, in fact, a huge loser. (1) Although she didn't say anything false, she clearly left out important information and likely did so on purpose. That's called a *half-truth which is not technically a lie, but it's just as dishonest. (174 words)

*beware「気をつける」 *comprehension「理解」 *lottery「（宝）くじ」 *buck「ドル」
*half-truth「一部だけが真実の話」

Let's try 本文の表現を参考にしながら，次の日本語を英語にしなさい。

「彼女に必要なのは，お金ではなく思いやりだ。」 (ℓ. 10)

____

____

日付　／　／

問 1　Answer the questions below.

(1) **According to the passage, how do people deceive you and others?**

① By unconsciously giving someone false information.
② By telling a lie which appears to be true.
③ By deliberately using aspects of the truth to uncover false information.
④ By telling the truth but deliberately cutting out important information.

(2) **The following is an example of deceit. Fill in the blanks（ア）―（ウ）with the correct set of numbers and words ①―④ below.**

A woman bought（　ア　）one-dollar tickets, one of（　イ　）turned out to be a winner. She got（　ウ　）dollars in return for that winning ticket. She just said that it was fantastic to have got（　ウ　）dollars, but actually she was a loser.

① ア：one hundred　イ：those　ウ：one hundred
② ア：one hundred　イ：those　ウ：two hundred
③ ア：two hundred　イ：which　ウ：one hundred
④ ア：two hundred　イ：which　ウ：two hundred

問 2　Put the underlined sentence (1) into Japanese.

____

____

問 3　Put ○ if the sentence is correct according to the passage, and put × if incorrect.

① Some people can deceive you by omitting important information from their story.　（　　　）
② The woman won more than she had spent on the state lottery.　（　　　）
③ The woman told the writer how many tickets she had bought.　（　　　）

44 真実を使ったうそ (2) [人間]

*Untrustworthy candidates in political campaigns often use such *deceptive communication strategies to trick voters into supporting them. Let's say that during Governor Smith's last term, her state lost one million jobs but gained three million new ones. Then she seeks another term in office and enters the election race. One of her opponents in that race subsequently begins a multimedia advertising campaign saying, "During Governor Smith's term, the state lost one million jobs!" (1) That is indeed true but, at the same time, it is intentionally deceptive. A more honest statement from her opponent would have been, "During Governor Smith's term, the state had a *net gain of two million jobs."

Advertisers sometimes use half-truths as well. Because it's illegal in many countries to openly make false claims about a product or service, some advertisers try to *mislead you with the truth. An ad might consequently *boast, "Nine out of ten doctors recommend Yucky Pills to cure nose *pimples." This is also a *factual statement but one which deliberately fails to mention that only ten doctors were asked about Yucky Pills and nine of these actually work for the Yucky Corporation.

(190 words)

*untrustworthy「信頼できない」 *deceptive「人をだますための」 *net「正味の」
*mislead「を誤解させる」 *boast「自慢する」 *pimple「吹き出物」 *factual「事実の」

Let's try 本文の表現を参考にしながら，次の日本語を英語にしなさい。

「彼女から一言あれば，問題の解決に役立ったでしょうに。」（ℓℓ. 9 ～ 10）

____

____

日付　　／　／

問 1　**Answer the questions below.**

(1)　**Which of the following is an example of an untrustworthy political strategy?**

① One governor said her state had lost one million jobs but gained three million new ones.

② One governor said her state had gained three million new jobs at the expense of one million jobs.

③ The governor's opponent said the state had lost one million jobs without mentioning the three million newly-gained jobs.

④ The governor's opponent said the state had gained three million new jobs in spite of the governor's poor political measures.

(2)　**How do advertisers use deceptive communication strategies?**

① By making false claims about a product or service.

② By boasting too much about the company's business performance.

③ By emphasizing the positive data without mentioning the negative.

④ By making the results of the research publicly available.

問 2　下線部 (1) を，**That** の内容を明確にして和訳しなさい。

____

____

問 3　**Put ○ if the sentence is correct according to the passage, and put × if incorrect.**

① Employment declined during Governor Smith's last term.　(　　　)

② We can accept as unbiased all ten doctors who were asked in Yucky Pill's ad about Yucky Pills.　(　　　)

③ It is not illegal to make half-true claims about a product or service.　(　　　)

45 個人主義と協調主義 [人間]

Have you ever noticed the different approaches people use to deal with problems? Some people, "individualists", generally try to work through problems on their own. Other people, "cooperators", tend to approach problem-solving as a group matter. Each approach has positive and negative points.

Individualists may often be the quickest to find an answer to a problem, and they tend to be willing to take responsibility. However, this approach is not perfect. They may be too committed to a particular position to be able to change their opinions. In this way, the individualists' approach may result in difficulties later.

Cooperators are valued as team members — in sports or school or work. (1) They tend to be flexible enough to recognize the importance of other points of view when problems arise. This approach, however, can take a long time, which may lead to delays in solving problems. Such difficulties sometimes cannot be avoided with the cooperators' approach.

We should learn to recognize the different approaches to dealing with problems. This knowledge can help us build smoother relations between people with different approaches to problem-solving.

(181 words)

日付　　／　　／

問 1　Answer the questions below.

(1) **Which of the following is true about individualists?**

① They take time and find the best answer to the problem.
② They sometimes find it difficult to change their opinions.
③ They don't mind what their position is.
④ They feel sorry about the difficulties their decision may cause.

(2) **Which of the following is true about cooperators?**

① They give weight to other people's opinions.
② They are too worried about various viewpoints to be flexible.
③ They are unwilling to take responsibility.
④ They take a long time and often fail to find the best answer.

問 2　Put the underlined sentence (1) into Japanese.

____

____

問 3　Put ○ if the sentence is correct according to the passage, and put × if incorrect.

① Individualists may often find an answer to a problem faster than cooperators. (　　　)
② Individualists tend to be willing to change their opinions. (　　　)
③ The cooperators' approach to dealing with problems can take a long time. (　　　)

Let's try 本文の表現を参考にしながら，次の日本語を英語にしなさい。

「この文字だと小さすぎて読めないかもしれない。」　(*ll*. 8 ～ 9)

____

____

46 テクノロジーは人間の職を奪うか（1）[科学]

In 1983, the Nobel Prize-winning economist Wassily Leontief highlighted the debate through a clever comparison of humans and horses. For many decades, horse labor appeared unaffected by technological change. (1) Even as railroads replaced the *stagecoach and the *Conestoga wagon, the U.S. horse population grew seemingly without end. The animals were vital not only on farms but also in the country's rapidly growing urban centers. But then, with the introduction and spread of the powerful and efficient engine, (2) the trend was rapidly reversed. As engines found their way into automobiles in the city and tractors in the countryside, horses became largely irrelevant. Then, the question is whether a similar outcome is possible for human labor. Are autonomous machines and supercomputers indicating a coming wave of technological progress that will finally sweep humans out of the economy? For Leontief, the answer was yes. However, he missed a number of important points. Humans, fortunately, are not horses and remain an important part of the economy. (162 words)

*stagecoach「駅馬車（各主要都市間を定期的に運行した馬車）」
*Conestoga wagon「大型ほろ馬車」

問 1　Answer the questions below.

(1) Which of the following is the closest to the meaning of (2) the trend was rapidly reversed?

① The railroads soon became the trend of the times.
② Other animals had rapidly taken the place of engines in the early 19th century.
③ At first, horse labor wasn't so rapidly affected by technological change.
④ The use of horse labor rapidly decreased both on farms and in the cities.

(2) What is the question the author mentions in the passage?

① whether or not technological progress will be a coming wave
② whether or not human labor might become unnecessary in the future
③ whether or not machines and supercomputers would be autonomous
④ whether or not mechanical horses would replace live ones

問 2　Put the underlined sentence (1) into Japanese.

____

____

問 3　Put ○ if the sentence is correct according to the passage, and put × if incorrect.

① Wassily Leontief was commended for the comparison of humans and horses. (　　　)
② Horse labor was rapidly affected by the powerful and efficient engine. (　　　)
③ Leontief would have agreed that autonomous machines and supercomputers will sweep humans out of the economy. (　　　)

Let's try 本文の表現を参考にしながら，次の日本語を英語にしなさい。

「問題は，リョウタが私たちにうそをついていたのかどうかだ。」（ℓ. 11）

____

47 テクノロジーは人間の職を奪うか（2）［科学］

Alfred Marshall, a British economist, in his foundational 1890 book, Principles of Economics, said, "Human wants and desires are countless in number and very various in kind." Ever since Marshall, people have linked unlimited wants to full employment. After all, who else but workers will be able to fulfill all those wants and desires? We humans are a deeply social species, and the desire for human connections carries over to our economic lives. We come together to appreciate human expression or ability when we attend plays and sporting events. Regular customers often visit particular restaurants, not only because of the food and drink, but because of the hospitality offered. In these cases, human interaction is central to the economic *transaction, not *incidental to it. Humans have economic wants that can be satisfied only by other humans, and (1) that makes us deny that we will go the way of the horse. (150 words)

*transaction「取引」 *incidental「偶発的な」

Let's try 本文の表現を参考にしながら，次の日本語を英語にしなさい。

「自身の努力だけでなく，家族の援助のおかげで，彼はビジネスで成功した。」 (ℓ. 10)

問 1　Answer the questions below.

(1) Which of the following is the idea of Alfred Marshall?

① Human wants and desires are so many that we cannot deal with all of them.
② Human beings cannot link unlimited wants, and so we need machines.
③ Human beings have tried to ensure all the employment for themselves.
④ Human beings alone can fulfill the countless number of human wants and desires.

(2) Which of the following is the main conclusion of the passage?

① Alfred Marshall made the correct assumption about human wants and desires.
② Economic transaction in the future will continue to center on human interaction.
③ All of us are aware that human beings alone can satisfy other humans' economic wants.
④ We need to come together to appreciate human expression or ability from now on.

問 2　下線部 (1) を，主語の **that** が指す内容を明確にして和訳しなさい。

____

____

問 3　Put ○ if the sentence is correct according to the passage, and put × if incorrect.

① Alfred Marshall wrote in his book that there was no end to human wants and desires. (　　　)
② Even in plays and sporting events, there may be no need for human interaction in the future. (　　　)
③ Even regular customers might stop visiting particular restaurants if those restaurants should replace human employees with robots. (　　　)

You are on your way to a concert. At an intersection, you encounter a group of people, all staring at the sky. Without even thinking about it, you look upwards, too. Why? *Social proof.* In the middle of the concert, when the *soloist is giving an excellent performance, someone begins to clap and suddenly the whole room joins in. You do, too. Why? *Social proof.* After the concert you go to the coat check to pick up your coat. You watch how the people in front of you place a coin on a plate, even though, officially, the service is included in the ticket price. What do you do? You probably leave a coin as well. Why? *Social proof.*

Social proof, sometimes roughly termed the *herd instinct*, dictates that individuals feel they are behaving correctly when they act the same as other people. In other words, if a large number of people follow a certain idea, others will find this idea truer or better. And (1) <u>the more people who display a certain behavior, the more appropriate others will judge it</u>. This is, of course, ridiculous. Social proof is the evil behind economic bubbles and stock market panic. It exists in fashion, management techniques, hobbies, religion and diets. In some cases, it can even negatively affect whole cultures.

(217 words)

*soloist「ソリスト；独奏者」

日付　／　／

問 1　**Answer the questions below.**

(1)　**Which of the following is NOT an example of so-called "*social proof*"?**

① You will join in if someone begins clapping at a concert.
② You will cross at a red light when there is no traffic.
③ You will leave a tip at a restaurant if other people leave one.
④ You will follow people's gaze if they are facing in the same direction.

(2)　**Which of the following is an example of the evil behind the so-called "*herd instinct*"?**

① You will plead your friend's innocence if your other classmates blame him.
② The *herd instinct* is what causes stock market panic.
③ We tend to worry about what to wear when invited to a party.
④ The *herd instinct* can deceive people during campaigns in an election.

問 2　**Put the underlined sentence (1) into Japanese.**

____

____

問 3　**Put ○ if the sentence is correct according to the passage, and put × if incorrect.**

① You will look upwards when people around you all look upward.　(　　　)
② You will clap at the concert only when you really appreciate the performance of the musician.　(　　　)
③ Social proof is sometimes wrongly termed the herd instinct.　(　　　)

Let's try　本文の表現を参考にしながら，次の日本語を英語にしなさい。

「人々が緊急事態にどう振る舞うかを見てみましょう。」　(*ll*. 7 ～ 8)

____

____

49 群集心理（2）［人間］

A simple experiment carried out in the 1950s by legendary psychologist Solomon Asch shows how common sense is influenced by peer pressure, the tendency to want to act the same as the members of one's social group. In Asch's experiment, a research participant is shown a line drawn on paper, and next to it three lines — numbered 1, 2 and 3 — one shorter, one longer and one of the same length as the original one. The participant must indicate which of the three lines corresponds to the original one. If that participant is alone in the room, he gives correct answers — unsurprising, because the task is really quite simple. Now five other people enter the room; (1) <u>they are all actors, a fact that the participant does not know</u>. One after another, they give wrong answers, saying "number 1," although it's very clear that number 3 is the correct answer. Then it is the participant's turn again. In one third of cases, he will answer incorrectly to match the other people's responses. Why do we act like this?

(177 words)

Let's try 本文の表現を参考にしながら，次の日本語を英語にしなさい。

「生徒たちは先生に選択科目（the optional subjects）のどれをとるつもりかを伝えなければならない。」 （ℓ.8）

____

____

日付　／　／

問 1　Answer the questions below.

(1) **Choose the most suitable word below to fill in the blanks (ア) — (エ). Write the number ① to ⑥ that corresponds to your answer.**

In an experiment, a participant can give (　ア　) answers when alone in the room. But with (　イ　) people in the room, in one case out of (　ウ　) he gives a (　エ　) answer when those people choose the wrong answer.

① another　② other　③ two　④ three　⑤ correct　⑥ wrong

(2) **Which of the following is true about Asch's experiment?**

① A research participant is shown 4 lines of different length.
② The five other participants are all good at acting because they are professional actors.
③ Some of the research participants answer incorrectly when others indicate the wrong answer.
④ Asch carefully chooses the questions he gives to the research participants.

問 2　下線部 (1) を，**they** が何を指すかを明確にして和訳しなさい。

____

____

問 3　Put ◯ if the sentence is correct according to the passage, and put × if incorrect.

① The experiment carried out by Solomon Asch reveals people's desire to be free from peer pressure. (　　　)
② Five other people are told to make intentional mistakes in Ash's experiment. (　　　)
③ In Asch's experiment, the research participant is given such a simple question that there is little possibility of his making a mistake. (　　　)

50 群集心理（3）[人間]

In the past, following others was a good survival strategy. Suppose that 50,000 years ago, you were travelling in the wild with your *hunter-gatherer friends, and suddenly they all fled at the sight of an animal. What would you have done? Would you have remained still, wondering about what you were looking at? Was it a lion, or something that just looked like a lion but was in fact a harmless animal? No, you would have followed your friends. Later on, when you were safe, you could have reflected on what the "lion" had actually been. Those who acted differently from the group did not pass their genes on to the later generations. We are directly descended from those who copied the others' behavior. This pattern is so deeply rooted in us that we still use it today, even when it offers no survival advantage, which is most of the time. (1) <u>Only a few cases come to mind where social proof is of value.</u> For example, if you find yourself hungry in a foreign city and don't know a good restaurant, it makes sense to pick the one that's full of local people. In other words, you copy the local people's behavior.

Comedy and talk shows make use of social proof by inserting sounds of people laughing at key moments, encouraging the audience to laugh along. (226 words)

*hunter-gatherer「狩猟採集民（の）」

日付　／　／

問 1　Answer the questions below.

(1)　Why did people in the past follow others?

① It was a good strategy to survive.
② They had to follow the leader of the group.
③ They had to pass their genes on to later generations.
④ Most of them could not decide by themselves what to do.

(2)　Which of the following is true about social proof?

① You must reflect on it after you follow it.
② It is deeply set in our genes and we still tend to follow it.
③ We still use social proof because we know it offers us a survival advantage.
④ Social proof is now a good strategy for a talk show audience.

問 2　Put the underlined sentence (1) into Japanese.

____

____

問 3　Put ○ if the sentence is correct according to the passage, and put × if incorrect.

① In the past, social proof was an indispensable survival strategy. (　　)
② When ancient people found later that they need not have followed others, they were sometimes disappointed. (　　)
③ Nowadays there are few cases where social proof is needed to survive. (　　)

Let's try　本文の表現を参考にしながら，次の日本語を英語にしなさい。

「君がエリのプレゼントにこの本を選ぶのは賢明だね。」　(ℓ. 16)

____

____

51 ゴミ0への挑戦（1）［環境］

Can we create a waste-free society? It would seem like an ideal goal to realize, since mass production has forced a shift in our way of living. (1) <u>Clothes have become 'fast fashion,' worn once and then thrown away like a finished bag of potato chips.</u> Sure, most people will recycle their cans and bottles, but that doesn't alter the fact that we are still throwing away pounds and pounds of waste every day. That will never change in a world where convenience is appreciated over all else. (2) will it?

Kamikatsu, a small town in Tokushima Prefecture, had been working for years to reduce waste. However, when they learned about zero-waste philosophy, an idea popped into the residents' minds: to become the first zero-waste town in Japan. The town doesn't collect domestic waste; instead the residents bring their waste to the waste collection site. There, they sort it into 45 very specific and detailed categories. Although some common stuff cannot be recycled, Kamikatsu has been able to recycle more than 80% of its waste. Kamikatsu is also encouraging residents to reuse goods. An area of its waste collection site offers used stuff for free. (194 words)

日付　／　／

問 1　**Answer the questions below.**

(1)　**Choose the most suitable answer from those below to fill in (　2　).**

① Or
② So
③ Still
④ Then

(2)　**Why did Kamikatsu decide to become a zero-waste town?**

① Because another zero-waste town at that time seemed attractive.
② Because it had been successfully reducing waste.
③ Because it had suffered from too much waste.
④ Because the residents were inspired by zero-waste philosophy.

問 2　**Put the underlined sentence (1) into Japanese.**

____

____

問 3　**Put ○ if the sentence is correct according to the passage, and put × if incorrect.**

① We are throwing away a lot of waste in pursuit of convenience.　(　　　)
② In Kamikatsu, the residents take turns collecting domestic waste instead of the town.　(　　　)
③ Kamikatsu sells used stuff at its waste collection site.　(　　　)

Let's try　本文の表現を参考にしながら，次の日本語を英語にしなさい。

「私は入浴中にいい考えをふと思いつくことが多い。」　(ℓ. 11)

____

____

(1)Recycling and reusing, however, are not enough to keep our world from becoming swallowed up in waste. Kamikatsu also makes an effort to get people to brush up their understanding of the environment and make society as a whole think 'why?' Why are you buying or selling the product? Is it good for the environment? (2)Will it become a favorite possession or will it be thrown away after one use? Whereas before some believed they had a sacred right to buy or produce whatever they desired, now they realize that their actions affect the world around them.

In recent years, Kamikatsu built a complex facility called the Zero Waste Center. A hotel located in the grounds of this facility is run on the understanding that creating a waste-free society applies not only to individuals, but also to businesses. (　3　), instead of offering an individual soap bar to each guest, it encourages them to cut off the amount of soap they need at the front desk. Fitting into a new strategy is not easy, but through its actions, Kamikatsu is leading the nation in finding ways to gain the prize of a truly waste-free society. (195 words)

問 1　Answer the questions below.

(1) **What is the purpose of the question on the underline (2)?**

① To encourage consumers to avoid buying unnecessary goods.
② To encourage consumers to get the most useful product.
③ To make consumers decide what their favorites are.
④ To push consumers to consider living with few possessions.

(2) **Choose the most suitable answer from those below to fill in (3).**

① In short
② For example
③ In addition
④ In contrast

問 2　Put the underlined sentence (1) into Japanese.

____

____

問 3　Put ○ if the sentence is correct according to the passage, and put × if incorrect.

① Some people have changed their opinions about purchase and production. (　　)
② People can stay the night at the Zero Waste Center. (　　)
③ Kamikatsu is becoming a role model in achieving a waste-free society. (　　)

Let's try 本文の表現を参考にしながら，次の日本語を英語にしなさい。

「ジェーン（Jane）はいつも難しい話題をわかりやすく説明するよう努めている。」 (ℓ. 3)

____

____

53 クローン技術の是非（1）[科学]

A basic rule of medical science is that no human life should be used for the benefit of another. Some people are against human cloning and related techniques for this reason. In cloning, an egg cell is used to develop ordinary cells. The opponents of cloning insist that this is killing, because it destroys the potential of the egg to develop into a human being.

Other people oppose cloning because at this stage it is unreliable. In animal experiments, for example, success rates are very low. Still others are concerned about the future that cloning might bring about. (1) <u>They are afraid that cloning will lead to the production of human beings for body parts.</u> They also fear that cloning might lead to attempts to create "superior" humans. (127 words)

日付　／　／

問 1　**Answer the questions below.**

(1) **Which of the following is NOT true about cloning?**

① No human life should be used to someone else's advantage.
② Some people don't accept human cloning at this stage.
③ Human egg cells are now being used to develop ordinary cells.
④ Cloning prevents the egg from developing into a human being.

(2) **Which of the following is a concern for people opposed to cloning?**

① Producing practically useful cloning technology will be very expensive.
② The value of the role that animal experimentation plays in cloning is questionable.
③ Through cloning human beings might be created in order to produce human body parts.
④ Cloning technology might promote body modification.

問 2　**Put the underlined sentence (1) into Japanese.**

問 3　**Put ◯ if the sentence is correct according to the passage, and put × if incorrect.**

① Medical science basically admits that human life must be used for the benefit of others. (　　　)
② Through cloning, an egg cell reaches its potential to turn into a human being. (　　　)
③ The success rates in experiments are so low that some people doubt the reliability of cloning. (　　　)

Let's try 本文の表現を参考にしながら，次の日本語を英語にしなさい。

「あなたはその計画に賛成ですか，それとも反対ですか。」　(ℓ. 2)

Not everyone is against human cloning, however. Some people support cloning if it is for the purpose of medical treatment, although they oppose the cloning of babies. The medical benefits of cloning and related techniques, they argue, could be huge. For example, if a heart can be developed from a patient's own cell, the body will not reject it. Furthermore, (1) he or she will not have to wait for someone to die to get a new heart.

Supporters claim that the use of such techniques is not killing. Just as ordinary store-bought eggs do not develop into chickens, the eggs used for cloning do not develop into human beings by themselves. They also argue that it is already practically impossible to stop a patient from receiving medical treatment that in some way depends on cloning and related techniques. Even if one country bans cloning, there will always be another country that promotes it. The supporters, therefore, maintain that scientists should have the freedom to experiment and that people should have the freedom to seek lifesaving treatments. In other words, they feel that cloning should be continued unless it is clearly shown to be harmful. The debate over this issue is likely to go on for some time. (207 words)

問 1　Answer the questions below.

(1) **Which of the following is NOT mentioned as a medical benefit of cloning?**

① We can develop an organ from a patient's own cell.
② Almost any kind of organ can be developed by cloning.
③ An organ developed from the patient's own cell will not be rejected after transplantation.
④ Patients won't have to wait for someone to die to get an organ.

(2) **Which of the following is NOT a claim made by supporters of organ cloning?**

① The use of techniques for developing an organ from a patient's own cell is not killing.
② A human egg cell never develops into a human beings.
③ It is not preferable to prevent scientists from using cloning techniques.
④ Cloning should be continued so long as it is not harmful to anyone.

問 2　下線部 (1) を，**he or she** が誰を指すかを明確にして和訳しなさい。

____

____

問 3　Put ○ if the sentence is correct according to the passage, and put × if incorrect.

① There are people who support human cloning. (　　　)
② The eggs people might use for cloning automatically turn into human beings in time. (　　　)
③ Supporters of the cloning of organs claim that scientists should be able to experiment freely. (　　　)

Let's try　本文の表現を参考にしながら，次の日本語を英語にしなさい。

「クラスの全員がその計画に賛成しているわけではない。」　(ℓ. 1)

____

55 ビタミンAの重要性とサツマイモ（1）[科学]

(1) <u>HarvestPlus, an agricultural research organization, is teaching people around the world how to grow what it calls "smart" crops.</u> Its project in Mozambique is having surprising effects. In 2006, HarvestPlus workers provided orange sweet potato plants to people in 24 villages in Mozambique. The workers taught these people how to grow the vegetables. They also explained the importance of Vitamin A to staying healthy.

Farmers in Mozambique had been planting white and yellow sweet potatoes, not the orange-colored ones. The white and yellow potatoes have very little Vitamin A. However, one small, orange sweet potato has a full day's supply of Vitamin A. A lack of Vitamin A is dangerous. Without enough Vitamin A, you face an increased risk of getting a serious disease or dying from infections.

The World Health Organization (WHO) reports that around the world, 190 million young children are not getting enough of this important vitamin in the foods they eat.

Economist Alan de Brauw is with the International Food Policy Research Institute and was involved with the project. He says about 70 percent of children there were Vitamin A deficient. They were not getting enough Vitamin A.

"About 70% of kids under the age of five were Vitamin A deficient. So, you have this huge need for new solutions. If you can do something through agriculture to increase the amount of vitamin in the diet... you're in much better shape because that's much more sustainable" than using vitamin supplements. (244 words)

問 1　**Which of the following is true about the project in which Alan de Brauw got involved?**

① His project could save 70 percent of children who were Vitamin A deficient.

② His project needs to be reconsidered in order to make it more sustainable.

③ His project helped raise the income of the farmers and lower the risk of disease.

④ His project will be of great benefit in reducing the risk of serious disease or infection in Mozambique.

問 2　**Put the underlined sentence (1) into Japanese.**

____

____

問 3　**Put ○ if the sentence is correct according to the passage, and put × if incorrect.**

① Before 2006, farmers in Mozambique had preferred the taste of white and yellow sweet potatoes to orange ones.　(　　　)

② Alan de Brauw is a staff member of the International Food Policy Research Institute.　(　　　)

③ About 70 percent of children in Mozambique were suffering from a shortage of Vitamin A.　(　　　)

Let's try　本文の表現を参考にしながら，次の日本語を英語にしなさい。

「私たちはお祭りで子供たちに温かいスープを提供した。」　(ℓ. 4)

____

____

56 ビタミンAの重要性とサツマイモ（2）[科学]

Anne Herforth, an expert on global food security and nutrition, calls supplements a short-term "solution to a more fundamental problem, which is people not having access to high-quality diets."

Mr. de Brauw says the potatoes had a surprising effect on the health of children. At the end of the three-year study, the researchers compared the health of children in villages growing orange sweet potatoes with those not growing them.

Children living in the sweet potato villages had 40% fewer cases of *diarrhea than other boys and girls. Among children under the age of three, the difference was 50%. According to Mr. de Brauw showing the effect of a food-growing project on health is very important, or as he says, "a big deal."

"This is a big deal because nobody has shown in the past that an agricultural production intervention can have big health impacts ... *any* health impacts."

Experts say that teaching farmers how to grow healthier food is one of the best ways to improve health. Ms. Herfoth says (1) <u>the findings do a good job making the link between food production and health.</u> It's important to show that if "you produce a food and it's available to people to eat and they like it, then it does good things for health."

HarvestPlus is now helping farmers in other countries. In India, the group is helping farmers grow iron-rich *millet. And in Bangladesh, it is helping farmers grow high-*zinc rice. (239 words)

*diarrhea「下痢」 *millet「キビ」 *zinc「亜鉛」

問 1　According to Anne Herforth, which of the following is a fundamental problem?

① Many farmers are reluctant to grow healthier food because they don't know how.
② Many people don't have enough knowledge about the nutrition in food.
③ People have difficulty getting healthy high-quality food on a day-to-day basis.
④ Vitamin supplements are just a short-term solution to a health problem.

問 2　下線部 (1) を，**the findings** の内容を明確にして和訳しなさい。

____

____

問 3　Put ○ if the sentence is correct according to the passage, and put × if incorrect.

① Almost all kinds of potatoes had a surprising effect on the health of children.　(　　)
② In the orange sweet potato villages, children under the age of three were 50% less likely to suffer from a certain health problem.　(　　)
③ All the farmers in some Asian countries are now aware of the importance of producing healthy food.　(　　)

Let's try　本文の表現を参考にしながら，次の日本語を英語にしなさい。

「私たちは都会にある学校と郊外にある学校の環境を比較した。」(ll. 6～7)

____

____

57 ダイエットに関する意外な論文（1）[人間]

No more TV dinners, no more snacking with Paul McCartney on the kitchen stereo and certainly no listening to the more intellectual bits of Radio 4 over breakfast. If you want to lose weight, the best accompaniment to a meal is the sound of your own chewing, a study suggests. Psychologists in the US have found that people consume less food when they can hear themselves eating. They believe the effect to be so powerful that even simply telling somebody that they are eating a crunchy snack makes them eat less. In a considerable benefit to those who cannot get through a packet of crisps without making the noise of a small gunfight, experiments show that the more people concentrate on the noise of their meal, the less they eat and they think the flavours are more intense.

Gina Mohr, assistant professor of marketing at Colorado State University, said the findings suggested that people who wanted to diet could cut down on distracting sounds. In one experiment, Dr Mohr and a colleague asked 71 students to sit in a room with a bowl of ten pretzels while wearing a pair of headphones. (1) <u>Half of the participants had their ears flooded with white noise, *drowning out the sound of their chewing.</u> They ate an average of four pretzels each. The other half, who were able to hear themselves eat much more distinctly, took 2.8 each. (234 words)

*drown out ～「～をかき消す」

問 1　Which of the following is true about the sound of your own chewing?

① It is the best accompaniment to a meal if you want to enjoy it.
② It has such a powerful effect that you want to tell somebody that you are eating something.
③ It makes you lose your appetite because it prevents you from concentrating on the food you want to enjoy.
④ It is helpful in cutting the amount of food you eat and letting you experience the flavours of the food more intensely.

問 2　Put the underlined sentence (1) into Japanese.

____

____

問 3　Put ○ if the sentence is correct according to the passage, and put × if incorrect.

① Listening to Radio 4 over breakfast is helpful if you want to lose weight. (　　)
② Psychologists in the US have found that those who can hear the sound of their own chewing eat more than those who cannot. (　　)
③ If you tell somebody that they are eating something that makes a noise, they will eat less. (　　)

Let's try 本文の表現を参考にしながら，次の日本語を英語にしなさい。

「子供たちはテレビゲームをして過ごす時間が多ければ多いほど，友達と遊ぶ時間が少なくなる。」　(*ll*. 10 ～ 12)

____

____

58 ダイエットに関する意外な論文（2）［人間］

The marketing psychologists also sat 156 undergraduates down in a room with eight baked crackers made from *pitta bread. One group read a piece of paper that said: “Our pitta crackers deliver the crunch you *crave. You’ll love the crispy sound of each bite.” They each ate an average of one fewer than the other group, who were shown an instruction that emphasised the taste instead.

The researchers believe that food manufacturers have long understood this phenomenon. When the company behind the Magnum brand of ice creams changed their chocolate coating to stop it slipping off the bar, they *were inundated with complaints. (1) It eventually emerged that people had largely been buying the bars precisely because they liked the brittleness of the chocolate and crackling noise it made when they ate it.

“To our knowledge, this relationship had not been examined in existing research despite the importance that food sound has in the consumer environment,” the authors wrote in the journal Food Quality and Preference.

(165 words)

*pitta bread「ピタパン（トルコなどでよく食べられる平焼きパン）」
*crave「をとても強く望む」 *be inundated with ～「～が殺到する」

Let's try 本文の表現を参考にしながら，次の日本語を英語にしなさい。

「悪天候だったにもかかわらず，リサは休暇を楽しんだようだ。」（ℓ. 15）

____

____

問 1 **Answer the questions below.**

(1) **Which of the following did the study mentioned in the passage suggest?**

① Consumers prefer pitta crackers because they are crunchy.

② Consumers loved the crispy sound the food made even more when they were told pitta crackers were crunchy.

③ Consumers who were told their pitta crackers made a crispy sound ate fewer than those who were not told.

④ Consumers put more emphasis on the taste of food than on the sound it makes.

(2) **Why did the company making Magnum ice creams receive a lot of complaints?**

① The chocolate coating needed improvement to stick more to the bar.

② The consumers had difficulty in eating the ice cream without making a crackling noise.

③ The improved chocolate coating wasn't as brittle and crispy as the one before the improvement.

④ The consumers didn't like the chocolate coating which easily slipped off the bar.

問 2 **Put the underlined sentence (1) into Japanese.**

____

____

問 3 **Put ○ if the sentence is correct according to the passage, and put × if incorrect.**

① Undergraduates preferred tasty crackers over crispy ones. (　　　)

② The company behind the Magnum brand of ice creams improved their products by referring to consumer feedback. (　　　)

③ How food sound affects consumer choice has not been fully examined so far. (　　　)

59 家族で食事をすることの重要性（1）[社会]

When it comes to eating, the United States has a lesson to learn from France. I'm not talking about the kind of elaborate dinners Americans often associate with the French. Many of the meals the French eat are quick and simple. The difference is that the French eat together. (1) They have managed to preserve a tradition that is good for everyone's health — the family meal.

According to the French government's Committee for Health Education, 75 percent of the French eat dinner together as a family and many French schoolchildren still go home for lunch.

These figures haven't changed much in decades. In the United States, on the other hand, national studies show that on average, only one family in three sits down for dinner together on a daily basis. Over the last two decades, there has been a steady decline in the number of American families that eat together regularly. It looks like the family meal is disappearing. (158 words)

問 1　**Answer the questions below.**

(1) **Which of the following is NOT a lesson the United States can learn from France?**

① The French cook elaborate dinners for their family.
② The French eat quick and simple meals but they eat together.
③ The French still preserve the tradition of the family meal.
④ Many French parents have their schoolchildren come home for lunch.

(2) **Choose the most suitable word to fill in the blank（ア）―（ウ）. Write the number ① to ⑥ that corresponds to your answer.**

In the United States, only（　ア　）of families sit down for dinner together. Over the last（　イ　）years, there has been a steady（　ウ　）in the number of American families that eat together regularly.

① increase	② twenty-four	③ decrease
④ one-third	⑤ shortage	⑥ twenty

問 2　下線部 (1) を，**They** が何を指すかを明確にして和訳しなさい。

問 3　**Put ○ if the sentence is correct according to the passage, and put × if incorrect.**

① One lesson that the United States should learn from France is the benefit of eating meals together.　（　　）
② Statistics show that only half of all French families eat dinner together.　（　　）
③ The number of American families that regularly eat together has increased steadily over the last two decades.　（　　）

Let's try　本文の表現を参考にしながら，次の日本語を英語にしなさい。

「今にも雨が降り出しそうだ。」　（ll. 14 ～ 15）

60 家族で食事をすることの重要性（2）［社会］

How and why did the family meal start to disappear in the United States? My friends in the United States have various explanations why meals together aren't an option for their families. Parents and children lead *hectic lives and there just isn't time for a sit-down meal. Kids' sports schedules run on into dinner hour. After a long day at work, parents are too tired to cook. Teenagers are off on their own after school. "Everyone likes different foods," they say, "so what is the point of eating together?"

Yet study after study shows that having meals together as a family is good for both adults and children. A University of Michigan study found that mealtime at home was the single strongest factor predicting better achievement scores and fewer behavioral problems for children. Mealtime was far more powerful than time spent in school, studying, worshiping, playing sports or doing arts activities.

Other studies show that children like family meals. In one report, (1) <u>nearly four-fifths of adolescents cited eating dinner at home as one of their top-rated family activities.</u> In a national YMCA poll in 2000, when teenagers were asked about their worries, 21 percent rated "not having enough time with parents" as their top concern. (205 words)

*hectic「大忙しの」

問 1　Which of the following best fits to fill in the blank below?

(1) **The family meal started to disappear in the United States because (　　　).**

① both parents and children are too busy to find time to eat at home
② schoolchildren have to take part in sports after school
③ parents are tired of cooking dinner
④ teenagers prefer to spend time with their friends rather than with their family

(2) **Studies show that having meals together as a family is good for everyone because (　　　).**

① it keeps children from causing trouble
② it is the most popular family achievement for everyone
③ it is a strong factor for better school achievement and behavior
④ it is more enjoyable than playing sports or doing arts activities

問 2　Put the underlined sentence (1) into Japanese.

____

____

問 3　Put ○ if the sentence is correct according to the passage, and put × if incorrect.

① In the US parents and children say they are too busy for a sit-down meal.　(　　　)
② Time spent in school is a more powerful factor in academic achievement than mealtime at home.　(　　　)
③ Nearly eighty percent of young people like to eat dinner at home.　(　　　)

Let's try　本文の表現を参考にしながら，次の日本語を英語にしなさい。

「卒業後の進路（course）について親と十分に話し合う時間がもてていない。」　(*ll*. 19 ～ 20)

____

61 スーパーの便利さと運搬燃料（1）［環境］

A modern supermarket is a thing of wonder. Even if it's snowing outside and summer is a distant memory, you can buy strawberries, peaches or grapes. If you want root vegetables in the middle of a *heatwave, you can have them. *Ex-pat Americans can have their Oreo cookies, while homesick New Zealanders can *console themselves with wine and kiwi fruit. Within days of being picked off the *vines, the fruit is in your *trolley, tasting of spring as the leaves are falling outside.

It's all great until you start *contemplating (1) the vast *mileage sitting in your shopping basket. Those kiwi fruits have travelled nearly 20,000 kilometers — or 12,000 miles. They've flown in a plane and travelled by road. (2) By the time they reach the supermarket, they're responsible for five times their own weight in greenhouse gases being pumped into the atmosphere. Increasingly, our food is coming from further and further away, and we're becoming more and more dependent on the fuel it takes to get them to us. (168 words)

*heatwave「熱波」 *ex-pat「国外在住の」 *console「を元気づける」 *vine「蔓（つる）」
*trolley「ショッピングカート」 *contemplate「をじっくり考える」
*mileage「総走行〔飛行〕マイル数」

Let's try 本文の表現を参考にしながら，次の日本語を英語にしなさい。

「ここから広島まで行くのにかかるガソリンを手に入れる必要がある。」

(ℓ. 15)

日付　／　／

問 1　**Answer the questions below.**

(1)　**Why does the writer describe a modern supermarket as a thing of wonder?**

① People can buy foods regardless of where they live and what season it is.

② People can get any kind of foods in all kinds of weather.

③ Americans can buy Oreo cookies even in a local supermarket.

④ New Zealanders can find wine and kiwi fruit on the same shelf.

(2)　**What kind of problem does (1) the vast mileage cause?**

① More and more people want to eat tropical fruits wherever they live.

② Some fruits must be transported either by plane or by road.

③ Some vegetables must be grown in a greenhouse to be transported long distances.

④ Huge amounts of fuel are used to transport fruit and vegetables long distances.

問 2　**Put the underlined sentence (2) into Japanese.**

____

____

問 3　**Put ○ if the sentence is correct according to the passage, and put × if incorrect.**

① Homesick New Zealanders cheer themselves up by picking kiwi fruits off the vines.　(　　　)

② The further away the food comes from, the more agricultural chemicals it includes.　(　　　)

③ By transporting a variety of food, we emit greenhouse gases because we consume a lot of fuel.　(　　　)

62 スーパーの便利さと運搬燃料（2）［環境］

This dependence was illustrated very clearly during the September 2000 fuel price protests in Britain. Inspired by similar actions in France, a group of farmers and *lorry drivers decided to *blockade the Stanlow oil *refinery in Cheshire. The protest quickly *snowballed, and *petrol tankers were unable to leave refineries. (1) Panic buying saw more than 90 per cent of petrol stations run dry. And with supplies unable to get through, supermarket shelves quickly emptied.

It's estimated that food now accounts for as much as 40 per cent of all UK road *freight, and the international food trade is increasing faster than the world's population and food production. In other words, food is moving around more than ever, and the environmental impact could be huge.

Despite the UK's cool climate being perfectly suited for growing apples, nearly three-quarters of the apples eaten in the UK are imported, and more than 60 per cent of Britain's apple *orchards have been destroyed in the past 30 years. We're now putting more energy into transporting some crops than we get out of eating them. For every calorie of lettuce imported to the UK from America's west coast, 127 calories of fuel are used. Put it another way: flying over a kilogram of Californian lettuce uses enough energy to keep a 100-watt light bulb glowing for eight days. (222 words)

*lorry「トラック」 *blockade「を封鎖する」 *refinery「精製所」
*snowball「雪だるま式に〔加速度的に〕増える」 *petrol「ガソリン」
*freight「運送貨物」 *orchard「果樹園」

日付　／　／

問 1　**Answer the questions below.**

(1)　**What happened in September 2000 in Britain? Put the sentences（ア）—（ウ）in chronological order.**

（ア）Most petrol stations ran out of stock because of panic buying.
（イ）Consumer goods disappeared from the supermarket shelves.
（ウ）Fuel price protests made oil refineries unable to supply fuel.

(2)　**Which of the following is the main conclusion of the passage?**

① Food now accounts for too large a part of all UK road freight.
② More than 60 per cent of Britain's apple orchards have been destroyed in the past three decades.
③ Transportation of food has a huge environmental impact.
④ We're putting as much energy into transporting crops as we get out of them.

問 2　**Put the underlined sentence (1) into Japanese.**

____

____

問 3　**Put ◯ if the sentence is correct according to the passage, and put × if incorrect.**

① During the protest, more than 90% of petrol stations ran dry because people bought petrol in panic.　(　　　)
② The international food trade is likely to have a big impact on the environment.　(　　　)
③ A great part of Britain's apple orchards have been destroyed and Britain is suffering from a shortage of apples.　(　　　)

Let's try　本文の表現を参考にしながら，次の日本語を英語にしなさい。

「私の兄は尊敬する作家に触発されて，小説を書くことにした。」(ll. 2～4)

____

____

63 熱湯の方がより速く氷になる？（1）[科学]

One of the most popular ways to demonstrate this year's severe US winter appeared to be tossing out a glass of boiling water and watching it freeze instantly in mid-air. Of course, (1) <u>the reason the fun experiment impressed viewers is because nobody expects boiling water to turn to ice that quickly</u>. It turns out that contrary to intuitive thinking, it actually freezes faster than cold water! Why? That's a mystery still waiting to be solved.

While this phenomenon has been observed for thousands of years, it was brought to the world's attention in 1963 by Tanzanian high school student, Erasto Mpemba.

It all began when the young boy was learning to make ice cream in cooking class. After dissolving the sugar in boiling milk, the students were instructed to allow the mixture to cool down, before putting it in the ice cream *churner. Too impatient to wait, Mpemba put his mixture in while it was still hot. To his and everyone's surprise, his ice cream was the first to freeze! His explanation appeared so unbelievable that even his teacher thought Mpemba must be mistaken. (184 words)

*churner「攪拌機（かくはんき）」

Let's try 本文の表現を参考にしながら，次の日本語を英語にしなさい。

「トムは最初に教室に来て，最後に教室を出ていった。」 (ℓ. 16)

問 1　Answer the questions below.

(1) What is the intuitive thinking about the result of tossing out a glass of water in mid-air?

① A glass of water cannot turn to ice just by tossing it out in mid-air.
② Cold water and boiling water will turn to ice at the same time.
③ Cold water will turn to ice more quickly than boiling water.
④ Boiling water will turn to ice more quickly than cold water.

(2) Which of the following is true about what Erasto Mpemba did in 1963?

① He put the hot mixture in the churner because he was mistaken in the procedure.
② He put the hot mixture in the churner because he wanted to see what would happen to the mixture.
③ He put the hot mixture in the churner because his classmates told him to.
④ He put the hot mixture in the churner because he could not wait for the mixture to cool down.

問 2　Put the underlined sentence (1) into Japanese.

____

____

問 3　Put ◯ if the sentence is correct according to the passage, and put × if incorrect.

① You can demonstrate how severe winter in the US was this year by tossing out a glass of boiling water in mid-air.　(　　　)
② Some people expected that boiling water might turn to ice more quickly than cold water.　(　　　)
③ The teacher couldn't believe that Mpemba's mixture had been put in the ice cream churner while it was hot.　(　　　)

64 熱湯の方がより速く氷になる？(2) [科学]

Convinced that he had discovered (1) something, Mpemba told a visiting physics professor about his accidental experiment. Like his teacher, the professor was a little doubtful, but invited him to test the theory.

The two began by filling 100 mL beakers with 70 mL samples of water of varying temperatures and placing them in the ice box of a normal refrigerator. (2) What they noticed was that it took longer for the water to freeze when the temperature was at 25°C than when it was at a much hotter 90°C. Since then, the phenomenon has been known as the Mpemba effect. However, while the two were able to demonstrate it, neither could find a scientific explanation for why it occurred. Over the years, researchers have come up with several theories.

The theory that most believe is fairly straightforward. It is a known fact that hot water *evaporates faster than cold. Hence, when boiling water is tossed into cold air, some of it turns into steam and disappears, leaving behind less to turn to ice! Sounds plausible, right? In fact, Mpemba had thought of this possibility and even tested it. Unfortunately, he found no difference in the volumes of the ice formed at different temperatures. (202 words)

*evaporate「蒸発する」

Let's try 本文の表現を参考にしながら，次の日本語を英語にしなさい。

「タバコが健康によくないというのは既知の事実である。」 (ll. 14 ~ 15)

____

____

問 1 **Answer the questions below.**

(1) **What does (1) something mean?**

① the phenomenon whereby a substance freezes more quickly when it is hot than when it is cold
② a way to show why boiling water turns into ice so quickly
③ a phenomenon no one has ever known before
④ a kind of supernatural phenomenon in which boiling water turns into ice so quickly

(2) **Which of the following is true about the experiment Mpemba and the professor did?**

① They filled 100 ml beakers with samples of water of varying temperatures.
② A beaker of water at a temperature of 90° C turned into ice more quickly than a beaker of colder water.
③ They thought the theory that hot water evaporates faster than cold could be applied to the experiment.
④ The professor alone was finally able to find a scientific explanation for the result of the experiment.

問 2 **Put the underlined sentence (2) into Japanese.**

____

____

問 3 **Put ○ if the sentence is correct according to the passage, and put × if incorrect.**

① At first, both Mpemba's teacher and the visiting physics professor were doubtful about what Mpemba said he had found. (　　　)
② Mpemba and the professor named the result of their experiment the "Mpemba effect." (　　　)
③ Mpemba found that the known fact that hot water evaporates faster than cold could not be a scientific explanation for the result of the experiment. (　　　)

65 熱湯の方がより速く氷になる？(3) [科学]

A more recent scientific study conducted by Xi Zhang at the Nanyang Technological University in Singapore attributes the phenomenon to the chemistry between the hydrogen and oxygen molecules that make up water. The researcher believes that as the temperature rises, it provides the molecules with a lot of *pent-up energy. When this water is tossed into a cold environment, (1) the energy 'jumps' out in a way similar to how a highly compressed spring would, when released. This results in the hot water cooling down much more rapidly than cold water, which does not contain as much energy.

While all these theories are plausible and explain the phenomenon under certain conditions, none seems to provide a satisfactory universal solution to this strange physical property that has confused scientists since Aristotle observed it in 380 BCE.

(134 words)

*pent-up「抑圧された」

Let's try 本文の表現を参考にしながら，次の日本語を英語にしなさい。

「運転者の不注意の結果としてこの事故が起きた。」 (ℓ.8)

問 1　**Answer the questions below.**

(1) **Which of the following is true about a recent scientific study by Xi Zhang?**

① Xi Zhang believes that as the temperature rises, the molecules lose a lot of pent-up energy.

② Xi Zhang found that a highly compressed spring would give out energy when jumping.

③ Xi Zhang tried to explain the phenomenon in terms of the chemistry between the hydrogen and oxygen molecules that make up water.

④ Xi Zhang doubted if his study fully explains the phenomenon because the results are not stable under certain conditions.

(2) **Which of the following describes our present understanding of the phenomenon?**

① There still is no plausible explanation of the phenomenon that is true under all conditions.

② Xi Zhang's explanation is true especially when we use only hot water in a cold environment.

③ Xi Zhang referenced many theories in his explanation of the phenomenon.

④ Xi Zhang's explanation of the phenomenon is similar to Aristotle's in 380 BCE.

問 2　**Put the underlined sentence (1) into Japanese.**

____

____

問 3　**Put ◯ if the sentence is correct according to the passage, and put × if incorrect.**

① Xi Zhang conducted a scientific study at the Nanyang Technological University to explain the phenomenon. (　　　)

② Cold water cannot give out as much energy as hot water. (　　　)

③ Aristotle tried to explain this strange phenomenon in 380 BCE. (　　　)

66 読書の重要性（1）[文化]

Even with the hard work and caring of many dedicated teachers and concerned parents, the U.S. continues to have a reading problem. According to the National Center for Educational Information, 38 percent of fourth grade students cannot read and understand a short paragraph of the type found in a simple children's book. Results from a 1998 study showed that 60 percent of U.S. teenagers could comprehend specific facts, but fewer than 5 percent could elaborate on the meanings of the material read.

No wonder many parents are discouraged, but they needn't be. By doing simple things like reading to their child, sharing their thinking about what they read, and telling their child stories, (1) they can help develop the foundation needed for children to become good readers and learn that reading is not a chore but a lifetime adventure.

(138 words)

Let's try 本文の表現を参考にしながら，次の日本語を英語にしなさい。

「日本人の平均寿命が世界一なのも当然だ。」 (ℓ. 9)

問 1　Answer the questions below.

(1) Which of the following is true about the reading problem in the U.S.?

① Children have trouble reading because teachers are indifferent toward them.

② Some school children cannot understand a short paragraph in a simple children's book.

③ Only 60 percent of U.S. teenagers can understand the meaning of the material read in detail.

④ Many fourth grade students cannot tell specific facts from the meaning of the material.

(2) How can parents help their children become good readers?

① By making reading their child's daily chore.

② By reading some difficult books to their child.

③ By talking with their child about what he or she reads.

④ By encouraging their child to become a good reader.

問 2　下線部 (1) を，**they** の指す内容を明確にして和訳しなさい。

____

____

問 3　Put ○ if the sentence is correct according to the passage, and put × if incorrect.

① The U.S. had and still has a reading problem.　(　　　)

② Results from a study showed that a large number of U.S. teenagers could not explain the precise meaning of the materials read.　(　　　)

③ There is nothing parents can do to help their children develop their reading skills.　(　　　)

Good readers follow a number of key strategies, whether they're reading a magazine or a textbook. Firstly, they create a wide range of mental and visual images as they read, to feel involved with what they are reading. Then, they use their background and relevant prior knowledge before, during and after reading to enhance their understanding of what they are reading. They also make and ask questions before, during, and after reading to *clarify meaning, make predictions, and focus their attention on what's important.

Good readers infer and determine the most important ideas or themes, and distinguish between these and unimportant information. Next, they track their thinking while reading, to get the overall meaning. Finally, (1) <u>if they have trouble understanding specific words, phrases, or longer passages, they use a wide range of problem-solving strategies</u> including skipping ahead, re-reading, asking questions, using a dictionary, and reading the passage aloud to "fix-up" their understanding.

Reading is fundamental to success in life. It's that simple. Reading opens the door to virtually all other learning. You have to be able to read to learn mathematics, science, history, engineering, mechanics, political science, not to mention to surf the web or figure out how to operate that new DVD player. Basically, you have to be able to read to succeed.

(214 words)

*clarify「を明らかにする」

問 1　**Answer the questions below.**

(1) **What are key strategies good readers follow? Put the following sentences in the right order.**

（ア）They determine the most important ideas or themes and try to get to the overall meaning.

（イ）They create various mental and visual images, use their knowledge, and ask questions.

（ウ）When they have trouble understanding something, they use problem-solving strategies.

(2) **Which of the following is the main conclusion of the passage?**

① Reading is a very simple and fundamental skill.

② Reading is something you need to be able to succeed in life.

③ Reading is important because you cannot operate anything without reading.

④ Reading is an indispensable skill for surfing the web.

問 2　下線部 (1) を，**they** が何を指すかを明確にして和訳しなさい。

____

____

問 3　**Put ○ if the sentence is correct according to the passage, and put × if incorrect.**

① Good readers don't use any strategies to understand when they're reading magazines.　（　　）

② Good readers can distinguish between the most important ideas or themes and unimportant information.　（　　）

③ You have to be able to read to learn a wide variety of things.　（　　）

Let's try　本文の表現を参考にしながら次の日本語を英語にしなさい。

「気に入ろうが入るまいが，コーチのアドバイスを聞くべきだよ。」(ℓℓ. 1 ～ 2)

____

____

68 AIについて（1）[科学]

How would you feel if a robot looked after your child? Worried? Anxious? (1) What if that robot was as intelligent as yourself, if not more so, and was able to react to every problem and *whim without ever tiring or wanting to scream? For those studying and working in artificial intelligence (AI), creating this kind of situation could so easily become a reality.

"AI is embedded in many educational applications," explains Janet Read, a professor in child computer interaction at the University of Central Lancashire, pointing to new gesture recognition and interpretation technologies. "Brain computer interfaces are detecting mood and emotion and in the near future robotic and virtual systems might be able to partially take on the care of children." (121 words)

*whim「気まぐれ」

Let's try 本文の表現を参考にしながら，次の日本語を英語にしなさい。

「英語を学習している人たちにとって，AI はスピーキングの練習に役立つかもしれない。」 (ℓ. 4)

問 1　**Answer the questions below.**

(1) **Which of the following is NOT true about what robots are expected to do in the near future?**

① Robots will be able to deal with many problems without any complaint.
② Robots will be able to look after your child.
③ Robots will be as intelligent as human beings.
④ Robot will even scream at whims of human beings.

(2) **Which of the following is NOT true about brain computer interfaces at present?**

① They can detect how we feel at the moment.
② They are embedded in many educational applications.
③ They can recognize our various gestures and interpret them.
④ They are able to take care of children just like their parents do.

問 2　**Put the underlined sentence (1) into Japanese.**

____

____

問 3　**Put ○ if the sentence is correct according to the passage, and put × if incorrect.**

① You might feel worried if a robot looked after your child. (　　　)
② Those studying and working in AI expect that it will take a long time to create robots which can deal with many problems in place of human beings. (　　　)
③ Creating robots that can take on the care of children is the goal Janet Read is aiming for now. (　　　)

AI is one of the most exciting fields of technological study, giving computers the ability to 'think', 'learn' and adapt when faced with a host of data. But it is not a technology of the future. It is all around us today, pervading our everyday lives and allowing us to take advantage of image and voice recognition software, intelligent web searching and medical advances, the latter made possible thanks to robot scientists formulating hypotheses and interpreting data. Modern video games use AI to generate intelligent behaviour in non-player characters. NASA's Mars Rover was designed to make its own decisions, stopping and analysing only the rocks it felt would be useful. And more is to come, with driverless cars and intelligent home systems on their way.

As a result, many universities have been promoting AI courses and modules for both undergraduate and postgraduate students. Each of them requires a solid background in computing, maths and physics and explores knowledge representation, planning and learning. "Studying AI is perfect for students who can solve problems in abstract ways and devise new angles," says Dr Richard Watson, senior lecturer in electronics and computer science at the University of Southampton. "But AI is also about learning techniques of advanced computer science, so students should have a broad education in computer science before they tackle it." For that reason, very few undergraduate degrees will concentrate entirely on AI. Instead, it tends to be offered as modules within an overall computer science degree.

(246 words)

日付　／　／

問 1　Answer the questions below.

(1) **Which of the following is true about AI?**

① AI will be used to give computers the ability to think, learn and adapt in future.
② AI today allows us to take advantage of image and voice recognition software.
③ AI made it possible for robot scientists to formulate hypotheses and interpret data.
④ Modern video games use AI to generate intelligent behavior in all the characters.

(2) **How have many universities been promoting AI courses and modules?**

① By requiring undergraduate students to gain a solid background in computing first.
② By inviting students who can solve problems in abstract ways and devise new angles.
③ By teaching students the techniques of advanced computer science.
④ By offering undergraduate degrees in overall computer science that include modules in AI.

問 2　Put ○ if the sentence is correct according to the passage, and put × if incorrect.

① Intelligent web searching and medical advances were both made possible thanks to robot scientists.　(　　　)
② NASA's Mars Rover was able to make its own decisions, and analyze only useful rocks.　(　　　)
③ In many universities, many undergraduate degrees concentrate entirely on AI.　(　　　)

Let's try 本文の表現を参考にしながら，次の日本語を英語にしなさい。

「インターネットは今日の私たちの周りの至るところにあり，役立つ情報もうその情報も提供している。」　(ll. 3 ～ 4)

____

____

70 ヒトの自然治癒力［医療］

Neglect of the mind-body link by technological medicine is actually a brief *aberration when viewed against the whole history of the healing art. In traditional *tribal medicine and in Western practice from its beginning in the work of Hippocrates, the need to operate through the patient's mind has always been recognized. Until the nineteenth century, (1) medical writers rarely failed to note the influence of *grief, despair, or discouragement on the *onset and outcome of illness, nor did they ignore the healing effects of faith, confidence, and peace of mind. (2) *Contentment used to be considered a *prerequisite for health.

The modern medicine man has gained so much power over certain diseases through drugs, however, that he has forgotten about the potential strength within the patient. One elderly physician friend recently told me of reading the diary of his uncle, also a doctor. In the early years, the *diarist always recorded what happened to the individual or the community prior to an illness or epidemic, but as medicine became more technological, this part of the history grew less and less important to him and finally was *omitted altogether. Awareness of the mind's powers was lost as medicine cast out all “soft” data, the information that's not easily *quantified or scientific.

(208 words)

*aberration「逸脱」 *tribal「部族の」 *grief「悲しみ」 *onset「始まり」
*contentment「心の安らぎ」 *prerequisite「必要条件」 *diarist「日記をつける人」
*omit「を除外する」 *quantify「を数量化する」

日付　／　／

問 1　**Answer the questions below.**

(1) **Which of the following is the closest to the meaning of (1) medical writers rarely failed to note?**

① medical writers almost always noted
② medical writers seldom noted
③ medical writers failed to write down
④ medical writers never wrote down

(2) **Which of the following is true about the modern medicine man?**

① He recognizes the need to operate through the patient's mind.
② He is aware of the potential strength within the patient.
③ He tries to consider all the information even though it is not scientific.
④ He tends to neglect the mind-body link, depending solely on technological medicine.

問 2　**Put the underlined sentence (2) into Japanese.**

問 3　**Put ○ if the sentence is correct according to the passage, and put × if incorrect.**

① In old times, people recognized the importance of the patient's mind in the process of healing.　(　　)
② Until the 19th century, medical writers ignored the effects of positive feelings.　(　　)
③ Modern medicine uses information that is not easy to quantify.　(　　)

Let's try　本文の表現を参考にしながら，次の日本語を英語にしなさい。

「結論が一番大切なところなのに，それを聞き逃しちゃった。」　(ℓ.6)

書籍のアンケートにご協力ください

抽選で**図書カード**を

プレゼント！

Z会の「個人情報の取り扱いについて」はZ会Webサイト(https://www.zkai.co.jp/home/policy/)に掲載しておりますのでご覧ください。

速単の英文で学ぶ **英語長文問題70** 速読英単語必修編［改訂第7版増補版］対応

改訂第7版対応第1刷発行……………2019年 3 月 1 日
改訂第7版増補版対応第1刷発行……2022年 7 月 10 日
改訂第7版増補版対応第4刷発行……2024年 1 月 20 日
編者……………Z会編集部
発行人……………藤井孝昭
発行……………Z会
〒411－0033 静岡県三島市文教町1－9－11
【販売部門：書籍の乱丁・落丁・返品・交換・注文】
TEL 055－976－9095
【書籍の内容に関するお問い合わせ】
https://www.zkai.co.jp/books/contact/
【ホームページ】
https://www.zkai.co.jp/books/
執筆協力……………濱村千賀子／三国正人
DTP・印刷・製本……………大日本法令印刷株式会社

ISBN978-4-86531-497-7 C7082

速単の英文で学ぶ

英語長文問題70

解答編

速単の英文で学ぶ

英語長文問題70

解答編

CONTENTS

1 オオカミの子育て [科学]

Wolves (S) have (V) an interesting way of raising their young (O).// When a female wolf is ready to give birth (「産む」), / she (= a female wolf) digs a hole.// Within this hole, / she (= a female wolf) has her babies.// While she (= a female wolf) is taking care of these babies, / other wolves (S) bring (V) her (O_1) food (O_2).// After they (= her babies) get a little older, / the mother can leave them (= her babies) / while she (= the mother) goes off to hunt / with other members of the group.// Then, instead of the mother, / another female will stay behind / <to guard the young wolves>.// (不定詞の副詞用法)

解答

問1 (1) ③　(2) ④

問2 母親の代わりに，他の雌が子供のオオカミを守るために後に残ることになる

問3 ① ○　② ×　③ ×

Let's try Are you ready to start?

解説

問1(1)　雌のオオカミは赤ん坊の世話をしている間，どのように食べ物を得るか。

①「より年長のオオカミが雌と食べ物を分け合う。」

②「つがいのオオカミが雌と食べ物を分け合う。」

③「他のオオカミが雌に食べ物を運んでくる。」(ll.3～4)

④「他の雌のオオカミが雌に食べ物を運んでくる。」

(2)　なぜ雌のオオカミは狩りに行っている間，赤ん坊を後に残していくことができるのか。

①「より年長のオオカミが赤ん坊の世話をする。」

②「他の動物が赤ん坊を守る。」

③「つがいのオオカミが赤ん坊の世話をする。」

④「他の雌オオカミの1匹が赤ん坊を守る。」(ll.6～7)

問2 instead of ～「～の代わりに」(ℓ.6) ／ stay behind「後に残る」(ℓℓ.6～7)
後に続く不定詞は‘目的’を表す。

問3 ①「オオカミは穴の中で赤ん坊を産む。」(ℓℓ.2～3)
②「オオカミはつがいで暮らし，雌のオオカミはつがいのオオカミと一緒に赤ん坊を育てる。」(ℓℓ.3～4)
③「ひとたび赤ん坊ができると，雌のオオカミは決して群れの他の仲間たちに赤ん坊を世話させない。」(ℓℓ.6～7)

Let's try 「…する用意ができている」be ready to *do*
「出発する」start〔go〕

概要を整理しよう

主題　オオカミの子育ての面白い方法

本論　その方法
- 雌のオオカミは穴を掘って子供を産む。
- 雌が子育て中→他のオオカミがその雌に食べ物を持ってくる。
- 子供が少し大きくなる→雌は他のオオカミとともに狩りに出かける。その間，他の雌が残って子供の世話をする。

背景知識　オオカミの生態

オオカミは子育てに入ると，所属する集団の別のオオカミが母親オオカミの代理をするが，これはよく用いられる「一匹狼」(lone wolf) という表現からは想像しにくいオオカミの生態だろう。ここで言う「オオカミ」はハイイロオオカミもしくはタイリクオオカミのことで，北半球に広く分布している。8～12頭の家族集団で暮らし，これが彼らの社会単位となる。この単位をパック (pack) と呼ぶ。パックには，中心となる雌雄がそれぞれ一頭いるが，残りのオオカミはすべてその子供たちだとされる。子供はある程度大きくなると，パートナーと出会うために群れを出て放浪することになる。「一匹狼」はこの状態にあるオオカミのことである。

2 お茶の種類 [文化]

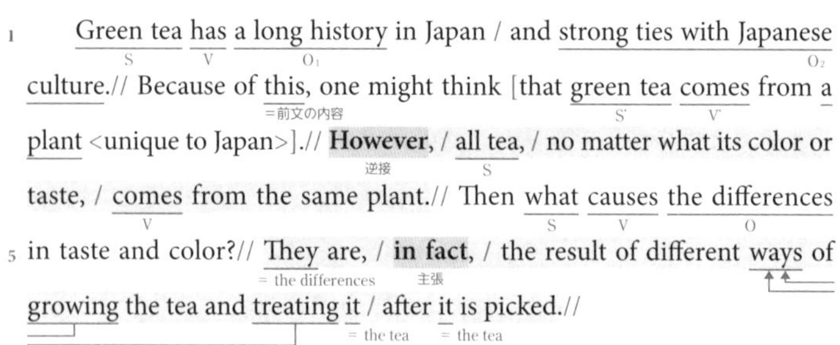

Green tea has a long history in Japan / and strong ties with Japanese culture.// Because of this, one might think [that green tea comes from a plant <unique to Japan>].// However, / all tea, / no matter what its color or taste, / comes from the same plant.// Then what causes the differences in taste and color?// They are, / in fact, / the result of different ways of growing the tea and treating it / after it is picked.//

解答

問 1　(1)　②　　(2)　①・③

問 2　緑茶には日本における長い歴史と，日本文化との強い結びつきがあるため，緑茶は日本に特有の植物から作られていると思う人がいるかもしれない。

問 3　①　○　　②　×　　③　○

Let's try　We have to carry out the plan, no matter what it may be.

解説

問 1 (1)　(1) strong ties に最も近い意味は次のうちどれか。

①「長く続く関係」

②「密接な関係」（*ll*. 1 ～ 2）

③「力強い束縛」

④「断ち切れない束縛」

(2)　緑茶の味と色における違いをもたらすのは次のうちどれか。選択肢は 1 つ以上選んでもよい。

①「異なる方法でお茶を育てること」（*ll*. 5 ～ 6）

②「日本に特有の植物を育てること」

③「摘み取られた後でお茶を異なる方法で処理すること」（*ll*. 5 ～ 6）

④「異なる種類の植物を育てること」

問2 thisは前の1文の内容を指しており，これが原因で緑茶に関する誤解が生まれるかもしれないと述べられている。
unique to ～「～に特有の」(ℓ.3)

問3 ①「日本人は古くから緑茶を楽しんできた。」(ℓ.1)
②「緑茶と他の種類のお茶は異なる種類の植物から作られている。」(ℓℓ.3～4)
③「茶葉を処理するさまざまな方法は異なる味や色をもたらす。」(ℓℓ.4～6)

Let's try 「Sがどんなものであろうと」no matter what S may be (ℓℓ.3～4)
「計画を遂行する」carry out the plan

概要を整理しよう

導入　緑茶は日本文化と密接な結びつきがある
→このため緑茶は日本独特の植物から作られるのかと思う人もいるかもしれない

主張　◆ However「しかし：逆接」(ℓ.3)
すべてのお茶は同じ植物から作られている。
・色や味の違いを生み出すもとは？
◆ in fact「実際には：主張」(ℓ.5)
お茶の育て方と収穫後の処理の仕方の違いから，差が生まれる。

背景知識 将軍様のお茶

緑茶と日本文化には密接な関係がある。江戸時代には庶民の間にも喫茶の習慣が浸透し，もちろん時の権力者もお茶に魅了されていた。大阪夏の陣（1615年：第二代将軍徳川秀忠の頃）での徳川方の勝利を祝って宇治の新茶が幕府に献上されて以来，宇治茶は将軍家御用達となった。その新茶を将軍に献上するため，京都から江戸への道中では新茶をおさめた茶壷（お茶壷様）をかごに載せた行列が通った。それを「お茶壷道中」と呼ぶ。この時，沿道の庶民は道をあけて土下座しなければならなかったともされる。「ずいずいずっころばし」という童謡に茶壷が出てくるが，当時横行していた「お茶壷道中」が庶民にとって迷惑だった様子を歌ったものだとも言われる。茶壷を運ぶ武士たちに威圧されることを嫌がった庶民が，茶壷が近くを通る際，家にこもってやり過ごそうと戸を「ピンシャン」と音を立てて閉めるさまが歌われているという。

3 ジェスチャーの違い［言語］

Physical gestures may have different meanings / in different cultures, / and misunderstanding these signals can sometimes be embarrassing.// I once had an experience [which I have never forgotten].// Some years ago, / I took a small group of foreign students to Kyoto.// I counted them with the index finger, [which is common in Japan].// **But** one of them became quiet / and looked puzzled.// When I asked him [what was the matter], / he replied, "In my country, / we count people with our eyes.// We use our fingers to count pigs."//

解答

問 1　(1)　②　　(2)　（ア）　②　　（イ）　③　　（ウ）　⑤

問 2　私は人差し指で外国人の学生たちを数えたが，これは日本では普通のことである。

問 3　①　×　　②　○　　③　×

Let's try　Making such a mistake may〔might〕be embarrassing.

解説

問 1(1)　身ぶりは（　　）ために異なる意味を持つことがある。

①「異なる文化の人々は決して同じ身ぶりを使わない」

②「身ぶりを異なった仕方で理解する人がいる」（ll. 1～3）

③「身ぶりを表現するのに慣れていない人がいる」

④「身ぶりを使うことは言葉を使うこととかなり異なる」

(2)　著者が人差し指で外国人の学生を数えた時，その１人が（　ア　）ように見えた。彼によると，彼の国の人は人を数えるのに（　イ　）を使う。というのも（　ウ　）はブタを数えるのに使うからだ。

①「困惑させる」②「困惑している」→（ア）（ll. 4～6）

③「目」→（イ）（ll. 7～8）④「頭」⑤「指」→（ウ）（l. 8）

問 2　them は前の文の foreign students を指している。関係代名詞 which は，I counted ～ finger の内容を修飾している（非制限用法）。

with ～「～を使って」（'手段' を表す前置詞）

問 3　①「身ぶりはあらゆる文化で同じことを意味する。」（ℓℓ.1 ～ 2）

②「日本の人々が人を数えるのに指を使うのは普通のことである。」（ℓℓ.4 ～ 5）

③「学生の 1 人は，彼の国の人は人を数える時，日本人と同じ身ぶりを使うと言った。」（ℓℓ.7 ～ 8）

Let's try　「ばつが悪い；気まずい」embarrassing（ℓ.3）
「間違いをする」make a mistake

概要を整理しよう

主張　身ぶりの意味は文化によって違う

具体例　著者の経験
著者は外国人学生の一団を引率していた時，指で生徒の人数を数えた。(日本のやり方)
↕
◆ But「しかし：逆接」（ℓ.5）
ある生徒はとまどった。
→指を使うのはブタを数える時（生徒の国のやり方）

背景知識　しぐさと社会

しぐさや身ぶり手ぶりは，周囲の人の模倣として幼児期を通じて無意識に学習されるため，社会の慣行になるのだと言われる。そのため，自分が当たり前だと思っているしぐさは，国や文化が異なると，別の意味でとらえられてしまうことに人は当惑する。同じ地理的・文化的圏内で一定の意味で通用するしぐさが，別の国ではまったく異なる意味となることも起こっている。たとえば，親指の先と人差し指の先とをくっつけて示すオーケーサインは，ヨーロッパの大半の人々にとっては「承認」の意味を持つとされる。これはフランスでも同じだが，そのフランスの一部の地域では「無価値」か「ゼロ」を意味してしまう。1 つの国の中でも，地域によって意味が違うという好例である。

4 ビタミンCの働き［医療］

Vitamin C plays an important role / in keeping us healthy.// Most mammals produce it / in their livers, / **so** they never suffer from a lack of it.// Curiously, / **however**, / some mammals, / **such as** humans and apes, / cannot do so.// What happens / when you lack this important vitamin? You might see black-and-blue marks / on your skin.// Your teeth could suffer, too: the pink area around them might become soft / and bleed easily.// These are just a couple of good reasons / <to eat plenty of fresh fruit>.//

解答

問 1　(1)　②　　(2)　④

問 2　ビタミンCは，私たちを健康な状態に保つことにおいて，重要な役割を果たしている。

問 3　①　○　　②　×　　③　○

Let's try　Fresh fruit is effective in〔has the effect of〕keeping us healthy.

解説

問 1(1)　なぜたいていの哺乳動物はビタミンCの不足に苦しむことが決してないのか。

①「自分の肝臓に蓄えることができる。」

②「自分の肝臓で作ることができる。」（ℓ.2）

③「たくさん新鮮なフルーツを食べる。」

④「他の何かをビタミンCに変えることができる。」

(2)　ビタミンCの不足の結果ではないものは次のうちどれか。

①「歯の周りのピンク色の部分が柔らかくなるかもしれない。」（ℓ.6）

②「歯の周りのピンク色の部分が容易に出血してしまうかもしれない。」（ℓ.6）

③「皮膚に青黒いあざを見つけるかもしれない。」(ℓ.5)

④「歯の周りのピンク色の部分に痛みがあるかもしれない。」

問 2 play a ～ role in …「…において～な役割を果たす」(ℓ.1)

問 3 ①「人間はビタミン C がなければ健康なままではいられない。」(ℓ.1)

②「人間や類人猿は自分の肝臓でビタミン C を作ることができる。」(ℓℓ.3～4)

③「たくさんの新鮮なフルーツを食べることは，歯の周りのピンク色の部分が出血するのを防ぐかもしれない。」(ℓℓ.6～8)

Let's try 「～を…の状態に保つ」keep O C（C には形容詞が入る）
「新鮮なフルーツ」fresh fruit
「～に効果的である」be effective in〔have the effect of〕～

概要を整理しよう

主題 ビタミン C は健康にとって重要である

本論 たいていの哺乳類はビタミン C を体内で作れる

◆ so「したがって：結果・結論」(ℓ.2)

・たいていの哺乳類はビタミン C が不足しない

◆ however「しかし：逆接」(ℓ.3)

・人間と類人猿などは体内でビタミン C が作れない

ビタミン C が不足した場合の症例

・皮膚に青黒いあざができる／歯ぐきが柔らかくなり，出血する場合がある
→たくさんのフルーツを食べるべきだという理由

背景知識 ビタミン C の基準値指標としてのレモン

皮膚に斑点が出たり，歯ぐきが腫れたり出血したりといった症状は，壊血病という病気の兆候である。1930 年代になって科学的に抗壊血病因子が特定された。この因子はビタミン C と名づけられ，壊血病の原因は食生活の欠陥にあるということがわかった。その後程なく，ビタミン C の必要摂取量を定める動きが起き，1930 年代中頃には経験知も手伝って，国際単位での必要摂取量が，新鮮なレモンの絞り汁 100㎎（ビタミン C20㎎に相当する）と定められた。1939 年から第二次世界大戦が始まる中，イギリスでビタミン C の 1 日の必要摂取量は最低限 15 ～ 20㎎であるとする論文発表があったが，大戦中に物資の不足などがなかったアメリカ合衆国では 1 日の必要摂取量は 75㎎とされるなど，各国でばらつきがあった。ちなみに現在の日本では成人のビタミン C 必要摂取量は 100㎎が推奨されている。

5 drugの定義［言語］

The word "drug" means anything / [that, / even in small amounts, / produces changes / in the body, the mind, or both].// This definition, **however**, does not clearly separate drugs / from [what we usually think of as food].// The difference between a drug and a poison is **also** unclear.// All drugs become poisons in large amounts, / and many poisons are useful drugs in carefully controlled amounts.// Is alcohol, **for instance**, a food, a drug, or a poison?// It can be any of the three, <depending on [how we use it]>.//

解答

問 1 (1) ③　(2) ③

問 2 しかし，この定義は，薬と私たちが通常食物とみなしているものとをはっきりと区別してはいない。

問 3 ① ×　② ×　③ ○　④ ×

Let's try The success of the project depends on when we ought to〔should〕start.

解説

問 1(1)　なぜ薬と食物の違いはあいまいなのか。

①「両方とも大量に摂取すると危険であると考えられている。」

②「両方とも少量だと益しかなさない。」

③「両方とも身体と心に変化をもたらし得る。」(*ll*.1～2)

④「両方とも注意深く調整された量であっても害をなし得る。」

(2)　なぜ薬と毒の違いはあいまいなのか。

①「両方とも少量だと益をなさない。」

②「両方とも大量に摂取することはできない。」

③「どちらもある程度の量で害をなし得る。」(*ll*.5～6)

④「両方ともさまざまな化合物から成る。」

問 2　separate A from B「A と B を区別する」(ℓ.3)

from の目的語に関係代名詞の導く節 what ～ as food「私たちが通常食物とみなしているもの」がきている。

問 3　①「薬と食物には明確な違いがある。」(ℓℓ.2～4)

②「薬は益をなすが，毒は害しかなさない。」(ℓℓ.5～6)

③「薬を飲みすぎると，その効果は毒と同類である。」(ℓ.5)

④「アルコールは薬としてのみ分類できる。」(ℓℓ.6～8)

Let's try　「プロジェクトの成功」the success of the project
「～にかかっている」depend on ～ (ℓ.8)
「いつ始めるべきか」when we ought to〔should〕start（間接疑問）

概要を整理しよう

導入　薬の定義：薬とは「身体や心に変化をもたらすもの」という意味

↕

本論　◆ **however「しかし：逆接」**(ℓ.3)

この定義では薬と食物の区別がはっきりしない。

◆ **also「また：列挙・追加」**(ℓ.5)

この定義では薬と毒の区別もはっきりしない。

◆ **for instance「例えば：例」**(ℓ.7)

アルコールは，使い方次第で食物・薬・毒のそのいずれにもなり得る。

背景知識　薬の作用を絞り込むことの効果

薬には副作用もあり，取り扱い方によっては人体に有害なものとなる。たとえば，がん治療薬の強い副作用や，身近な例では，熱や咳などの症状を抑えるための風邪薬を飲むと，眠くなったり胃腸障害を招いたりすることなどである。一方で，がん治療に絞って見てみると，副作用の減少を狙って新たな薬が開発されている。がん細胞の周りの正常細胞を傷つけずにターゲットを絞って攻撃する「分子標的薬」などである。これは，がん細胞の増殖や転移に必要な分子に限ってそれらを押さえ込むものである。そうすることで，従来の投薬よりも副作用を減らして治療効果を上げることができるとされている。

6 皮膚の役割 ［医療］

Have you ever thought about [what skin does for us]?// **Most of us** are aware [that skin protects us from liquid, heat, cold, dirt, and bacteria].// **But** that is not its only job.// **For instance**, the skin is ∧[where our bodies make the vitamin D [that we need]].// **Another** function has to do with the sense of touch.// Without that sense, / we could not feel any difference / between rough and smooth surfaces.// Skin can even help us <determine [if someone is sick]>.// The wrong color — slightly gray or very pale — / may be a sign of disease.// Skin may reflect a person's mental state, too.// Unusual sweating, / **for example**, / may be a sign [that a person is nervous or under stress].//

解答

問 1 (1) ②　(2) ③

問 2 触覚がなかったら，（私たちは）ざらざらした表面となめらかな表面の違いをまったく感じ取ることができないだろう。

問 3 ① ×　② ○　③ ×

Let's try I couldn't determine at that time if〔whether〕Lisa was tired.

解説

問 1(1) 皮膚の働きについて当てはまらないものは次のうちどれか。

①「私たちを多くの好ましくない状態から守る。」(*ll.* 2～3)

②「私たちがいつビタミン D を作るべきかを判断する助けになる。」

③「様々な表面の状態の違いを私たちに知らせる。」(*ll.* 5～6)

④「人の精神状態を表す可能性があるしるしを伝える。」(*ll.* 8～9)

(2) 私たちは（　　）時，誰かが病気であるかどうか判断できるかもしれない。

①「その人が不快な表情をしている」

②「その人の皮膚の表面がなめらかでない」

③「その人が少し灰色か非常に青白い色に見える」（ll.7～8）

④「その人が異常に汗をかいている」

問2 without ～「～がなかったら」（l.5）以下は仮定法過去になっている。

問3 ①「私たちは骨でビタミンDを作ることができる。」（ll.3～4）

②「私たちは皮膚の色を見ることで誰かが病気かどうか推測できる。」（ll.6～8）

③「異常な発汗はある人が心地よいかうれしいことを意味するかもしれない。」（ll.9～10）

Let's try 「…かどうか判断する」determine if〔whether〕…

概要を整理しよう

主題　皮膚の働きの紹介

→皮膚は液体，熱，寒さ，汚れ，細菌から私たちを守ってくれる。

◆ But「しかし：逆接」（l.3）

それだけではない。

具体例 ◆ For instance「例えば：例」（l.3）

・皮膚はビタミンDを作る

◆ Another ～「別の～は：列挙・追加」（l.4）

・触覚という機能　／病気の判断に役立つ　／精神状態を表す

背景知識　メラニン色素によって左右される肌の色

太陽光に含まれる紫外線は，ビタミンを作る皮膚の働きを促すが，その一方で有害な作用も持つ。したがって，紫外線にさらされすぎないようにするため，メラニン色素が作られ，これが表皮全層へ行き渡るようになっている。

メラニン色素の種類は大きく分けて黒褐色のユーメラニンと赤っぽいフェオメラニンがある。ユーメラニンは紫外線を遮断する働きを持ち，フェオメラニンは紫外線をたくさん取り込むように薄い色となっている。アフリカなど人体に入り込んでくる紫外線が強い環境に生まれた人は，ユーメラニンが多い黒色の肌になる。一方イギリスなどでは紫外線がもともと弱く，ビタミンDを十分に生産するためには紫外線をむしろ取り入れなければならないので，人々はフェオメラニンの多い白い肌となっている。

7 紳士服と婦人服でボタンが違う理由 ［社会］

Western clothes have buttons on the right for men.// This（＝前文の内容）is convenient / because the majority of men are right-handed.// It（形式主語）is easier <for them to use the right hand>（真主語）/ when ∧（they are）buttoning up.// Why, then, / do women's clothes have buttons on the left,（対比）/ even though most women are also right-handed?// Is this（＝前文の内容）a kind of discrimination?// **In fact**（主張）, / there is a reason / [why（関係副詞）women's buttons are on that side（＝the left）].// In the past, / buttons were quite expensive / and only very rich people could afford them（＝buttons）.// Women in such wealthy families（S）had（V）servants（O）[who（関係代名詞）dressed them（＝women）].// **Therefore**（結果・結論）, / <to make it easier for the servants>（不定詞の副詞用法）, / buttons were put on the left.//

解答

問１ (1) ③　(2) ②

問２ 右利きの男性にとって，ボタンをかける時に右手を使う方が簡単なのだ。

問３ ① ○　② ×　③ ○

Let's try Tom made the problem more difficult to solve.
〔別解〕Tom made it more difficult to solve the problem.

解説

問１(1) 女性の衣服の（　A　）側にボタンがついているのは，昔のとても裕福な女性は（　B　）利きの召使いによって服を着せられたからである。

A：左，B：右（ll. 8～10）

(2) (2) afford them に最も近い意味のものは次のうちどれか。

①「高価な服を手に入れる」　②「高価なボタンを買う」（ll. 6～7）
③「召使いを雇う」　④「高価なボタンを持ち続ける」

問2 it is ～ for（人）to *do*「(人) が…することは～だ」(ll.2～3)
them は前文の the majority of men の「男性」を指している。「右手を使う方が簡単」な男性なので，「右利きの男性」とした方がよい。

問3 ①「ボタンが衣服の右側についていると，男性の大多数にとってボタンをかけるのが簡単だ。」(ll.2～3)
②「昔は大部分の女性が左利きだったので，女性の衣服は左側にボタンがついている。」(ll.4～5)
③「ボタンが左側についていると，召使いにとって女性の衣服のボタンをかけるのを助けるのがより簡単だ。」(ll.9～10)

Let's try 「O を C の状態にさせる〔する〕」make O（名詞）C（形容詞）

概要を整理しよう

導入	男性の衣服のボタンは右側についている →大多数の男性が右利きなので便利 ↕ 対比
疑問	なぜ女性の洋服のボタンは左側についているのか →大多数の女性もまた右利き
理由の開示	◆ **In fact「実際には：主張」**(l.5) 昔，ボタンは高価なものだった。 →裕福な女性だけがボタンのついた服を着られた 富裕層の女性は召使いに服を着せてもらっていた。
結論	◆ **Therefore「したがって：結果・結論」**(l.9) 召使いがやりやすいようにボタンは左側についていたのだ。

背景知識 高価な装飾品としてのボタン

ヨーロッパでは，ある時代では富裕層の女性だけがボタンを買うことができたと言われている。ある時代とは，中世～近代までの長い間，すなわち服を留め合わせるひもにかわって，ボタンが使用されるようになった 13 世紀以降，婦人の服装に現在のボタンが用いられるようになった 19 世紀までである。

ボタンがこのように富裕層だけしか買えないほど高価だった理由は，中世ヨーロッパではボタンが私たちの知っているいわゆる「ボタン」ではなく，金・銀・ルビーやエメラルドなどの宝石がボタンとされていたことにある。宝石そのものがボタンの機能を果たしているので，高価なのは当然だろう。

8 紫色のもと［文化］

The color purple has often been regarded as a symbol of wealth and power, / **but** the dye <used to produce it> did not have an elegant beginning.// An ancient people <living along the coast of the Mediterranean Sea> / first discovered <how to make the dye / from Murex snails, small sea animals with hard shells>.// Unlike other snails, / Murex snails give off a strong-smelling liquid [that changes color / when it comes into contact / with air and light].// From this liquid / the people produced the purple dye.// If we visit the places [where the dye was produced], / we might still be able to see the shells of Murex snails.// Let us hope [∧we cannot smell them].//

but：逆接／used to produce it：過去分詞の修飾／it = the color purple／An ancient people：S／living：現在分詞の修飾／discovered：V／how to make the dye：O how to *do*「～の仕方」／Murex snails, small sea animals with hard shells：同格／that：関係代名詞／changes：V'／color：O'／it = a strong-smelling liquid／the people = an ancient people living ～／we：S'／visit：V'／the places：O'／where：関係副詞／the dye：S'／was produced：V''／we：S／might be able to see：V／the shells of Murex snails：O／∧ (that)／them = the shells of Murex snails

解答

問 1　(1)　②　　(2)　①

問 2　地中海の海岸に沿って〔沿岸に〕住んでいた古代の人々は，染料を作る方法を最初に発見した

問 3　①　×　　②　○　　③　×

Let's try　Hokkaido is a place where I have long wanted to live.

解説

問 1 (1)　古代の人々はどのように紫色の染料を作ったか。

①「アクキガイの硬い殻を使って」

②「空気や光にさらされると色を変える液体を使って」(*ll.* 6 ～ 8)

③「地中海の海岸沿いにある岩を使って」

④「強いにおいのする液体を放出する巻き貝の膜を使って」

(2) なぜ紫色の染料には優雅な始まりがあったとは言えないのか。

①「その染料は小さな海洋動物が作る臭い液体から作り出された。」(ll.6～8)

②「その染料を作るために巻き貝の殻を割るのがとても難しかった。」

③「その染料を作るために使われる液体は簡単に色を変えた。」

④「その染料を作るために使われる小さな海洋動物は暗い場所を好んだ。」

問2 名詞＋現在分詞「…している（名詞）」(l.3)

An ancient people ～ Mediterranean Sea までがこの文の主部。

how to make the dye「染料の作り方」

問3 ①「人々はしばしば紫色を知恵の象徴とみなしてきた。」(ll.1～2)

②「紫色の染料は巻き貝の一種から作られた。」(ll.4～5)

③「地中海の海岸に沿って住んでいた古代の人々が最初にアクキガイを発見した。」(ll.3～5)

Let's try 「…する〔した〕場所」the place where ...

「ずっと住みたいと思っている」は現在完了で表すとよい。

概要を整理しよう

導入 紫色は富と権力の象徴

◆ **but「しかし：逆接」**(l.2)

その染料の起源は優雅ではなかった。

本論 紫色の染料の起源

・地中海沿岸に住む古代の人々がアクキガイから染料を作る方法を発見

・アクキガイは悪臭を放つ液体を分泌する。これが空気や光に触れると，発色して染料になる

・染料を作っていた場所に行けば，アクキガイの殻を見ることができるかもしれない

(筆者の本音) その匂いはしないといいが。

背景知識 古代日本の貝紫染め

地中海のアクキガイから取れた染料を使った染色法は，メキシコや古代の日本でも行われていたとされる。日本最大規模の弥生時代の遺跡，吉野ヶ里遺跡（佐賀県神埼市・吉野ヶ里町）にある，弥生中期～後期の墓から出土した染色布がまさしくこの染色法に従ったものだ。さらに，大森貝塚を発見したことで有名なエドワード・S・モースは，チリメンボラという貝の貝殻の一部分が砕かれた状態で発見されたことと，チリメンボラがアクキガイの仲間であることに着目して，縄文時代の日本において早くも貝紫染めがなされていた可能性があると推理した。

9 本当のほほえみと偽りのほほえみ［人間］

The smile may no longer be an effective way / <to mask one's true feelings>.// **Some** psychologists have claimed [that true smiles and false smiles use different muscles].// **For example**, / in the true smile, / the muscles <surrounding the eyes> tighten, / **while** the cheek muscles pull the corners of the lips upward.// **On the other hand**, / in the false smile, / the muscles between the eyebrows move slightly, / **while** the muscles around the mouth pull the corners of the lips downward.// If the psychologists' claim is proven <to be true>, / perhaps people will worry less about [what they say] / and ∧ more about <which muscles to use / when they smile>.//

解答

問 1 (1) ② (2) ③

問 2 人々は，自分が何を言うかを気にすることがより少なくなり，ほほえむ際にどの筋肉を使うべきかをもっと気にするようになるだろう

問 3 ① ○ ② × ③ ○

Let's try Tom worries about the past, while Jack thinks about the future.

解説

問 1(1) (1) mask one's true feelings に最も近い意味のものは次のうちどれか。

①「本当に感じていることを見過ごす」②「本当に感じていることを隠す」

③「本当に感じていることを示す」④「本当に感じていることを指摘する」

(2) （　　）を確認することで，あるほほえみが本当のほほえみであると見分けられると主張している心理学者もいる。

①「目の間の筋肉と唇の端」②「まゆの間の筋肉と口の周りの筋肉」

③「目を囲んでいる筋肉と唇の端」(ℓℓ.3～5)

④「まゆを囲んでいる筋肉と口の周りの筋肉」

問2 worry less about ～ and more about ...「～についてあまり気にしなくなり，…についてもっと気にする」という文の構造。

which ～ to *do*「どの～を…するべきか」(ℓ.9)

問3 ①「本当にほほえむ際に使う筋肉は偽ってほほえむ際に使う筋肉とは異なる。」(ℓℓ.2～3)

②「偽りのほほえみの場合，唇の端は上方に引っ張られる。」(ℓℓ.5～7)

③「ほほえむ際にどのように筋肉が動くかを人々が知っていれば，あなたはほほえんで本当の気持ちを隠すことはできないだろう。」(ℓℓ.1～3)

Let's try 「～を気にする」worry about ～／「一方…」while ...
「～のことを考える」think about ～

概要を整理しよう

主題　ほほえみでは，もはや本当の気持ちを隠せなくなるかもしれない
→ある心理学者が，本当のほほえみと偽りのほほえみでは使う筋肉が異なると主張

具体例
◆ **For example「例えば：例」**(ℓ.3)
・本当のほほえみ：目の周りの筋肉が張る。ほおの筋肉が唇の端を上に引っ張る。

◆ **On the other hand「他方で：対比」**(ℓ.5)
・偽りのほほえみ：眉間の筋肉が少し動く。口の周りの筋肉が唇の端を下に引っ張る。

→これが本当なら，人々はほほえむ際にどの筋肉を使うべきかをもっと気にするようになるだろう

背景知識　筋肉と表情－ほほえみと泣き顔の対比－

ヒトの笑い顔は表情筋の運動によって生み出される。この際，目尻の横から唇の両端にかけてのびる大頬骨筋の動きが重要となる。ほほえみの時に唇の両端（口角）が上に吊り上がるのは，この大頬骨筋の収縮による。これに伴い，目尻が下がり，目の横にしわもできるようになる。一方，泣き顔の場合，表情筋の下唇下制筋が収縮することによって口角が下方と外側に引っ張られる。口の形を形成する表情筋の動作の初めの段階では，笑いの場合は大頬骨筋，泣きの場合は下唇下制筋，と収縮する筋肉が異なっているものの，いずれの場合も口角が横に引っ張られることは共通する。

10 「熱い」か「辛い」か［言語］

When English-speaking people talk about "hot" food, / are they saying
[∧the food is spicy like curry], / or are they talking about its temperature, /
(that)
as in "hot" coffee?// These two different meanings of "hot" / **may** seem
= spicy, high temperature 譲歩
confusing / to Japanese students, / **but as a matter of fact**, / the word is the
逆接 主張 = "hot"
right one / for describing the way [the body responds to spice and heat].//
= word
A simple explanation would go something like this: / when we eat or
仮定を含む S V =コロン以下
drink, / the same nerves in the mouth react both to spicy chemicals
S V
in the food and to a rise in temperature.// The English expression, /
= "hot"
therefore, / reflects this fact about the human body.//
結果・結論 =前文のコロン以下（= when ... temperature）

解答

問 1 (1) ① (2) ③

問 2 こうした"hot"という単語の 2 つの異なる意味は，日本人の学生にとってはややこしいように思われるかもしれないが，実際のところ，その単語は適切なものである

問 3 ① ○ ② × ③ ○

Let's try A frank talk would lead to the solution of the problem.

解説

問 1(1) なぜ"hot"という英単語は日本人の学生を混乱させるのか。

①「"hot"は『香辛料がきいている』と『高温の』の両方の意味を表す。」(ll. 1 ～ 3)

②「カレーのようないわゆる"hot"な食べ物を説明する時，"spicy"という単語を使う。」

③「温度について話す時のみ"hot"という単語を使う。」

④「体が香辛料に反応する方法を言い表すのに"hot"という単語を使わない。」

(2) 英語を話す人たちが，カレーは"hot"な食べ物だと言う時，"hot"という単語は（ ）方法を言い表すのに使われている。

①「人体が体温の変化を感じる」

②「人体が高い温度のカレーに反応する」

③「口の中にある神経が香辛料の化学物質に反応する」(*ll*.7～8)

④「口の中にある神経が高い温度のカレーに反応する」

問2 may seem ＋形容詞, but ...「～に思われるかもしれないが，しかし…」

as a matter of fact「実は；実際のところ」(*l*.4)

the word (*l*.4) は "hot" という単語のことを指している。

問3 ①「"hot" という単語には2つの異なる意味がある。」(*ll*.1～3)

②「私たちの体は香辛料の化学物質に対してと温度の上昇に対してではまったく異なる方法で反応する。」(*ll*.7～9)

③「"hot" という単語は香辛料のきいた食べ物と温度の上昇の両方に使われる。なぜなら，両方の場合で同じ神経が反応するからだ。」(*ll*.7～9)

Let's try 「率直な話し合い」a frank talk

「もしSならば…だろう」仮定を含むS ＋ would *do*

主語 A frank talk に「率直な話し合いであれば」という仮定の意味を含んでいる。

概要を整理しよう

主張	"hot" の持つ2つの意味；「香辛料のきいた」／「熱い」 →この単語は適切だ
理由の説明	口の中の同じ神経が，香辛料の化学物質と温度上昇の両方に反応する ◆ therefore「したがって：結果・結論」(*l*.9) → "hot" という表現は，人体のこの事実を反映している

背景知識 神経での刺激の伝わり方から説明できる英語のhot

実は，「熱い」と感じる刺激と「辛い」と感じる刺激は，いずれも同じ刺激として伝わる。胡椒や唐辛子などを口にした時に「辛い」と感じる刺激である「辛味」は，基本五味（「苦味」「酸味」「甘味」「塩味」「旨味」）とは異なるものとされている。そして辛味は，味を感じる器官である舌の味蕾を通さず，温度や痛みを感じる温痛覚を刺激してそれが脳に伝わる，ということが通説となっている。したがって，この説に準ずる限り，「辛味」は温痛覚で感じられるので，「熱さ」を感じるのと同じ伝導路を通ることになり，その両者を hot と表現するのはむしろ自然であると言える。

1 People today are worried about food safety.// **As a result**, / the popularity of "organic" farming of fruits and vegetables is increasing.// But / what exactly does organic farming mean?//

2 It is probably easier <to explain [what organic farming is not]>.// Organic farming does not use pesticides or fertilizers.// **Instead**, / this style of farming uses natural methods <to protect plants and help them grow>.// **So**, / organic agricultural products are thought <to be generally safer / than non-organic ones>.//

3 In the United States, / about two percent of all food is grown / <using organic methods>.// The U.S. government officially licenses farms as "organic" / if they pass an examination.// Presently, / there are about 10,000 licensed farmers in the U.S., / and this number is growing by about 20% a year.//

解答

問1 (1) ④ (2) ②

問2 おそらく，何が有機農業ではないかを説明する方が簡単だろう。

問3 ① ○ ② × ③ ×

Let's try Electric cars〔vehicles〕are thought to be more eco-friendly than gasoline cars〔vehicles〕.

解説

問 1(1)　有機農業では，合衆国の農場経営者は（　　）。

①「できるだけ少量の農薬を使って植物を育てている」

②「有機栽培の方法を使う前に試験に合格しなければならない」

③「認可を受けた農薬か化学肥料を使わなければならない」

④「自然な方法を使ってすべての食物の約 2%を育てている」（ll. 9 ~ 10）

(2)　合衆国で認可を受けた有機栽培の農場経営者は今から 2 年後に何人になるか。

①「約 12,000 人」②「約 14,000 人」③「約 16,000 人」④「約 20,000 人」

10,000 人が 1 年間で 20% ずつ増加（ll. 11 ~ 13）→ 10,000 × 1.2 × 1.2 = 14,400

問 2　it is ～ to *do*「…するのは～だ」

explain の目的語 what 以降は，What is not organic farming? という疑問文が間接疑問になっている。

問 3　①「人々が食物の安全について懸念しているため，有機農業の人気が高まっている。」（ll. 1 ~ 2）

②「有機栽培の生産物は農薬で保護されているためにより安全であると考えられている。」（l. 5）

③「約 20% の合衆国の農場経営者が農業において有機栽培の方法を利用している。」（ll. 11 ~ 13）

Let's try　「O を～と考える」think + O + to be ～（l. 7）

「環境にやさしい」eco-friendly；be good〔safe〕for the environment

概要を整理しよう

導入　今日の人々は食物の安全について懸念している

主題　◆ **As a result「その結果：結果・結論」**（l. 1）

→有機農業に対する人気が上昇している

具体的説明　有機農業は殺虫剤や農薬を使わない

◆ **Instead「その代わりに：逆接」**（l. 5）

植物を保護し，成長を助けるのに，自然な方法を使う。

◆ **So「したがって：結果・結論」**（l. 7）

→有機農業の生産物は安全だと考えられる

・合衆国では，認可を受けた有機栽培農場経営者は約 1 万人で，毎年 20% 程度増加中

12 食の安全と有機農業（2）［環境］

1 **In addition to** food safety, / **another** reason for the popularity of organic fruits and vegetables is [that they taste better].// This is [why many restaurants only buy organic products].//

2 A lot of people think [∧organic farming is not competitive / <compared to other methods> / because it cannot grow the same quantity of food]. **However**, / new research has shown [that organic farming only grows, / on average, / about five percent less than non-organic methods].// Still, / organic food today is more expensive / than non-organic food.// **But** / when the environmental and health costs of non-organic farming are considered, / **such as** the pollution of water by pesticides, / most people would agree [that the higher price of organic farming is **in fact** a small price <to pay for our health and safety>].//

解答

問 1　(1) ③　(2) ④

問 2　食物の安全に加えて，有機栽培の果物や野菜が人気であるもう 1 つの理由は，それらの方が味がよいということだ。

問 3　① ○　② ×　③ ×

Let's try　I forgot to call her. This is why she's still angry with me.

解説

問 1(1)　なぜ多くの人々は有機農業に競争力がないと考えているのか。

①「例えば有機栽培の果物や野菜は大きさがより小さいことが多い。」

②「非有機農法も食の安全を考慮して使われている。」

③「有機農業は非有機農法より少量の食物しか栽培しない。」(ll. 4 ～ 5)

④「有機栽培の果物や野菜が多くのレストランで人気である。」

(2) なぜ人々が有機食品が高価格であることに同意するのか。

①「有機農業は天然資源を大量に消費する。」

②「有機食品が高級レストランでますます人気である。」

③「有機農業は非有機農法よりも栽培する量がずっと少ない。」

④「有機食品は健康や環境に配慮してつくられている。」(ll. 9 ~ 12)

問2 another reason for ~ is that …「~のもう1つの理由は…ということだ」 thatが導く名詞節が補語になっている。that節内の they = organic fruits and vegetables。

問3 ①「非有機栽培の生産物よりも味がよいために，有機栽培の生産物のみを購入するレストランがある。」(ll. 2 ~ 3)

②「有機農業は非有機農法よりもはるかに少量の食物しか生産しないために，有機食品の価格は高い。」(ll. 6 ~ 7)

③「筆者は，その恩恵にもかかわらずほとんどの人が有機農業のより高い価格について不満を言うだろうと考えている。」(ll. 10 ~ 12)

Let's try 「…するのを忘れる」forget to *do*／「こういうわけで…だ」this is why …
「~（人）に怒っている」be angry with ~

概要を整理しよう

・有機農産物の人気には，安全性に加えてもう1つ別の理由がある。

→味が他のものよりもよい。

・有機農産物の価格は高い。

◆ **But「しかし：逆接」**(l. 8) ／◆ **in fact「実際には：主張」**(l. 11)

環境や健康のことを考えると，それほど高くはないと言える。

背景知識　有機農産物の需要とマーケット開拓

ある調査によれば，有機農産物の小売販売高を高い順に並べると，アメリカ>ドイツ>フランスとなる。こうした有機農産物への需要は，人々の，健康と環境問題への意識の高まりを背景に著しく伸びている。有機農産物をはじめとする，いわゆるオーガニック食品を好む消費者層は「LOHAS 消費者層」と言われる。LOHAS とは Lifestyles of Health and Sustainability の略で，この名称は本来は環境や健康に対して意識の高い人々から成る社会集団に着目して名づけられたものであった。しかし昨今では，この層にあたる人々を対象としたマーケットを意味するものへとその意味が変化している。

13 数学の歴史（1）[歴史]

1 The knowledge of mathematics developed rapidly / in Europe and North America / after the industrial revolution.// **But** / the study of mathematics was carried out / many centuries before in other countries, **like** China.//

2 Over two thousand years ago, / the Chinese began their study of numbers, / <mostly related to astronomy and the perfection of a calendar>.// Already as early as 200 B.C. / they had written a textbook on mathematics / [that was called *The Nine Chapters on the Mathematical Art*].// Interestingly, / the ideas in this book seem to have been developed in China / without any influence from Europe or other regions.//

解答

問 1　(1)　①　　(2)　④

問 2　興味深いことに，この書籍の中の考え方は，ヨーロッパやその他の地域からのいかなる影響も受けることなしに，中国で発展してきたようだ。

問 3　①　×　　②　○　　③　○

Let's try　Akira had finished (writing) his paper as early as two weeks before the deadline.

解説

問 1 (1)　中国人はなぜ 2000 年以上前に数について研究を始めたのか。

① 「星とその動きについてもっと理解するため」(ll. 5 ～ 7)

② 「数学を芸術の一部にするため」

③ 「最初の暦を世界中に広めるため」 ④ 「数学についての教科書を記すため」

(2) 早くも紀元前200年に中国人によって記された数学についての教科書の中の考え方には，どの地域が影響を与えたか。

①「ヨーロッパの地域」②「北アメリカの地域」③「アジアの地域」

④「他のどの地域でもない」(ℓℓ.9～10)

問2 seem to have＋過去分詞「…だったようだ」(ℓ.9)

in this book は前の文で述べられている数学の教科書を指している。

without any influence from ～「～からのいかなる影響も受けずに」

問3 ①「中国は産業革命前に数学を研究した唯一の国だ。」(ℓℓ.2～4)

②「中国人は2000年以上前に暦の完成に関心を持っていた。」(ℓℓ.5～7)

③「紀元前200年に記された数学についての教科書の考え方に，ヨーロッパからのいかなる影響も見つけられない。」(ℓℓ.9～10)

Let's try 「早くも～には」as early as ～

「締め切り」が過去の時点であり，それよりもさらに2週間前のことなので過去完了で表す。

「書き上げた」→「書き終えた」had finished (writing) his paper〔report〕

概要を整理しよう

導入　産業革命後，ヨーロッパと北アメリカで数学の知識が急速に発展した

本論　◆ But「しかし：逆接」(ℓ.2)

他の国々では，その何世紀も前から数学の研究が行われていた。

◆ like「～のような：例示」(ℓ.4)

2000年以上前に中国では数学の研究が始まった。

・紀元前200年…『九章算術』の執筆

→ヨーロッパやその他地域の影響をまったく受けていない

背景知識 『九章算術』と，その時代

『九章算術』は紀元前1世紀から紀元後2世紀頃に中国で制作されたと考えられている。9章から成り，例えば田畑の面積の測量に必要な，長方形・円・台形の面積の算出法，土木・建築に関わる体積の算出法，租税の計算法など，主に行政の場において必要な知識を，246題の問題集形式で集めたものである。そこにはすでに，分数，平面，立体の求積，比例算，利息計算，ピタゴラスの定理の数学的証明，一次多元方程式，二次一元方程式などが含まれ，「方程」の章では，正負を用いた連立方程式も含まれていた。

14 数学の歴史（2）［歴史］

1 Various other books on mathematics appeared / in the following centuries.// **But**, / by the 5th century, / it seems [that the Chinese already had the concept of negative numbers / and perhaps **also** had the concept of “zero”].// Around the 13th century, / Chinese mathematicians were solving equations / <using methods [that Europeans would not discover / until 500 years later]>!//

2 Unfortunately, / near the end of the 14th century, / the leaders of China began to be critical of math and science.// Because of this change in attitude, / people turned away from the study of math / <to study plants and medicine instead>.// It wasn't until the 19th century / that the Chinese would become interested in math again, / **but** this time ∧ under the influence of European mathematical knowledge.//

解答

問 1 (1) （ア） ① （イ） ④ （ウ） ⑥ (2) ④

問 2 5 世紀までには，中国人はすでに負の数の概念を持ち，またおそらく「ゼロ」の概念も持っていただろうと思われる

問 3 ① × ② ○ ③ ○

Let's try It wasn't until Friday that I realized I had〔would have〕an exam on Monday.

解説

問 1(1)　ヨーロッパ人たちが方程式を解く方法を発見したのは500年後（　ア　）だった。のちに（　イ　）には，ヨーロッパの数学の知識（　ウ　）中国人は数学に再び関心を持つようになった。

①「～になって初めて」→（ア）(ll. 4 ～ 6) ②「～前に」③「14 世紀」

④「19 世紀」→（イ）(ll. 10 ～ 11) ⑤「～に影響を与えて」

⑥「～に影響されて」→（ウ）(ll. 11 ～ 12)

(2)　なぜ中国の人々は一度数学の研究に背を向けたのか。

①「人々が植物や医学のみに関心を持った。」

②「中国の指導者たちがもはや数学を研究することを許さなかった。」

③「中国の指導者たちが植物や医学のみを研究するよう命じた。」

④「中国の指導者たちが数学の研究に対する姿勢を変えた。」(ll. 7 ～ 10)

問 2　it seems that ...「…だと思われる」(l. 2)

that 節内の主語 the Chinese に続いて，had the concept of ～と also had the concept of ～の 2 つ動詞があることに注意。

問 3　①「中国人が 13 世紀頃に用いた方法は 14 世紀にヨーロッパ人たちによって発見された。」(ll. 4 ～ 6)

②「中国は 14 世紀の終わり近くには数学への関心を失い始めた。」(ll. 7 ～ 9)

③「19 世紀には，ヨーロッパの数学の知識から学んだ中国人が少なくなかった。」

(ll. 10 ～ 12)

Let's try　「～になって初めて…」it isn't until ～ that …

「試験がある」have an exam〔an examination ; a test〕

概要を整理しよう

中国の数学の歴史

・5 世紀までに…負の数の概念を持ち，さらにはおそらく「ゼロ」の概念も持っていた

・13 世紀頃…ヨーロッパでは 500 年後まで発見されなかった方法で方程式を解いていた

・14 世紀の終わり…指導者たちが数学や科学に対し批判的になった

→人々が数学から離れた

・19 世紀…中国人は再び数学に関心を持つようになった

◆　**but「しかし：逆接」**(l. 11)

→ヨーロッパの数学の影響を受けていた

15 遺伝子と行動 [科学]

Genes, the basic parts of cells / [which are passed down from parents to children], / may have something <to do with human behavior>.// In an experiment, / scientists put flies into a glass tube / and placed a light at the end of it.// **Some** of the flies began flying toward the light, / **some** began walking, / and **some** did not move at all.// On the basis of the flies' actions, / they were separated into different groups: / flies [that love light], flies [that like light], and flies [that like the dark].// The researchers found [that these three groups of flies had variations / in a particular set of genes]. This suggested to the researchers [that the variations in these genes might explain the differences in the flies' behaviors].// If genes influence behaviors in flies, / why not in humans too?//

解答

問 1 (1) ③ (2) ②

問 2 遺伝子は親から子供へと伝えられる細胞の基礎的な部分であるが，人間の行動と関係があるかもしれない。

問 3 ① × ② ○ ③ ○

Let's try Some students like〔prefer〕paper books, and some like〔prefer〕e-books.

解説

問 1(1) ハエの行動（　　）。

①「における違いを，光との距離が引き起こしたかもしれない」

②「に光の種類が強い影響を与えたかもしれない」

③「における違いを，遺伝子の変異が引き起こしたかもしれない」（ll. 9 ～ 10）

④「における違いを，特定の遺伝子の欠如が引き起こしたかもしれない」

(2)　下線部 (2) に最も近い意味のものは次のうちどれか。

①「遺伝子は人間の行動に影響を与えないだろう。」

②「遺伝子は人間がすることにも影響を与えるかもしれない。」(*ll.* 10 ~ 11)

③「私たちは人間の遺伝子の影響を研究すべきである。」

④「私たちの行動への遺伝子の影響は説明できない。」

問 2　have something to do with ～「～と関係がある」(*l.* 2)

the basic parts ～ children が Genes の同格表現となっている。

問 3　①「実験の後，科学者たちは大きさと重さによってハエを 3 つのグループに分けた。」(*ll.* 5 ~ 6)

②「ハエの遺伝子の研究は特定の 1 組の遺伝子に違いがあることを明らかにした。」(*ll.* 7 ~ 9)

③「科学者たちは特定の 1 組の遺伝子がハエの異なる行動を説明するかもしれないと考えた。」(*ll.* 9 ~ 10)

Let's try　「～するものもいれば，…するものもいる」some ～ , and some … some ..., others ～の表現も可。「電子書籍」e-books ; electronic〔digital〕books

概要を整理しよう

主題	遺伝子と人間の行動は，何か関係があるかもしれない
実験の経緯	ガラスの管にハエを入れ，管の先端に明かりを置く。 →ハエの行動に 3 つのパターンがあった →遺伝子を調べると，遺伝子のある特定の組に差異があった
結論	人間の行動の差異も，遺伝子に影響されているのでは

背景知識　遺伝子が人間の行動を規定する？

ヒトの行動についても遺伝子の何らかの影響を受けていると推論するのは，「遺伝子決定論」もしくは「生物学的決定論」と呼ばれる。これに対して，ヒトの行動については環境など非遺伝的な要因が関わるため，そのようには言えないとする非決定論もある。遺伝子決定論もしくは生物学的決定論に立つと，遺伝子こそがヒトひいては生物の行動を規定するものとなり，ヒトあるいは生物自身の意思的な要素にはまったく自由がないという杓子定規な世界観にもなりかねない。このようなことから，どちらの立場を取るかが議論の的となるのである。

16 風邪に関する常識［医療］

Ben Hemmens is the father of three children, / including four-year-old Sophie.// According to medical experts, / it is normal <for kids around this age to catch colds four to five times a year>.// In adults, / the ratio is about two to three times a year, / for reasons [that are not completely clear].// **However**, / says Dr. Ranit Mishori of Georgetown University Hospital, / [∧ many people believe [that it is possible to become immune to the common cold / so that one gets fewer and fewer colds as he ages]].// "There are about 200 types of virus / [that cause the common cold], / **yet** people think [that once you get infected one time, / you develop immunity for the rest of your life].// This is entirely wrong," / she claims.// There are simply too many different viruses, / [many of which change in slight ways / as they pass from person to person].//

解答

問 1 (1) ③ (2) ③

問 2 多くの人々が，風邪に対して免疫をつけることが可能なので，人は歳を取るにつれてどんどん風邪を引くことが少なくなる，と考えている

問 3 ① × ② ○ ③ ○

Let's try Once you get into the habit of being lazy, it's difficult to get rid of it.

解説

問 1(1) 多くの人々が知らない事実は次のうちどれか。

① 「成人は子供よりも風邪を引きにくい。」

② 「風邪を引き起こすウイルスは人から人へと広がる。」

③「風邪を引き起こすおよそ 200 種類のウイルスがある。」(ℓℓ.8 ~ 10)

④「1 回風邪を引くと免疫ができる。」

(2)　ラニ・ミショリ博士の発言によると，次のうち正しいものはどれか。

①「いかなる風邪にも免疫をつけることはできない。」

②「風邪を引き起こすウイルスの種類は多すぎて数え切れない。」

③「様々なウイルスの多くはわずかに変化するかもしれない。」(ℓℓ.11 ~ 12)

④「いくつかの風邪に免疫ができると風邪を引きにくくなる。」

問 2　believe の目的語となる that 節に it is ～ to *do* 構文「…することは～だ」が含まれている。

so that …「その結果…」(ℓ.7) ／ as he ages の as …「…するにつれて」

問 3　①「一般に，4 歳くらいの子供は年に 2 ~ 3 回風邪を引く。」(ℓℓ.2 ~ 3)

②「なぜ成人は子供よりも風邪を引くことが少なくなるのかは，誰にもはっきりとはわからない。」(ℓℓ.2 ~ 5)

③「ラニ・ミショリ博士によると，あまりに多くの種類のウイルスがあるので，風邪に対して免疫をつけることは不可能である。」(ℓℓ.9 ~ 11)

Let's try　「いったん…すれば」once + S + V

「…する癖がつく〔習慣になる〕」get into〔have ; become〕a habit of *doing*

「(習慣など) をやめる」get rid of ～〔give up ～ ; stop ～〕

概要を整理しよう

導入　大人の方が子供よりも風邪を引きにくいが，その理由は明らかになっていない

本論　◆ **However「しかし：逆接」**(ℓ.5)

一般の人の考え …風邪に対する免疫をつけることが可能

医者の反論 …風邪の原因となるウイルスは約 200 種類もある

→その多くが人々の間で伝染するうちにわずかに変化する

(風邪を引けば風邪にかかりにくくなるという一般的な見解を否定)

17 英単語はいくつあるか（1）［言語］

1 English is a language with an enormous number of words, / but how many English words are there?// Most dictionaries <used by college students> have about 200,000 words, / **while** most full-length dictionaries have about 300,000 to 600,000.// **Meanwhile**, / an organization <called the Global Language Monitor> positively claims [that there are exactly 1,019,729 English words].//

2 **But** counting the number of words in English is not an easy task.// **First of all**, / many words [that we use in English today] were originally words in other languages.// Should the words *sushi* or *tsunami* be considered English words / now that they are frequently used?// Then there is the question of words [that were used centuries ago / but are no longer used today].// Should they be counted too?// What about words [that are only used in certain regions of a country]?//

解答

問1 (1) （ア） ③　（イ） ⑤　（ウ） ⑥　（エ） ⑧
(2) ①, ③, ④

問2 「スシ」や「ツナミ」という単語は今や頻繁に使われているので，それらは英単語であるとみなされるべきだろうか。

問3 ① ×　② ○　③ ○

Let's try In my neighborhood there is a big pool which is no longer used.

解説

問 1(1)　大学生用のたいていの英語の辞書にはほぼ 20 万語が載っているが，大部分の標準的な辞書には約（　ア　）から（　イ　）の語が載っていて，ある団体は正確な語数は約（　ウ　）の（　エ　）数であると主張している。

①「3 分の 1」　②「3 分の 2」　③「1.5 倍」→（ア）（*ll.* 3 ～ 4）
④「2 倍」　⑤「3 倍」→（イ）（*ll.* 3 ～ 4）　⑥「5 倍」→（ウ）（*l.* 6）
⑦「多い」　⑧「大きい」→（エ）（number を修飾する形容詞）

(2)　英単語の数を数えることをより難しくするものは次のうちどれか。選択肢は 1 つ以上選んでもよい。

①「英語は他の言語から多くの単語を借用してきた。」（*ll.* 8 ～ 9）
②「英単語を数える団体がある。」
③「数世紀前に使われていた単語で，今日ではもう使われていない単語がある。」（*ll.* 11 ～ 12）
④「一国のある地域の人々しか話していない単語がある。」（*ll.* 12 ～ 13）

問 2　now that S V…「今や…なのだから」（*l.* 10）
consider A（to be）B「A を B とみなす」→受動態の形で，the words *sushi* or *tsunami* should be considered English words が疑問文になった状態。

問 3　①「大学生用のたいていの辞書には約 2 万語が載っている。」（*ll.* 2 ～ 3）
②「英単語の正確な数を数えたと主張している団体がある。」（*ll.* 4 ～ 6）
③「今日英語で使われている多くの単語は英語以外に起源を持つ。」（*ll.* 8 ～ 9）

Let's try　「もはや…ない」no longer ...
否定の not を使った not ... any longer も同様の意味を表す。

概要を整理しよう

疑問の提示　英単語はいくつあるか

具体例
・大学生の使う辞書に載っている語：約 20 万語
・標準的な辞書に載っている語：約 30 万～ 60 万語
・ある団体の主張：101 万 9,729 語

課題①
◆　**But「しかし：逆接」**（*l.* 7）
英単語を数える作業は簡単ではない。
◆　**First of all「最初に：列挙」**（*l.* 8）
外来語／今日使われていない古い語／方言などをどう見なすか

18 英単語はいくつあるか (2) [言語]

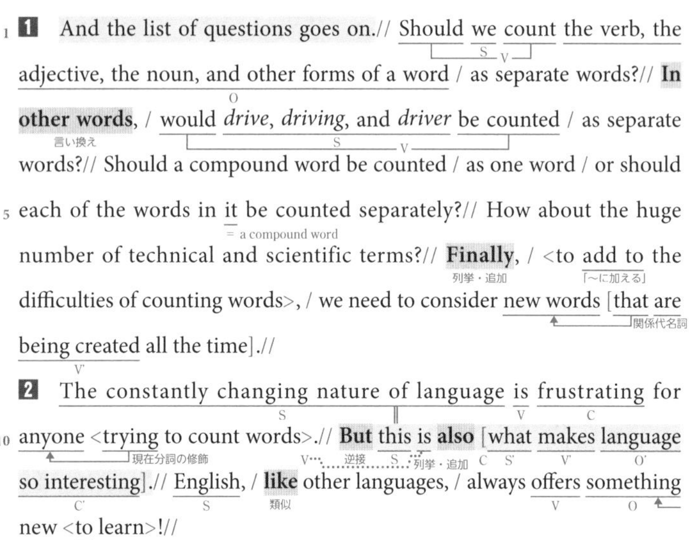

1 And the list of questions goes on.// Should we count the verb, the adjective, the noun, and other forms of a word / as separate words?// **In other words**, / would *drive*, *driving*, and *driver* be counted / as separate words?// Should a compound word be counted / as one word / or should each of the words in it be counted separately?// How about the huge number of technical and scientific terms?// **Finally**, / <to add to the difficulties of counting words>, / we need to consider new words [that are being created all the time].//

2 The constantly changing nature of language is frustrating for anyone <trying to count words>.// **But** this is **also** [what makes language so interesting].// English, / **like** other languages, / always offers something new <to learn>!//

解答

問 1 (1) (ア) ② (イ) ① (ウ) ④ (2) ④

問 2 単語を数えることの難しさに加えて，私たちは絶えず生み出されている新語を考慮に入れる必要がある

問 3 ① × ② ○ ③ ○

Let's try Mr. Yamada provides us with something interesting to learn.

解説

問 1(1) 単語を数えるのを難しくしているのは，1 つの単語に多くの形があることである。例えば，'attend' という語は (ア) だが，'attendance' と 'attention' という 2 つの (イ) 形がある。さらに，'attendant' という (ウ) 形は人の世話をする人という意味の名詞としても使うことができる。

①「名詞」→（イ）②「動詞」→（ア）③「副詞」④「形容詞」→（ウ）

(2)　単語を数えることをいらいらさせる要素でないのは次のうちどれか。

①「膨大な数の専門用語や科学用語がある。」(ll.5〜6)

②「複合語は1語として数えるか2語として数えるかが難しい。」(ll.4〜5)

③「言語はそれ自体絶えず変化する。」(ll.7〜8)

④「言語は学ぶべき新しいことをいつも提供してくれる。」

問2　to add to 〜「〜に加えて」

be動詞＋being＋過去分詞「…されている〔されていた〕」(l.8)受動態の進行形。

関係代名詞 that 以降が new words を修飾している。

問3　①「私たちは絶えず生み出されている新語を無視できる。」(ll.7〜8)

②「単語を数えようとしている人は，言語が変化を止めることが決してないのでいらいらするかもしれない。」(ll.9〜10)

③「私たちは言語についていつも新しいことを学ぶことができる。」(ll.11〜12)

Let's try　「何か〜な…するもの」something＋形容詞＋to *do*

「AにBを提供する」provide A with B〔offer B to A〕

「学ぶ興味がわくもの」something interesting to learn

概要を整理しよう

課題②　英単語を数える際のさらなる問題

1つの語の語形／複合語／専門用語・科学用語／新語などをどう見なすか

主張　◆　But「しかし：逆接」(l.10)

◆　also「また：列挙・追加」(l.10)

その性質が言語の面白いところだ。

→英語はどんどん学ぶべき新しいことが出てくるため

背景知識　辞書に載せるべき単語についての争い

ノア・ウェブスターは，アメリカ自前の最初の辞書となる『アメリカ英語辞典』を編纂した。しかし，これは出版当初，アメリカ国内のジャーナリズムなどから大いに批判を受けた。当時，『ウェブスター新国際英語辞典第2版』（1934年）がアメリカで「最高の権威」を持つ辞書ととらえられていたこともあり，例えば，ain't (am not ／ aren't ／ isn't などの略) の収録など，「『正しくない英語』を権威ある辞書に載せるとは何事か」，などという批判を浴びた。辞書の規範性を重視するか，現代語の記述を重視するかでこのような論争が起こったのである。

19 結婚式の慣習（1）［文化］

1 Traditions and customs <based on superstitions and religion> / have been an important aspect of weddings / in all cultures.// They vary greatly from one country to another / and sometimes ∧ even between different ethnic groups / in a particular country.//

2 **Though** many traditions and customs have been forgotten through the years, / many of today's wedding ceremonies have their beginnings / in ancient beliefs and customs / [that originated / in medieval times].// In a Christian wedding, / the bride usually wears a white wedding gown / <to show [that she is pure]>.// White was a color [that was once believed to keep evil spirits away].// **On the other hand**, / in Hinduism, white signifies the color of death.// A Hindu bride usually wears a red dress with gold stitching.// In China, both the bride and groom are dressed in red, / [which is a color <associated with celebration and good fortune>].//

解答

問 1 (1) ③　(2) ③

問 2 中国では，新郎新婦の両人が赤い色に身を包むが，これは祝賀と幸運に結び付けられている色なのである。

問 3 ① ○　② ○　③ ×

Let's try The number 7 is believed to be a lucky number.

解説

問 1(1)　今日の結婚式について正しくないのは次のうちどれか。

① 「古くからの信仰や慣習と結び付いている。」(*ll*. 6 ~ 7)

② 「結婚式の伝統や慣習は国ごとに異なる。」(*ll*. 2 ~ 4)

③ 「結婚式の慣習は長い年月を経て大きく変化した。」

④「人々は結婚式の古い伝統や慣習のいくつかに従っている。」(ℓℓ.6 ~ 7)

(2) ウエディングドレスの色について正しいのは次のうちどれか。

①「赤いドレスは血液を意味するので，中国の新婦は赤いドレスは着ない。」

②「白いドレスは死を意味するので，中国の新婦は白いドレスは着ない。」

③「キリスト教徒の新婦は純潔であることを示すために白いドレスを着る。」(ℓℓ.7 ~ 9)

④「ヒンドゥー教徒の新婦はセレブであることを示すために赤いドレスを着る。」

問2 , which is a color ~ fortune の部分は，先行詞 red について補足的な情報を加えている。(関係代名詞の非制限用法)

associate A with B「A で B を連想する；A と B を結び付ける」(ℓ.13)

問3 ①「あらゆる文化で伝統や慣習は結婚式の重要な一部である。」(ℓℓ.1 ~ 2)

②「キリスト教信者は，純潔の象徴と考えて，結婚式に白色を好む。」(ℓℓ.7 ~ 9)

③「ヒンドゥー教では，赤色はよいことを意味しないが，中国では意味する。」(ℓℓ.11 ~ 13)

Let's try 「…すると信じられている」be believed to *do*

「幸運な数字」a lucky number

概要を整理しよう

主題　あらゆる文化において，伝統と慣習は結婚式の重要な側面だ

具体例　今日の結婚式の多くには，古くからの信仰や慣習に発端がある

・キリスト教…新婦は白いドレスを着る　→白は純潔を表す

↕ ◆ On the other hand「一方：対比」(ℓ.10)

・ヒンドゥー教…新婦は赤いドレスを着る　→白は死の色を表す

・中国…新郎新婦は赤い衣装を着る　→赤は祝賀と幸運を表す

背景知識　現代の結婚式の慣習

ブライダル産業の企業戦略も手伝って，海外から現代日本の結婚式に取り入れられつつあるものも多い。No.20 の本文に出てくる，ライスシャワーやフラワーシャワーも，日本でもよく見られる。ライスシャワーには人生の豊かさと子宝に恵まれることを願う意味が，フラワーシャワーには新婚の 2 人の幸せをねたむ悪魔から守るという意味が込められている。一方，日本で一般的に行われている「お色直し」は，日本だけの慣習である。お色直しは，古くは白一色の白無垢から，嫁ぎ先の用意した色打掛に着替えていた武家の慣習に由来する。これには結婚して相手の家に染まるという意味が込められている。

1 In many cultures, / after the wedding / it is traditional for the groom <to carry the bride / over the threshold of their new home>.// This custom originated from the belief / [that bad luck may fall on the bride / if she enters a new home with her left foot first].// The custom of throwing rice or flowers at the newly married couple / <to wish them fertility and prosperity> / originated in Asia / and later became popular in America.// At a traditional Japanese wedding, / it is considered unlucky / <to use words like "cut", "separate", or "leave">.//

2 **Though** weddings in many parts of the world / still continue to be rituals / [that reflect ethnic, cultural, and social backgrounds], / contemporary weddings incorporate more meaningful customs / <better suited to today's values>.//

解答

問 1 (1) ① (2) ②

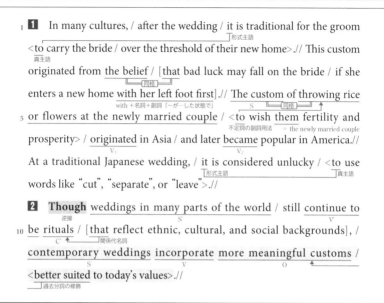

問 2 現代の結婚式は，今日の価値観により適した，より有意義な慣習を取り入れている

問 3 ① ○ ② × ③ ○

Let's try Japanese people have the custom of eating mochi〔rice cakes〕during the New Year's holidays.

解説

問 1 (1) 多くの国で，なぜ新しい家に入る時，新郎は新婦を抱えるのか。

① 「そうしないと不吉な出来事が彼女に起こるかもしれない。」（ll. 2～4）

② 「彼は新しい家に入る時，主導権を握るべきだと考えている。」

③ 「彼は彼女に前を歩いてほしくないと思っている。」

④「彼女は疲れすぎて自力で新しい家に入れなくなっている。」

(2)　現代の結婚式ににについて正しいのは次のうちどれか。

①「民族的，文化的，社会的背景を反映する必要がない。」

②「近年の価値観に対応する新しい慣習を取り入れている。」(ℓℓ. 11 ~ 12)

③「人々はいつも結婚式のいくつかの部分を変えようとする。」

④「人々はいつも断固として自身の伝統や慣習を守ろうとする。」

問 2　better suited to ～「～により適した」(ℓ. 12)

better は過去分詞 suited を修飾する副詞。better suited ～ values が more meaningful customs を修飾している。

問 3　①「新婦が左足から最初に新しい家に入ることは不吉だと考えられている。」(ℓℓ. 2 ~ 4)

②「アメリカ人が初めて米あるいは花を新婚の 2 人に投げた。」(ℓℓ. 4 ~ 6)

③「今日の結婚式は伝統的な側面と新しい慣習を組み合わせている。」(ℓℓ. 9 ~ 12)

Let's try　「…する慣習」the custom of *doing*

同格の of を使って「…という慣習」という意味を表す。「餅」は rice cakes と表すが，最近は *mochi* という表現もよく使われる。

概要を整理しよう

具体例　結婚式に影響を与えている信仰や慣習

多くの文化…結婚式の後，新郎が新婦を抱えて新居の敷居を越える

アジア　…多産や繁栄を願って，米や花を新郎新婦に投げる

→後にアメリカで広まった

日本　…結婚式では「切る」，「離れる」などの言葉は不吉

→結婚式は，民族的・文化的・社会的背景を反映する儀式

展開　◆ Though「しかし：逆接」(ℓ. 9)

現代では，今日の価値観により合った，より有意義な慣習を取り入れている。

21 遊びを通して学ぶこと（1）［教育］

1 When we watch kittens and puppies playing, / we realize [that through play / they are learning <how to live>].// They learn various physical skills, / **such as** <how to jump over barriers / without getting hurt>.// They **also** learn social interaction.// **For example**, / if a kitten bites his sister too hard, / she will get angry / and bite him back.// These physical and social skills form part of the training [that young animals need / <in order to grow up>].//

2 **Just as** kittens and puppies learn about <how to live through play>, / so do children.// **But** in present-day Japan, / especially in cities, / there is not much space for children <to play in>.// Children need to release their energy / for their mental and physical health.// They need space, / especially outdoors, / so that they can run, jump, and yell.//

解答

問 1 (1) ④ (2) ③

問 2 子猫や子犬が遊びを通して生きるすべについて学ぶのと同じように，（人間の）子供も学ぶ。

問 3 ① × ② ○ ③ ○

Let's try I left home early in the morning so that I wouldn't get caught in a traffic jam.

解説

問 1(1) 子猫や子犬が遊びを通して学ぶ教訓ではないのは次のうちどれか。

① 「他の子猫や子犬との交流の方法」（ℓ. 4）

② 「けがをすることなく障害物を跳び越える方法」（ℓ. 3）

③ 「さまざまな技能を身につけて成猫や成犬に成長する方法」（ℓℓ. 6 ～ 7）

④「きょうだいをかまないようにする方法」

(2)　筆者によると，なぜ子供たちには生きるすべを学ぶために十分な屋外の空間が必要なのか。

①「走り，跳び，そして大声で叫ぶことができるようになるため」

②「危険から身を守れるようになるため」

③「エネルギーを発散することで健康でいるため」(ll. 10 ～ 11)

④「さまざまな身体的技能を向上させるため」

問 2　so do〔does〕S「～ (S) もまた同じである」(l. 9)

so do の内容は文の前半「遊びを通して生きるすべについて学ぶ」ことを指す。

問 3　①「子猫や子犬は遊びを通して敵と戦う方法を学ぶ。」(ll. 1 ～ 4)

②「日本の都市の子供には遊ぶための空間が多くない。」(ll. 9 ～ 10)

③「生きるすべを学ぶために，子供には特に屋外の空間が必要だ。」(ll. 8 ～ 12)

Let's try　「～ (S) が…するために」so that S can〔will〕*do*

「交通渋滞」a traffic jam

「～ (渋滞など) に巻き込まれる」get caught in ～

概要を整理しよう

導入　子猫や子犬は遊びを通して生きるすべを学ぶ

身体的技能や社会的な交流も学ぶ。

課題①　◆ Just as ～「ちょうど～のように：類似」(l. 8)

人間の子供も動物の子供のように，遊びを通して生きるすべを学ぶ

◆ But「しかし：逆接」(l. 9)

現在の日本では遊ぶ場所がない。

結論　子供はエネルギーを発散させるために屋外の遊び場が必要だ

背景知識　「遊び」を通じた子供の発達－社会性を身に付ける

子供の遊び方は，成長とともに変わっていく。遊び相手として両親だけが必要であったところから，1 歳～ 3 歳の間に同年齢の子供へと遊び相手が変わってゆく。そして 5 歳～ 8 歳という時期を迎えて，同年齢の仲間同士の関係性を重視するようになり，さらに 8 歳～ 11 歳になると，親友関係が生まれ，両親との関係よりも親友関係を大事にするようになる。この時期を経て小学校高学年～中学生頃までの時期になると，4 人～ 8 人の同年代の仲間との結びつきを強くし，そのような仲間同士でグループを作って行動する。子供は集団内での自分の役割を得ることで，責任感や義務感，忠誠といったさまざまな社会性を学ぶ。

22 遊びを通して学ぶこと (2) [教育]

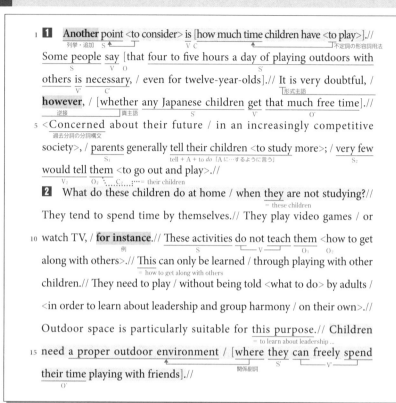

1 Another point <to consider> is [how much time children have <to play>].// Some people say [that four to five hours a day of playing outdoors with others is necessary, / even for twelve-year-olds].// It is very doubtful, / however, / [whether any Japanese children get that much free time].// <Concerned about their future / in an increasingly competitive society>, / parents generally tell their children <to study more>; / very few would tell them <to go out and play>.//

2 What do these children do at home / when they are not studying?// They tend to spend time by themselves.// They play video games / or watch TV, / for instance.// These activities do not teach them <how to get along with others>.// This can only be learned / through playing with other children.// They need to play / without being told <what to do> by adults / <in order to learn about leadership and group harmony / on their own>.// Outdoor space is particularly suitable for this purpose.// Children need a proper outdoor environment / [where they can freely spend their time playing with friends].//

解答

問 1　(1)　④　　(2)　②

問 2　しかし，どの日本の子供にもそれほど多くの自由時間があるかどうかは非常に疑わしい。

問 3　①　×　　②　×　　③　○

Let's try　Mr. & Ms. Smith enjoyed their dinner without being disturbed by their children.

解説

問 1(1) なぜ今日の親は子供の将来を心配するのか。

①「子供が統率力やグループの調和を学ぼうとしない。」

②「子供がもう他の子供と外に行って遊ばないかもしれない。」

③「社会がテクノロジーに依存しすぎるようになっている。」

④「社会がますます競争が激しくなってきている。」(ℓℓ. 5 ～ 6)

(2) 子供はどのように他人との付き合い方を学べるのか。

①「家で一緒にテレビゲームをしたりテレビを見たりすることによって」

②「屋外で自由に他の子供と一緒に遊んで過ごすことによって」(ℓℓ. 10 ～ 13)

③「より競争的な方法で他の子供と勉強することによって」

④「他の子供とさまざまな話題について自由に話すことによって」

問 2 it is ～ whether …「…かどうかは～である」(ℓℓ. 3 ～ 4)

It の真主語は不定詞や that 節で示されることが多いが，このように whether の節が真主語になることもある。whether は「…かどうか」という意味を表す。

問 3 ①「日本の平均的な 12 歳の子供は 1 日に 4，5 時間遊ぶ。」(ℓℓ. 3 ～ 4)

②「テレビゲームをしたり，テレビを見たりすることは他人との付き合い方を教える。」(ℓℓ. 10 ～ 11)

③「統率力やグループの調和について学ぶために，子供は友達と遊ぶ必要がある。」(ℓℓ. 11 ～ 13)

Let's try 「…することなく」without *doing*

「～に邪魔される」なので，be disturbed by ～ → without being disturbed by ～となる。

概要を整理しよう

課題② もう 1 つの重要な点：遊ぶ時間の長さ

→ 4，5 時間外で遊ぶことが必要という人もいる

◆ **however「しかし：逆接」**(ℓ. 4)

日本の子供にはそんな時間はなさそうだ。

具体例 子供は家の中で勉強していない時何をしているか

◆ **for instance「例えば：例示」**(ℓ. 10)

1 人でテレビゲームをしたりテレビを見たりする。

→これでは統率力やグループの調和は学べない

結論 こうした技能の獲得のためにも子供には屋外の遊び場が必要だ

23 サッカーの起源（1）［歴史］

1 There is much debate / on the origin of the game of football.// The Japanese and Chinese claim to have invented a sport ∧ similar to modern soccer many centuries ago.//

2 **In comparison to** modern soccer, / the Japanese game of *kemari* was a game [that used a large ball <stuffed with sawdust>].// This version used a field [which was set up by choosing four trees].// These trees were usually cherry, maple, pine and willow.// Many large houses in Japan would grow these trees <to make a field for *kemari*>.// *Kemari* was normally played with two to twelve players.//

3 China's version, *tsu chu*, involved players <hitting a leather, fur-stuffed ball into a small hole>.// As ∧ in soccer, no player could use his hands during play.// It was considered an honor <to be part of a team>.// The first international soccer or *tsu chu* match is believed <to have been held in China around 50 B.C.>//

解答

問 1 (1) ③ (2) ②

問 2 チームの一員になることは，名誉であると考えられていた。

問 3 ① × ② ○ ③ ×

Let's try Mika seems to have had a fight with Kana yesterday.

解説

問 1(1) 日本の蹴鞠競技で通例必要としなかったものは何か。

① 「通例，サクラ，カエデ，マツ，ヤナギの，4 本の木」（ll. 6 ~ 7）

② 「2 名から 12 名の競技者」（ll. 8 ~ 9） ③ 「競技場の小さな穴」

④ 「おがくずを詰め込んだ大きな鞠」（ll. 4 ~ 5）

(2) 紀元前50年頃に中国で名誉であると考えられていたことは何か。

①「中国で蹴鞠の国際的な試合を行うこと」

②「蹴鞠のチームの一員としてプレイすること」(ℓ.12)

③「毛を詰めた革製の鞠を小さな穴の中に入れること」

④「手を使わずに蹴鞠をプレイすること」

問2 it is considered 〜 to *do*「…することは〜と考えられている」(ℓ.12)

問3 ①「日本の蹴鞠の方が中国の蹴鞠よりも早くに確立したことは疑いない。」(ℓℓ.1〜3)

②「蹴鞠競技の競技者の数は柔軟だ。」(ℓℓ.8〜9)

③「中国の蹴鞠は，競技者がおがくずを詰め込んだ大きな鞠を小さな穴の中にたたき込まなければならない。」(ℓℓ.10〜11)

Let's try 「…したこと」to have 過去分詞（完了不定詞の表現）
「けんかをする」have a fight〔an argument ; a quarrel〕

概要を整理しよう

導入　日本と中国が，自国のスポーツこそがサッカーの起源と主張。

日本起源の蹴鞠

・道具はおがくずを詰めた大きな鞠
・競技場は4種の木を選んで設営
・競技者数は2人〜12人

中国起源の蹴鞠

・毛を詰めた革製の鞠を蹴って小さな穴に入れる
・サッカーと同じく，プレイ中は手を使えない
・紀元前50年頃に最初の国際的な試合

背景知識　中国の蹴鞠（*tsu chu*）

tsu chu は，中国古代の神話上の統治者とされる黄帝（紀元前2500年頃の人物とされる）が創始であるという説がある。帝の治世，蚩尤（しゆう）という人物がいたが，この人物は帝に取って代わろうと自分の親族や武器を駆使して戦をしかけたとされる。これに対抗し，戦いを続けた黄帝はついに勝利を収めるところとなり，首謀者である蚩尤を捕えて斬首し，その首を鞠のように蹴ったことが *tsu chu* の始まりとされる。

24 サッカーの起源（2）［歴史］

1 The Emperor of the Han Dynasty was an avid, early player and fan of *tsu chu*.// This spread the popularity of *tsu chu* all over China.// Some people in China claim [that it is even possible [∧*tsu chu* could go back to 5000 B.C.]]//

2 The British claim [that soccer was created in the 8th century in Britain].// It was not a recreational sport at the time, / but a war game.// It was a violent game / and serious injury and even death were not uncommon.// It was not until 1815 [when Eton College set up a series of rules for the game] / that it became a less violent sport.// At that time, / colleges began to play /<using similar rules>.// In 1848, the rules were set by Cambridge University.// In the Cambridge rules, / shin-kicking and carrying the ball were forbidden.// This is ∧[where rugby and soccer developed into two different sports].//

解答

問 1 (1) ② (2) ④

問 2 イートン校が競技の一連のルールを設けた 1815 年になって初めて，サッカーはそれほど暴力的ではないスポーツになったのである。

問 3 ① ○ ② × ③ ×

Let's try This is where many Japanese come to see cherry blossoms〔cherry trees〕in full bloom.

解説

問 1(1)　蹴鞠について正しくないものは次のうちどれか。

①「蹴鞠の歴史は 7000 年以上であり得る。」(ll. 3 ～ 4)

②「漢の皇帝が軍事演習として蹴鞠を広めた。」

③「かつて中国の皇帝自身が蹴鞠の競技者だった。」(ll. 1 ～ 2)

④「皇帝が蹴鞠を愛したため蹴鞠は中国全土に広まった。」(l. 2)

(2)　英国で 8 世紀にサッカーが生み出された時，それはどのようなスポーツだったか。

①「人々が娯楽として競技することが許された唯一のスポーツだった。」

②「競技中に深刻な負傷をする競技者はほとんどいなかった。」

③「競技者は脛蹴りやボールを手で持って移動することができなかった。」

④「死にさえする競技者もいる軍事演習だった。」(ll. 6 ～ 8)

問 2　it is not until ～ that …「～になって初めて…する」(ll. 8 ～ 9)

when ～ for the game（イートン校が競技の一連のルールを設けた）は，関係副詞 when の導く節が先行詞 1815 を修飾している。

問 3　①「漢の皇帝は蹴鞠の大ファンなだけでなく，競技者でもあった。」(ll. 1 ～ 2)

②「一部のイギリスの人々は，サッカーの起源は紀元前 5000 年にさかのぼりうると主張している。」(ll. 5 ～ 6)

③「19 世紀の最初にケンブリッジ大学が競技中にボールを手で持って移動できるルールを定めた。」(ll. 10 ～ 12)

Let's try　「ここで…する」this is where …　ある時点や場所について説明する表現
「満開の桜」cherry blossoms in full bloom〔at their best〕

概要を整理しよう

中国での蹴鞠の歴史　→紀元前 5000 年にさかのぼるという主張

漢の皇帝が蹴鞠の競技者でありファン→蹴鞠が中国全土に広まった

英国でのサッカーの歴史　→ 8 世紀に生みだされたという主張

もとは娯楽ではなく，軍事演習だった。

・1815 年，イートン校がルールを定め，以前ほど暴力的な競技ではなくなった

・1848 年，ケンブリッジ大学がルールを定め，脛蹴りや，ボールを手で運ぶことが禁止された

→ここから，ラグビーとサッカーが，別々の発展を遂げた

25 ハエの超能力（1）［科学］

1 A fly can do one thing extremely well: fly.// Recently / a team of British scientists declared [that the common housefly is the most talented aerodynamicist on the planet, / <(being) superior to any bird, bat, or bee>].// A housefly can make six turns a second; / hover; / fly straight up, down, or backward; / land on the ceiling; / and perform various other show-off maneuvers.// And it has a brain /<smaller than a sesame seed>.//

2 Michael Dickinson, / [who studies fly flight in his lab at the California Institute of Technology], / says [(that) the housefly isn't actually the best flier].// "Hoverflies are the be-all and end-all," / he says.// They can hover in one spot, / dash to another location, / and then race back to their original hovering point / — precisely.//

3 Scientists, engineers, and military researchers want to know [how creatures with such small brains can do that].// Maybe they could reverse-engineer a fly <to make a robotic device / [that could reconnoiter dangerous places, / **such as** earthquake zones or collapsed mines]>.//

解答

問1 (1) ②　(2) ①

問2 科学者，技術者，そして軍の研究者は，これほど小さな脳しか持たない生き物が，どうしてそのようなことができるのか知りたがっている。

問3 ① ×　② ○　③ ×

Let's try Kota, who is my best friend, is familiar with〔knows a lot about〕computers.

解説

問 1(1)　どこにでもいるイエバエについて正しくないものは次のうちどれか。

①「1 秒間に 6 回転できる。」(ℓ.4)

②「空中にとどまり，前方に飛び，初めにとどまっていた地点に戻ることができる。」

③「垂直方向に飛ぶことができる。」(ℓℓ.4 ～ 5)

④「天井にさえとまることができる。」(ℓ.5)

(2)　科学者，技術者，軍の研究者はなぜハエの飛行を研究したいのか。

①「ハエの飛行技術をロボットの装置に応用したい。」(ℓℓ.13 ～ 15)

②「ハナアブが一番飛行能力があるのかどうか知りたい。」

③「ハエのように極小の軍事用機器を開発したい。」

④「ハエよりも有能な新種を発見したい。」

問 2　how creatures with such small brains can do that「これほど小さな脳しか持たない生き物が，どうしてそのようなことができるのか」(ℓ.13)
疑問詞が導く名詞節。do that は前文の内容（ハナアブの飛行能力）を指す。

問 3　①「英国の科学者たちが，どこにでもいるイエバエをある種のショーで芸をするように訓練できることを明らかにした。」(ℓℓ.1 ～ 3)

②「マイケル・ディキンソンは，ハナアブはどこにでもいるイエバエよりもうまく飛ぶと考えている。」(ℓℓ.7 ～ 9)

③「中には危険な場所でハエを飛ばす可能性を研究している科学者や技術者もいる。」(ℓℓ.12 ～ 15)

Let's try　「その人は…なのだが」, who ...　関係代名詞の非制限用法。
「(人が) ～ (ものごと) に詳しい」be familiar with ～

概要を整理しよう

・英国の科学者たちのハエに対する見解
どこにでもいるイエバエは地球上で最も有能な空気力学者である。

・マイケル・ディキンソンの見解
ハナアブは，イエバエよりもさらに飛行能力が高い。
→この飛行技術を解析・模倣できれば危険な地域を偵察する装置の開発に役立つ

26 ハエの超能力（2）[科学]

1 Dickinson's laboratory works with fruit flies.// Researchers put them in chambers and manipulate the visual field, / <filming the flies in super-slow motion, 6,000 frames a second>.// Dickinson is interested in knowing [how flies avoid collisions].// He has found [that certain patterns, / **such as** 90-degree turns, / are triggered by visual cues and two equilibrium organs on their backs [that function like a gyroscope]].//

2 Flies have only a dozen muscles for maneuvering, / **but** they're loaded with sensors.// **In addition to** their compound eyes, / [which permit panoramic imagery and are excellent at detecting motion], / they have wind-sensitive hairs and antennae.// They **also** have three light sensors on the tops of their heads, [which tell them [which way is up]].// Roughly two-thirds of a fly's entire nervous system is devoted / to processing visual images.// They take all this sensory data / and boil it down to a few basic commands, / such as "go left" and "go right."//

解答

問1 (1) ③　(2) ②

問2 全景が見渡せる画像を可能にし，動きを探知するのに秀でた複眼に加え，（ハエは）風に敏感な体毛と触角を持っている。

問3 ① ○　② ×　③ ×

Let's try Students ran up to the window(s), pointing at the big rainbow.

解説

問 1 (1)　ディキンソンの研究室の研究者たちは，ミバエの体のセンサーの使い方を知るために何をするか。

① 「ハエを非常にゆっくり飛ばして撮影する。」

② 「障害物を置いてハエがどのように衝突を避けるかを調べる。」

③ 「視野を操作してハエがどのように反応するかを調べる。」（*ll*. 1 ～ 4）

④ 「ハエに頭頂部のジャイロスコープのような器官を使わせる。」

(2)　ミバエについて正しいものは次のうちどれか。

① 「複眼を使ってどの方向が上かを知る。」

② 「神経系統の 3 分の 2 を使って視覚映像を処理する。」（*ll*. 12 ～ 13）

③ 「頭の上に，動きを探知する 12 の筋肉がある。」

④ 「すべての感覚情報を光を感じ取るセンサーを使って取り込む。」

問 2　in addition to ～「～に加えて」

, which ...「そしてそれは…」（*l*. 8）関係代名詞の非制限用法。which ～ motion が their compound eyes を修飾している。

問 3　① 「ディキンソンはスーパースローモーション撮影を使ってハエが衝突を避ける仕組みを分析する。」（*ll*. 1 ～ 4）

② 「筋肉量が非常に少ないので，飛ぶときには代わりに敏感な体毛と触覚を使う。」（*ll*. 7 ～ 10）

③ 「他の筋肉とともに，ハエには背中に 3 つの光を感じ取るセンサーがある。」（*ll*. 10 ～ 11）

Let's try　付帯状況を表す分詞構文を用いて表すことができる。
「～に駆け寄る」run up to ～／「～を指差す」point at ～

概要を整理しよう

・ディキンソンの研究
（方法）ミバエを小室に入れて視野を操作し，スーパースローモーションで撮影する
（発見）特定の飛行の型は，背中にある 2 つの平衡器官によって引き起こされる
・ハエの飛行の仕組み
複眼に加え，風に敏感な体毛と触角がある。頭頂部に 3 つの光センサーがある。
神経系統の約 3 分の 2 が視覚映像を処理している。
→これらのすべての情報を取り入れて飛行する

27 アレルギーが増加する背景（1）［医療］

1 The past thirty to forty years have seen a huge increase in the number of children / [who suffer from allergies], and scientists are still looking for the explanation.// Some have blamed increased air pollution, / **but** it has also been found / [that allergies are common not only among children in the city / but also among children in the countryside, / [where pollution is typically much lower]].//

2 A currently popular explanation for the rise in allergies is the so-called "hygiene hypothesis." // The basic idea is [that young children <brought up in an environment [which is too clean]> / are more at risk of developing allergies].// Nowadays, / people bathe and wash their clothes more frequently / than in the past, / and thanks to vacuum cleaners / homes are less dusty, too.// **One result** of all these changes is / [that in their early lives / children are exposed to fewer allergens / — substances [that can cause allergies]] — and this means [that their bodies cannot build up natural immunity to them].// Simply put, / exposure to allergy-causing substances is necessary / <for natural protection against them to develop>.//

解答

問1 (1) ③　(2) ①，④

問2 簡単に言うと，アレルギーを誘発する物質にさらされることは，それらに対して自然に備わる抵抗力を発達させるために必要なことなのである。

問3 ① ○　② ×　③ ×

Let's try It has been found that smartphone users are at a high risk of developing sleep disorder.

解説

問 1(1)　アレルギーに苦しむ子供の数が近年増加していることに関して，科学者から出された考えではないものは次のうちどれか。

①「この増加は悪化する大気汚染による面がある。」(ℓ. 3)
②「子供が育てられる環境が清潔すぎる。」(ℓℓ. 8 ～ 10)
③「都市の子供は田舎の子供よりもアレルギーになりやすい。」
④「アレルゲンにさらされない限り，子供の体がアレルゲンに対する自然免疫を作り上げることができない。」(ℓℓ. 15 ～ 16)

(2)　近年，子供がアレルゲンに対する自然免疫を作り上げることができないのはなぜか。選択肢は1つ以上選んでもよい。

①「頻繁に入浴するため，体を清潔に保っている。」(ℓ. 10)
②「着替えをしすぎる。」
③「部屋を清潔に保つために頻繁に掃除サービスを使う。」
④「さまざまなアレルゲンから子供を遠ざけようと努力する。」(ℓℓ. 12 ～ 15)

問 2　副詞＋ put〔speaking ; talking〕, S ＋ V …「～に言うと…」(ℓ. 15) 独立分詞構文。natural protection against them は to develop の意味上の主語。

問 3　①「ここ 30 ～ 40 年で，アレルギーがある子供の数が増えてきた。」(ℓℓ. 1 ～ 2)
②「アレルギーは都市の子供にのみよく見られる。」(ℓℓ. 4 ～ 5)
③「幼い子供がアレルギーを誘発する物質にさらされる必要はない。」
(ℓℓ. 15 ～ 16)

Let's try　「…ということがわかる」it is found that …が現在完了になった形。
「～の危険性がある」be at (a) risk of ～
smartphone users は people who use smartphones としてもよい。

概要を整理しよう

導入　アレルギーの子供が増加している
原因 1　大気汚染とする説
⇔空気のきれいな田舎の子供にもアレルギーがある
原因 2　清潔すぎるためとする説
→清潔すぎる環境で育った子供は，アレルギーを発症しやすい
アレルゲンにさらされる量が減り，免疫を作り上げることができない。
→アレルゲンにさらされることは，抵抗力をつけるために必要

28 アレルギーが増加する背景（2）［医療］

1 The trend towards smaller families **also** means / [that young children encounter fewer allergens in the home].// **In fact**, / it is known [that children [who have older brothers and sisters] are more resistant to allergies].// The same is true of children / [who share their home with a pet].// Such children are much less likely to develop the very common allergy / to cat or dog hair, / **for example**.//

2 Scientists agree [that being exposed to a wider range of allergens early in life / helps children <to develop greater immunity>].// There is, / **however**, / **also** some data <suggesting [that genetics, family income, and even the parents' level of education may play a part in [how likely a child is to suffer from allergies]]>.// **Thus**, / **although** the hygiene hypothesis is an important area for research, / we cannot yet be sure / [that too much attention to cleanliness is the only explanation / for the enormous rise in the number of allergy victims].//

解答

問 1 (1)（ア）⑥　（イ）⑤　（ウ）②　(2) ②

問 2 家にペットがいる子供は，ネコやイヌの毛に対する非常によく見られるアレルギーになる可能性がはるかに低い。

問 3 ① ○　② ×　③ ×

Let's try Lack of sleep is not healthy. The same is true of too much sleep.

解説

問 1 (1) アレルギーの激増のもう１つの原因は，（　ア　）家族化の傾向のために，幼い子供に（　イ　）きょうだいがおらず，家庭で（　ウ　）アレルゲンに遭遇するためかもしれない。

①「より多い」②「より少ない」→(ウ)(ll. 1～2) ③「より少ない」

④「年下の」⑤「年上の」→(イ)(ll. 3～4) ⑥「より小さい」→(ア)(ll. 1～2)

(2) アレルギーの激増について，科学者は(　　)ということに同意している。

①「清潔さに注意することが唯一の説明である」

②「遺伝的性質のためにアレルギーに苦しむ人がいる」(ll. 9～11)

③「家庭の収入は子供がアレルギーにかかる可能性に影響を与えない」

④「親の教育のレベルは無関係である」

問2 Such children は前文の children who share their home with a pet（ペットと家を共有する子供）を指す。

be less likely to *do*「…する可能性が低い；…しそうでない」(l. 5)

問3 ①「小家族化の傾向は幼い子供が家庭でアレルゲンに遭遇する量を減らす結果となった。」(ll. 1～2)

②「自分の子供をアレルギーに対してより抵抗力があるようにしたいのなら，1人だけ子供を持つべきだ。」(ll. 3～4)

③「幼少期にアレルゲンにさらされる量を減らすことで，子供はより強い免疫をつけることができる。」(ll. 7～8)

Let's try 「～についても同じことが当てはまる」the same is true of〔for；with〕～／「睡眠不足」lack of sleep

概要を整理しよう

・小家族化の傾向による幼い子供のアレルギーへの抵抗力の低下

・遺伝，家庭収入，親の教育レベルもアレルギー発症に関係するというデータも

結論　◆ Thus「したがって：結果・結論」(l. 11)

衛生への過剰な注意がアレルギーの唯一の原因とは確信できない。

背景知識　「衛生仮説（hygiene hypothesis）」提唱者のアプローチ

アレルギーとは，免疫反応が激しすぎたために身体に異変が起こった状態を言う。その引き金となるのがアレルゲンで，例えばスギ花粉やダニなどがある。アレルゲンとなるダニが増加すると，アレルギーの増加につながるという考え方がある。これに対し，逆の説もある。1989年，イギリスのストレイハン博士は，同居家族の数が多いほど花粉症の発症例が少ないという観察結果から，アレルゲンにさらされていないことがアレルギーの原因だとする説を発表した。これが「衛生仮説」であり，アレルギーの原因解明の新たな手法として注目されている。

29 外国語を学ぶ際に必要なもの（1）［言語］

People may decide to study foreign languages / for various reasons.// They may do so / for the immediate purpose of satisfying the requirements of some public examination / **or** of getting greater fun and enjoyment out of a holiday abroad.// Business people may have to deal / directly or indirectly / with various kinds of information from abroad.// Research workers may realize the importance of being able to read the latest reports of advances <made in their studies> / as soon as they are published in foreign journals, / without waiting for a translator, / [who may or may not have the ability <to make an exact translation / with one hundred percent accuracy>].// People may be keenly interested / in the activities of a foreign nation / for political reasons.// They may need information about current affairs [that foreign newspapers and journals alone can deliver].// Students of literature must surely be able to read great works / first hand.//

解答

問 1　(1)　③　　(2)　④

問 2　彼らは何かの公的試験の必要条件を満たす，あるいは海外で休暇を過ごす際により大きな喜びや楽しみを得る，といった目の前の目的のために外国語を学習しようと決めるかもしれない。

問 3　①　○　　②　×　　③　○

Let's try　Many people were waiting for the singer, who arrived at the concert hall an hour late.

解説

問 1(1)　なぜ人々が外国語を学習しようと決心するかについて言及された理由の1つではないものは次のうちどれか。

①「外国語で試験を受けなければならないかもしれない。」(ll. 2 ~ 3)

②「旅行中に現地の言葉を話せたら楽しいだろう。」(ll. 3 ~ 4)

③「その言語を話せる能力が職場での昇進に必要である。」

④「さまざまな種類の情報を海外から直接得られる。」(ll. 4 ~ 5)

(2)　外国語を学習しないと人々にどのような問題が起こる可能性があるか。

①「海外の情報を扱う翻訳者を見つけられない。」

②「公開された時に最新の情報を見つけられない。」

③「外国の活動への関心を失うかもしれない。」

④「外国の時事問題について情報を得られないかもしれない。」(ll. 11 ~ 13)

問 2　do so は前文の decide to study foreign languages を指している。

for the purpose of *doing*「…する目的で」(l. 2)

of satisfying the requirements ~ examination と of getting greater fun ~ abroad の 2 つが目的として挙げられている。

問 3　①「人々が外国語を学習するさまざまな理由がある。」(l. 1)

②「研究者は海外の専門誌に発表された研究報告の正確な翻訳が出るのを待つ方がよいと考える。」(ll. 6 ~ 10)

③「文学の研究者は名作をそれが最初に書かれた言語で読めなければならない。」(ll. 13 ~ 14)

Let's try　「その人は…なのだが」, who … (l. 8)

単純に and で文をつなげてもよいが，関係代名詞の非制限用法を用いる場合，先行詞を the singer にして , who を続ける。

概要を整理しよう

・外国語を学習する理由

例 1　目の前の目的：(1) 公的試験の必要条件 (2) 海外での休暇をより楽しむ

例 2　実業家：海外の情報を直接的・間接的に扱う必要がある

例 3　研究者：海外の専門誌で発表された最新の研究報告を翻訳が出るのを待つことなく読みたい

例 4　外国の時事問題はその国の新聞や雑誌でしか知り得ない

例 5　文学の研究者：名作を原文で読めなくてはならない

30 外国語を学ぶ際に必要なもの（2）［言語］

1 Learning a new language implies entering a new world, / and it inevitably leads to a widening of intellectual experience.// Learning a new language <well enough to be able to understand it when ∧ heard>, / <to speak it, ∧ read it, and ∧ write it>, / is such hard training / that we certainly need some strong urge <to drive us on>.// The four distinct and separable activities <just mentioned> / — listening, speaking, reading, and writing — call for constant, preferably daily, exercise.// These activities are concerned / in varying degrees / with four aspects of language study / — pronunciation, grammar, vocabulary, and idiom.// It is useful / <to keep these four activities and four aspects clearly in mind>.//

2 Learning a new language calls for no great originality of mind or critical talent, / **but** it does demand an eager intellectual curiosity and a constant and lively interest / in the endless ways [in which human ideas may be expressed].// It demands quick observation **first of all**, / reasonable ability <to mimic and imitate>, / good powers of association and generalization, / and a good memory.//

解答

問 1 (1) ③ (2) ③

問 2 聞くこと，話すこと，読むこと，書くことという活動は，言語学習の 4 つの側面と，それぞれ異なる度合いで，関連している

問 3 ① ○ ② ○ ③ ×

Let's try It was such a noisy room that we couldn't hear what we were saying to each other.

解説

問 1(1)　新たな言語を学ぶことについて正しいのは次のうちどれか。

①「それを習得する強い願望は常に必要ではない。」

②「聞くこと，話すこと，読むこと，書くことの 4 つの活動のみが必要である。」

③「毎日新たな言語を聞き，話し，読み，書く方がよい。」(*ll*. 5 ~ 7)

④「それを学ぶ努力を続ける人はほとんどいない。」

(2)　新たな言語を学ぶのに必要でないものは次のうちどれか。

①「別々の知識の項目を一般化する能力」(*ll*. 14 ~ 16)

②「鋭い観察力とまねしたり模倣したりする能力」(*ll*. 14 ~ 15)

③「新たな人間の考えに対して常に批判的である特別な才能」

④「旺盛な知的好奇心と不変で強い関心」(*ll*. 12 ~ 13)

問 2　These activities は前文の listening, speaking, reading, and writing を指す。

be concerned with ~「~と関連している」(*ll*. 7 ~ 8)

挿入されている in varying degrees は「それぞれ異なる度合いで」という意味。

問 3　①「新たな言語を学ぶためには，聞くこと，話すこと，読むこと，書くことの継続的な訓練が必要とされる。」(*ll*. 5 ~ 7)

②「本文中の『言語学習の 4 つの側面』は文法と熟語を含む。」(*ll*. 7 ~ 9)

③「新たな言語を学ぶことは，卓越した創造性と決定的な才能を必要とする。」(*ll*. 11 ~ 12)

Let's try　「…ほどの~；大変~なので，…」such 形容詞＋名詞 that ...
the room を主語にした場合は，The room was so noisy that we couldn't hear ~となる。「私たちの話していること」は関係代名詞 what を使うとよい。

概要を整理しよう

・新しい言語を学ぶこと＝新しい世界に入ること

→新しい言語を「聞く・話す・読む・書く」という活動は，継続的な訓練を必要とする

・新たな言語を学ぶために必要なもの

→卓越した創造性や決定的な才能は不要

◆　**but「しかし：逆接」**(*l*. 12)

旺盛な知的好奇心や，人間の考えの表現方法に対する強い関心が必要。

→そのために（1）鋭い観察力（2）まねをする能力（3）連想や一般化の能力（4）記憶力が必要

31 ディズニーの大きな決断（1）［社会］

1 On April 4, 2003, / Glen Keane, / one of Walt Disney's most respected animators, / called for a meeting / <to discuss the war breaking out at the studio>.// Disney's animators had settled into two opposing camps: those [who were skilled in computer animation] / and those [who refused to give up their pencils].//

2 Keane, a 31-year veteran [who created the beast for "Beauty and the Beast" and Ariel for "The Little Mermaid,"] was a Disney traditionalist.// **But** after a series of experiments / <to see [whether he could create a computer-animated ballerina]>, / his opposition softened.// **So** he invited the 50 animators <to discuss the pros and cons of both art forms>, / <calling his seminar "The Best of Both Worlds.">//

解答

問 1 (1) ①　(2) ③

問 2 ウォルト・ディズニー社の最も尊敬されているアニメ制作者の 1 人，グレン・キーンは，スタジオで起きている争いについて話し合うための会議を召集した。

問 3 ① ○　② ×　③ ○

Let's try I'm not sure whether my younger brother attends cram school (or not).

解説

問 1(1) グレン・キーンについて正しくないのは次のうちどれか。

① 「彼は世界で最も才能のあるアニメ制作者だった。」

② 「彼は『美女と野獣』の野獣を創り出した。」(ℓℓ.6 ~ 7)

③ 「彼は自身の研究会を『2 つの世界の最高のもの』と呼んだ。」(ℓ.11)

④「彼は最初は鉛筆を手放したくなかった。」(ℓℓ.6～8)

(2) (2) his opposition softened は何を意味しているか。

①「彼はコンピューターのアニメにやんわりと反対し始めた。」

②「彼はより言葉少なにコンピューターのアニメに反対した。」

③「彼は徐々にコンピューターのアニメの利点を認めるようになった。」(ℓℓ.8～9)

④「彼の反対はもはや一貫していなかった。」

問2 call for ～「～を招集する；～を要請する」(ℓ.2)

Glen Keane と one of Walt ～ animators は同格で，グレン・キーンがどのような人物かを説明している。現在分詞 breaking out ～は the war を修飾→「スタジオで起きている争い」。

問3 ①「ウォルト・ディズニー社には互いに対立する2つのグループがあった。」(ℓ.3)

②「グレン・キーンはコンピューターのアニメに熟練したアニメ制作者だった。」(ℓℓ.6～8)

③「キーンは2つの技法形態を評価するために会議を招集した。」(ℓℓ.10～11)

Let's try 「…かどうか」whether ... (or not)
「わからない」I'm not sure（I don't know は意味が強い）
「塾」は cram school（日本のいわゆる「塾」を指す）などで表す。

概要を整理しよう

当初の状況	ディズニー・スタジオ内の対立（コンピューター・アニメ派と手描き派） →グレン・キーンは手描きを主張する伝統派
状況の変化	◆ **But「しかし：逆接」**(ℓ.8) コンピューター・アニメの制作を試して，対立感情が和らいだ。 ◆ **So「したがって：結果・結論」**(ℓ.10) 双方の良し悪しを話し合うために50人のアニメ制作者を召集した。

背景知識 『白雪姫』でディズニーが築いた伝統

1937年に公開されたディズニー制作の『白雪姫』は，世界初のカラー長編アニメである。それまでアニメスタジオが制作してきたアニメ映画といえば短編であり，大手映画会社の配給する劇映画の添え物的な役割しか果たさなかった。そこでウォルト・ディズニーは『白雪姫』を制作し，ストーリー性をアニメの世界に持ち込んで成功を収め，アニメ映画のこれまでの扱いから脱却する道筋を開いた。『白雪姫』は当時の興行成績総収入の記録を更新し，これまでの短編アニメよりも大きな収益を見込めることを立証したのである。

32 ディズニーの大きな決断（2）［社会］

1 For an hour, / Keane listed the pluses and minuses of each technique / while the other animators listened quietly.// After a few questions, / the crowd burst into chatter / as animators shouted over one another, / <some arguing [that computers should not replace people] / and others expressing fears [that they would be forced to draw by hand]>.//

2 In a recent interview, / Keane recalled [that Kevin Geiger, a computer animation supervisor, then stood up and demanded of him, / "If you can do all this cool stuff [that you're talking about] — [that you want to see in animation] — but you have to give up the pencil <to do it>, / are you in?"]// Keane hesitated / before answering, "I'm in." //

3 Three weeks later, / the company's animators were told [that Disney would concentrate on making computer-animated movies, / <abandoning a 70-year-old hand-drawn tradition / in favor of a style <popularized by newer and more successful rivals like Pixar Animation Studios and DreamWorks Animation>>].//

解答

問1　(1) ③　(2) ④

問2　もしあなたが，今話題にしている，つまりアニメで見たいと思っている，このすごい内容のすべてができるが，それを行うためには鉛筆を手放さなければならないとすると，あなたは（こちらへ）加わりますか。

問3　① ×　② ×　③ ×

Let's try　I'm left-handed, and I had fears that I would be forced to write with my right hand.

解説

問 1(1)　アニメ制作者の議論の間に何が起きたか。

①「アニメ制作者は全員手描きで絵を描くことを愛していることを認めた。」

②「ほとんどのアニメ制作者は常に話し手に静かに耳を傾けていた。」

③「アニメ制作者の中には，手描きで絵を描くことを強いられることを恐れる者もいた。」(ℓℓ. 4 ～ 5)

④「すべてのアニメ制作者は，コンピューターは人間に取って代わるべきではないと考えた。」

(2)　議論の結果として正しくないのは次のうちどれか。

①「ディズニーはコンピューター・アニメに専念することを決めた。」(ℓ. 12)

②「アニメ制作者は 70 年に及ぶ手描きの伝統を捨てると告げられた。」(ℓℓ. 11 ～ 13)

③「キーンはコンピューター・アニメ映画の制作に加わることに同意した。」(ℓ. 10)

④「ディズニーは何人かのアニメ制作者に手描きの伝統を維持させてやった。」

問 2　If 節の中に you can do ～ animation と but you have to ～ to do it の 2 文が含まれている。that you're talking about と that you want to see in animation は，all this cool stuff を修飾している。

be in「(グループなどに) 加わる」(ℓℓ. 9 ～ 10)

問 3　①「結論に至るまで，議論は非常に平和的に進んだ。」(ℓℓ. 2 ～ 5)

②「コンピューター・アニメーションの技術はとても印象的だったので，アニメ制作者たちはすぐに決心した。」(ℓ. 10)

③「キーンはディズニーがアニメ制作の伝統的な方式をやめることを決めた時 70 歳だった。」(ℓℓ. 11 ～ 13)

Let's try　「…することを強いられる」be forced to *do*
「…という不安を感じる」have fears that ... 〔be afraid that ...〕

概要を整理しよう

・2 つの対立するグループの激しい議論
(1 つのグループの主張) コンピューターが人間に取って代わるべきではない。
(もう 1 つのグループの主張) 手で描くことを強いられるのは不安だ。
→ディズニーはコンピューター・アニメ制作に専念することを決めた

33 ディズニーの大きな決断（3）［社会］

1 The results were nothing short of a cultural revolution at the studio, [which is famous for the hand-drawn classics <championed by its founder, Walt Disney>, / like "Snow White and the Seven Dwarfs" and "Peter Pan]."//

nothing short of ～「～にほかならない」　関係代名詞の非制限用法　過去分詞の修飾　同格

2 Two years and a half after that decision, / Disney released "Chicken Little," the first of four computer-animated films <developed at the newly reorganized studio>.// The company hoped [that this movie, / along with others / like "Meet the Robinsons," "American Dog," and Keane's "Rapunzel Unbraided," / would return Disney to its past glory].//

同格　過去分詞の修飾　S　V　O　S' = "Chicken Little"　= other movies　V'　O'

3 There was a lot more than pride, **however**, <riding on its success>.// Animation was once Disney's heart, a profitable lifeline [that fed the company's theme park, book, and home video divisions].// And restoring profit was as essential to Disney in those days / as regaining its reputation.//

逆接　There is S＋分詞　同格　関係代名詞　V'　O'　S　V　C

解答

問 1　(1)　②　　(2)　④

問 2　しかし，誇りよりももっと多くの事情がその成功に乗っかっていた。

問 3　①　○　　②　○　　③　×

Let's try　Eating regular meals is as important as doing〔taking〕moderate exercise.

解説

問 1(1)　ディズニーの『チキン・リトル』について正しくないのは次のうちどれか。

①「ディズニースタジオにおける文化的な革命に他ならなかった。」(ll. 1～4)

②「ウォルト・ディズニーのようなアニメ制作者によって擁護された映画だった。」
③「ディズニーの最初のコンピューター・アニメ映画だった。」(ll.5～7)
④「ディズニーを過去の栄光に戻すことが意図された映画だった。」(ll.7～9)
(2) ディズニーは手描きのアニメをやめるという決断とともに何を目指していたか。
①「スタジオを再編成すること」
②「コンピューターを使って新しい方式を開発すること」
③「テーマパークを含むディズニーの生命線を養うこと」
④「収益を回復し，名声を取り戻すこと」(ll.13～14)

問2 ride on ～「～にかかっている」(≒ depend on ～)
a lot more は名詞に近い扱いで，「もっと多い何か，事情など」を表す。There is 名詞＋分詞の構文で，現在分詞 riding ～ success が a lot more を修飾している。

問3 ①「『ピーターパン』はディズニーの有名な手描きアニメである。」(ll.2～4)
②「ディズニーが最初のコンピューター・アニメ映画を公開するのに２年半かかった。」(ll.5～6)
③「ディズニーにとって名声を取り戻すことは収益を取り戻すことほどには重要ではなかった。」(ll.13～14)

Let's try 「…と同様に～」as ～ as
「規則正しい食事」regular meals
「適度な運動」moderate〔appropriate〕exercise

概要を整理しよう

・決定がもたらした結果
コンピューター・アニメ映画制作への転換はスタジオにおける文化的な革命だった。
・最初のコンピューター・アニメ映画『チキン・リトル』の公開
会社は，新しいアニメ映画で再び栄光に輝きたいと思っている。
・新しいコンピューター・アニメ映画に会社が期待するもの
◆ **however「しかし：逆接」**(l.10)
誇りよりももっと多くの事情が新しい映画の成功にかかっていた。
→会社の名声を取り戻すだけでなく，収益の回復が期待されている

34 ネコの習性 [科学]

Although cats appear to perform most actions instinctively, / they **also** seem to react to human behavior / and adapt themselves to it.// **For instance**, / some cats behave / as if they understood their owners' feelings.// One cat owner told of the time [when she lay <crying and exhausted> on her bed, / and her cat put its front legs around her head and comforted her].// Cats **also** sometimes appear to be able to understand the function of many of the things [∧ human beings use].// **For example**, / some cats, / when they bring a captured bird or mouse into the house, / put it on a plate or in a dish.// There are **also** cats [who know <how to open a door / by turning the handle>].// **Furthermore**, / a lot of cats seem to understand [what their owners say].// A writer tells a story of her cat [who used to sleep on top of her word processor].// **At first**, / when the cat's tail got in the way of the screen, / the owner would push its tail away and say, "Move your tail, please."// **Eventually**, / she didn't have to push the tail / but only had to tell the cat <to move it>.//

解答

問 1 (1) ①　(2) ③

問 2 例えば，まるで自分の飼い主の感情を理解しているかのように行動するネコもいる。

問 3 ① ×　② ○　③ ○

Let's try The teacher told us not to enter this room with our shoes on.

解説

問 1(1)　どのようにネコが人間の行動に反応してそれに合わせるかについて，正しくないのは次のうちどれか。

① 「飼い主に与えるために捕まえた鳥やネズミを持って来るネコがいる。」

② 「平皿が食べ物を載せるためのものと知っているようなネコがいる。」(ll. 8～9)

③「あるネコの飼い主が，ネコが自分を慰めようとしていると感じた。」(ll. 4～6)

④ 「ドアを開けるために取っ手を回すことのできるネコがいる。」(ll. 9～10)

(2)　どのようにある作家は彼女のネコが彼女の言っていることを理解できるとわかったか。

①「彼女がネコに話をした時，ネコは彼女のワープロの上で眠るのが常だった。」

② 「彼女がネコにしっぽを動かすよう言った時，しっぽを画面に押しつけた。」

③ 「彼女がネコにしっぽを動かすよう言った時，彼女が言った通りにした。」

(ll. 14～15)

④ 「彼女がワープロを使うと言った時，ネコはワープロから離れた。」

問 2　as if S V「まるで…するかのように」(l. 3) あとに仮定法が続く。

このtheyはsome catsを指している。

問 3　① 「ネコは飼い主の感情を理解することができないように見える。」(l. 2)

② 「あるネコは捕まえた鳥を平皿の上に載せた。これはネコが平皿の機能を理解していたことを示唆する。」(ll. 6～9)

③ 「ある作家のネコは，そうするように言われてしっぽを画面の前から動かした。」(ll. 12～15)

Let's try　「O に…するように言う〔命令する〕」tell O to *do*

「…しないように」と否定形にする。→ told us not to enter this room

「靴をはいたまま」with one's shoes on

概要を整理しよう

主題　ネコは人間の行動に反応して合わせているようにも見える

具体例

◆ For instance「例えば：例示」(ll. 2～3)

・飼い主の感情を理解しているかのように行動する

◆ also「また：列挙・追加」(l. 6)

・人間の使う物の機能を理解できるようにも見える

◆ Furthermore「そのうえ：列挙・追加」(l. 10)

・飼い主の言うことを理解しているようである

1 Touching is the language of physical intimacy.// Because of this, touch can be the most powerful of all the communication channels.// In May 1985, / Brigitte Gerney was trapped for six hours / beneath a collapsed construction crane / in New York City.// Throughout her ordeal, / she held the hand of a rescue worker, / [who stayed by her side / as heavy machinery removed the tons of twisted steel / from her crushed legs].// A stranger's touch gave her hope and the will <to live>.//

2 Touch appears to affect the sexes differently.// Women sometimes react much more favorably to touch / than men.// In an interesting study, / psychologists asked a group of nurses <to lightly touch a patient once or twice> / shortly before the patient underwent surgery.// The touching produced a strongly positive reaction / — but only among women.// It appeared to lower their blood pressure and anxiety levels / both before and after surgery.//

3 For men, / **however**, / the touching proved to be very upsetting.// Their blood pressure and anxiety levels both rose.// The psychologists suspect [that / because men are taught <to be more stoic>, / **that is**, / <to hide their feelings and to ignore their fears>, / the touching rattled them / by reminding them [that life is fragile]].//

解答

問1 (1) ② (2) ④ **問2** しかし，男性にとっては，触れることは非常に動揺させることだとわかった。

問3 ① ○ ② × ③ ○

Let's try Yuko asked me to wait (for her) in the classroom.

解説

問 1 (1)　ブリジット・ガーニーに何が起きたか。

①「彼女は建設用クレーンによって助けられた。」

②「**彼女は建設作業の事故で閉じ込められた。**」(ℓℓ.3～4)

③「彼女は災害時に救助隊員を支援した。」

④「彼女は救助隊員と一緒にいるのを拒絶した。」

(2)　触れることの研究の結果は何か。

①「男女ともに触れられることに好ましい反応をした。」

②「ほとんどの男性は触れられると冷静になった。」

③「ほとんどの女性は触れられると不安を感じた。」

④「**女性は男性よりも触れられることに好ましい反応をした。**」(ℓℓ.8～9)

問 2　prove to be ～「～だと判明する」

upsetting は upset「～を動揺させる」が形容詞化したもの。

問 3　①「触れることがすべてのコミュニケーション手段の中で最も強力なものであり得る。」(ℓℓ.1～2)

②「触れることに対する反応の仕方に男女差はないように思われる。」(ℓ.8)

③「手術の前に女性の患者にそっと触れることで彼女の血圧と不安の度合いが下がった。」(ℓℓ.10～14)

Let's try　「O に…するように頼む」ask O to *do*

tell O to *do* にすると,「指示する」という意味になる。

概要を整理しよう

主題	触れることはコミュニケーション手段の中で最も強力なものになり得る
具体例	建設機械の下敷きになった女性 →救助隊員に触れていることで，希望と生きる意志を得た
展開	女性の方が触れられることに好意的に反応する
具体例	手術前に女性の患者に軽く触れる→血圧が下がり，不安の度合いが下がった ◆　however「しかし：逆接」(ℓ.15) 男性は触れられると非常に動揺することがわかった。 (原因) 生命はもろいものだということを思い出させてしまうため

36 「触れること」の作用 (2) [人間]

1 How do you feel about touching and being touched?// Salespeople think [∧they know∧] — research shows [that it is harder <to say "no" to someone [who touches you] / when ∧ making a request>] — **but** not everyone is happy about being touched by a stranger.// Think about your own comfort level / when you find yourself in a crowd.// Are you relaxed and loose, / or does physical contact make you feel awkward and tense?//

2 In some situations, / we can't help touching each other.// **Take** a crowded elevator, / **for instance**.// Normally, / people stand / shoulder to shoulder and arm to arm, / <accepting such close contact / without complaint>.// The rule seems to be "Touch only from shoulder to elbow, / but nowhere else."// Even though the Japanese are regarded as a nontouching society, / their crowded cities force them <to be jammed into subways and trains>.// Edward T. Hall, / an anthropologist, / says [∧the Japanese handle their uneasiness about being packed into public places / by avoiding eye contact and drawing within themselves emotionally, / thus "touching without feeling]."//

解答

問 1 (1) ④ (2) ③

問 2 たとえ日本人は人の体に触れない社会だと考えられているとしても，混雑した都会では，人は地下鉄や電車に無理やり詰め込まれる。

問 3 ① ○ ② ○ ③ ×

Let's try Mika couldn't help crying when she read the letter from her mother.

解説

問 1(1)　触れられることに対する人々の感じ方について，どの文が正しいか。

① 「人々は触れられると頼みごとを断りやすく感じる。」

② 「人々は身体的接触があるとリラックスして落ち着く。」

③ 「人々は人込みで触れられる時のみ居心地が悪く緊張した思いをする。」

④ **「すべての人が知らない人に触られるのを好むわけではない。」**(*ll.* 3 ~ 4)

(2)　(2) touching without feeling に最も近い意味のものは次のうちどれか。

① 「触れられていることを感じることなく触れること」

② 「触れることを強いられていると感じることなく触れること」

③ **「感情的に自分の中に引きこもりながら触れること」**(*ll.* 15 ~ 17)

④ 「お互いを見るのを避けながら触れること」

問 2　regard A as B「A を B とみなす」

A にあたる the Japanese を主語にして受動態になった形。

force O to *do*「O に無理やり…させる」(*l.* 13)

問 3　① 「販売員は頼みごとをしている人に触られている時に，頼みごとに『ノー』と言うのがより難しいと思っている。」(*ll.* 1 ~ 3)

② 「人々は満員のエレベーターでは肩同士の接触を受け入れているようだ。」(*ll.* 9 ~ 11)

③ 「知らない人との密接な接触を受け入れなければならない時，日本人は周りの人と視線を合わせようとする。」(*ll.* 15 ~ 17)

Let's try　「…せざるを得ない」cannot〔can't〕help *doing*

cannot〔can't〕help but *do* も同様の意味を表す。

「泣く」cry →「(突然) 泣き出す」burst into tears も可。

概要を整理しよう

導入	接触に対する好悪 ・販売員の考え方：自分に触れている相手には「ノー」と言いにくい ◆ **but「しかし：逆接」**(*l.* 3) ・皆が知らない人に触れられてうれしいわけではない
具体例	満員のエレベーター／日本の満員電車 →「感情を持たずに触れる」状態を保ち，不快さをうまく処理

1 The Internet is very much **like** television / in that it takes time away from other pursuits, / provides entertainment and information, / **but** in no way can ∧compare with the warm, personal experience of reading a good book.// This is not the only reason [why the Internet will never replace books], / **for** books provide the sufficient knowledge of a subject [that sitting in front of a computer monitor cannot provide].// We can transfer text from an Internet source, / **but** the artistic quality of sheets of transferred text leaves much <to be desired>.// A well-designed book makes the reading experience important.//

2 The book is still the most compact and economical means / of conveying a lot of knowledge / in a convenient package, / and this is [what makes it popular].// The idea [that one can carry in one's pocket a play by Shakespeare, a novel by Charles Dickens or the Bible in a small book with a stiff, paper cover] is incredible.// We take such uncommon convenience for granted, / <not realizing [that the book itself has undergone quite an evolution / since the production of the Gutenberg Bible in 1455 and Shakespeare's book of plays in 1623]>.//

(注) like：類似 / in that：「…という点で」 / but：逆接 / ∧ (it = the Internet) / why：関係副詞 / for：理由 / that：関係代名詞 / to be desired：不定詞の形容詞用法 / that：同格 / take A for granted「A を当然だと思う」 / not realizing：付帯状況を表す分詞構文

解答

問 1　(1)　①　　(2)　③

問 2　（本は）便利なパッケージでたくさんの知識を伝える最もコンパクトかつ経済的な手段なので，本は人気があるのだ

問 3　①　×　　②　×　　③　○

Let's try　Men〔Human beings ; Humans〕are quite different from other animals in that they can speak a language.

解説

問 1(1)　インターネットはどのようにテレビにとてもよく似ているのか。

①「使っている間は他の仕事に十分な時間をかけられない。」(ℓℓ. 1 ～ 2)

②「観ることで個人的な体験を得られる。」

③「前に座るだけで十分な知識を得られる。」

④「情報源から直接情報を得られる。」

(2)　なぜ筆者は本が今もなおインターネットよりよいと考えているのか。

①「本は娯楽や情報をより多く提供する。」②「本には便利な硬い紙表紙がある。」

③「本はそれが含むたくさんの知識に対して経済的である。」(ℓℓ. 10 ～ 11)

④「本は長い年月をかけて進化を経たためコンパクトである。」

問 2　make O (名詞) C (形容詞)「O を C の状態にさせる〔する〕」(ℓ. 12)
it は the book を指し, This は本が人気の理由になる事柄を指している。つまり, 前文の the most compact ～ convenient package の部分。

問 3　①「筆者はテレビがインターネットよりはるかによい経験を与えると考えている。」(ℓℓ. 1 ～ 4)

②「筆者はインターネットソースから転送されるテキストは非常に望ましいと考えている。」(ℓℓ. 7 ～ 8)

③「筆者が本を好きな理由の 1 つは, 本が運ぶ情報量の割にとてもコンパクトだからである。」(ℓℓ. 10 ～ 12)

Let's try　「～と異なる」be different from ～／「…という点で」in that ...

概要を整理しよう

導入　インターネット：娯楽や情報を与えてくれる。

主張　◆ **but「しかし：逆接」**(ℓ. 3)
良書を読むという心温まる個人的な体験とは比べものにならない。

理由　・本はインターネットが与えることのできない知識を与えてくれる
・本は多くの情報を伝える, 最もコンパクトで経済的な手段である。
→本そのものも, 昔と比べて進歩している
→私たちはその進歩に気づかず, 便利さを当然のことと考えている

38 インターネット時代の印刷物の役割（2）［社会］

1 Not only has the art and craft of printing and making books been greatly improved / over the centuries, / but ∧ (also) the great variety of subject matter now available in books is surprising, / to say the least.// **In fact**, / the Internet requires the constant entry of authors and their books / <to obtain the information [that makes it a useful tool for research and learning]>.//

2 **Another important reason** [why the Internet will never replace books] / is [because those [who wish to become writers] want to see their works permanently published as books / — something [you can hold, see, feel, look through, and read at your leisure / without the need for an electric current apart from a lamp]].// The writer **may** use a computer / instead of a pen and pad, / **but** the finished product must eventually end up as a book / if it is to have value to the reading public.// The writer **may** use the Internet / in the course of researching a subject / **just as** he may use a library for that purpose, / **but** the end product will still be a book.//

解答

問 1 (1) ③　(2) ②

問 2 完成した作品が一般読者にとって価値あるものでありたいなら，結局最後には本になる必要がある

問 3 ① ○　② ○　③ ×

Let's try Not only did my boyfriend forget my birthday, but he (also) didn't even apologize for forgetting it.

解説

問1(1)　筆者によると，何が本をそこまで驚くべきものにしているのか。

①「作家が本を研究や学習のために非常に便利な道具にできる。」

②「本を印刷して製作するという技術やわざがすばらしい。」

③「さまざまな題材が本で得られる。」(*ll*. 2～3)

④「本は著者とその著書が絶えず掲載されることが求められない。」

(2)　なぜ筆者はインターネットが決して本に取って代わることがないと考えているのか。

①「インターネットは費用が多くかかる電流を消費する。」

②「人は暇な時に手に持ったり，触れたり，読んだりできるものを欲しがっている。」(*ll*. 7～10)

③「好きな時にいつでもペンで本に書き込むことができる。」

④「作家は普通，題材を調べるために図書館で本に頼る。」

問2　end up ～「結局～になる」／be 動詞＋ to *do*「…したい」(*l*. 13) ここでは‘意図’を表す。the reading public は「読書をする大衆」→「読者」ととらえるとよい。

問3　①「今，非常に多くの題材についてあらゆる種類の本が利用できる。」(*ll*. 2～3)

②「筆者によると，本のいいところは，手に持ったり触れたりできることである。」(*ll*. 7～10)

③「作家はインターネットユーザー向きの本を調査するために図書館を利用する。」(*ll*. 13～15)

Let's try　「A だけでなく B」not only A but (also) B
「…したことを謝る」apologize for *doing*

概要を整理しよう

・本で得られる題材の豊富さ

◆ **in fact「実際には：主張」**(*l*. 3)
インターネットが研究や学習に役立つためには，常に著者とその著書の内容の掲載が求められる。

・インターネットが本に取って代わらないもう１つの理由

◆ **Another important reason「もう１つの重要な理由：理由」**(*l*. 7)
著者は，その作品が永久的に出版されているのを見たいから。
→読者にとって作品が価値のあるものになるには，本になる必要がある

39 つらい経験について書くことの効用（1）［人間］

1 Why is it that many people [who have suffered a major shock, / **such as** divorce or the death of a family member], / seem to be weaker / against a variety of major and minor illnesses?// One common idea among psychologists has been [that people could deal with suffering more effectively / if they were able to understand and accept it].// **Indeed**, / many experts emphasize the value <of expressing thoughts and feelings <associated with upsetting events>>.//

2 Recently, / a team of medical researchers investigated the links / between describing psychologically painful events / and long-term health.// In one experiment / healthy college students were asked <to write about either personally disturbing experiences / or ordinary topics / over a period of four days>.// In the months afterwards, / students [who had chosen <to reveal their inner thoughts and feelings / in their writing>] visited the health center for illness / much less often than those [who had written about everyday topics].//

解答

問 1　(1)　②　(2)　（ア）　③　（イ）　①　（ウ）　⑤

問 2　人々が苦しみを理解し受け入れることができれば，もっと効果的にそれに対処できるかもしれない

問 3　①　×　②　〇　③　×

Let's try　Why is it that Tom was late for class today?

解説

問1(1)　なぜ気持ちをかき乱すような出来事に関連した考えや感情を表現することが重要なのか。

①「気持ちをかき乱すような出来事のつらさを和らげるかもしれない。」

②「病気にかかりやすくなることを防ぐかもしれない。」(ll. 12～15)

③「そのような出来事に対する本当の気持ちを隠す助けになるかもしれない。」

④「そのような出来事の原因を理解する助けになるかもしれない。」

(2)　ある実験で，健康な大学生が，個人的に心をかき乱す経験か日常の話題の（　ア　）について書いた。数カ月後，（　イ　）思いや感情を明らかにした学生たちは，ごく普通の話題について書いた学生たちよりも，病気で医療センターを訪れる回数がはるかに（　ウ　）ことが明らかになった。

①「心の中の」→(イ)(ll. 12～15) ②「両方」③「どちらか」→(ア)(ll. 10～12)

④「より多い」⑤「より少ない」→（ウ）(ll. 12～15)

問2　deal with ～「～に対処する」／ if S' ＋過去形 ～, S would〔could〕*do*「もしもS' が～ならば，S は…だろうに」(ll. 4～5) 仮定法過去。

問3　①「人々は苦しみを理解していなくてもより効果的にそれに対処できる。」(ll. 4～5)

②「医療研究者は精神的につらい出来事が長期間でみる健康状態にどのように影響するのかを調査した。」(ll. 8～10)

③「心理的に問題を抱えた学生が調査実験に選ばれた。」(ll. 10～12)

Let's try　「いったいなぜ…なのか。」Why is it that ...?
「～に遅れる」be late for ～

概要を整理しよう

導入　大きなショックを受けた場合，苦しみを理解し受け入れると，人は効果的に対処できる

実験　つらい出来事を言葉で表現することと長期的健康との関連について調査
→学生たちに4日間にわたって，つらい経験と日常生活の話題のどちらかを書くよう求める

結果　前者の学生の方が，後者の学生よりも，その後病気で医療センターに行く回数が少なかった

40 つらい経験について書くことの効用（2）［人間］

1 In an experiment [that followed], / another group of healthy students were given the four-day writing exercise.// Some chose to write about highly personal and upsetting experiences / (**including** loneliness, problems with family and friends, and death).// When ∧questioned (they were) immediately afterwards, / they stated [that they did not feel any better].// **However**, / their blood samples <taken before and after the experiment>/ showed evidence of an improved resistance to illness.// The white cells [that fight off bacteria and viruses] / had increased their reaction and sensitivity to these "invaders."// This trend continued over the following six weeks, / [when another blood sample was taken].// Individuals [who showed the best results] / were those [who wrote about topics [that they had actively refrained from telling others about]].//

2 The researchers propose [that failure <to face up to painful experience> / can be a form of stress itself, / and can increase the possibility of illness].// It follows, / then, / [that actively dealing with a major shock makes possible its understanding and acceptance].// The answer is <not to suffer in silence>.// It **may** not always be possible <to talk about personal problems>, / **but** writing them down will help the body <to fight disease in the long run>.//

解答

問1 (1) ①　(2) ③　**問2** それなら，積極的に大きなショックに立ち向かっていけば，それを理解し，受け入れることができるようになる。

問3 ① ×　② ○　③ ○

Let's try At seven I was taking a bath, when the lights suddenly went out.

解説

問 1(1)　個人的で気持ちをかき乱す経験について書いた学生について正しくないのは次のうちどれか。

①「彼らは体の調子がよくなったと気づいた。」

②「彼らの血液サンプルは，彼らが病気に対してより抵抗力がついたことを示していた。」(ll. 6 ~ 7)

③「文章を書く課題の直後は少しも気が楽にならなかった。」(ll. 4 ~ 5)

④「彼らの白血球の反応や感度が改善した。」(ll. 7 ~ 9)

(2)　研究者からの提案は次のうちどれか。

①「苦しい経験を理解して受け入れれば，積極的に対処することになる。」

②「積極的に大きなショックに立ち向かわなければ，沈黙して苦しむだろう。」

③「苦しい経験を直視しないと，ストレスが生じて病気にかかりやすくなる。」

(ll. 13 ~ 15)

④「個人的な問題について書くことは，それについて話すことよりも効果的に体が病気と闘う助けになる。」

問 2　it follows that ...「(以上のことから) 当然…という結果になる」(l. 15)

makes の目的語にあたる its understanding and acceptance が補語の possible より長いため，本来 SVOC の語順が SVCO になっている。

問 3　①「気持ちをかき乱す経験について書いた学生ははるかに気分がよくなったと言った。」(ll. 4 ~ 5)

②「苦しい経験を直視できないと，病気になる可能性が高まるかもしれない。」

(ll. 13 ~ 15)

③「個人的な問題について話したり書いたりすれば，体が病気と闘う助けになる。」(ll. 16 ~ 18)

Let's try　「…，そしてその時～」時を示す語句＋，when ～

「(明かりがなどが) 消える」go out

概要を整理しよう

実験　4日間学生に作文を書かせた

結果　血液検査の結果，病気への抵抗力が改善

→苦しい経験を直視できないこと自体がストレスになり病気を招く

→積極的に大きなショックに立ち向かっていけば，理解し，受け入れられる

結論　個人的な問題を話したり書いたりすることで，体が病気と闘う助けになる

41 テレビゲームの影響力（1）[社会]

1 "The impact of exposure to violent video games has not been studied as extensively / as the impact of exposure to TV or movie violence," / the researchers write in *Psychological Science in the Public Interest*.// "**However**, / on the whole, / the results <reported for video games to date> / are very similar / to those <obtained in the investigations of TV and movie violence>."// Among the effects of violent game playing / are increases / in physiological arousal and physically aggressive behavior, / **such as** hitting, kicking, and pulling clothes or hair.// Studies **also** have found a reduction / in helpful behavior among youths <exposed to violent video games>.//

2 Males tend to prefer action-oriented video games <involving shooting, fighting, sports, action adventure, fantasy role-playing, and strategy>, / according to the Michigan State survey.// Females prefer classic board games, trivia quizzes, puzzles, and arcade games.// Electronic game playing gets young people involved with technologies / and opens up opportunities in high-paying tech careers, / notes communications professor / Bradley Greenberg of Michigan State.//

解答

問1 (1) ③ (2) ②

問2 暴力的なゲームを行うことによる影響の中には，生理的な興奮や，身体的に攻撃性のある行動が増加する，ということがある

問3 ① × ② ○ ③ ○

Let's try His passion got many people involved in the project.

解説

問 1(1)　暴力的なテレビゲームにさらされることで受ける影響について正しいのは次のうちどれか。

①「広く研究されてきているが，結果はまだ報告されていない。」

②「研究者たちが心配するほど深刻ではない。」

③「テレビや映画の暴力シーンにさらされることとほぼ同じ影響を示している。」(ll.4 ~ 6)

④「暴力的なテレビゲームにさらされた若者は他の人よりも人の助けになる行動を見せた。」

(2)　男の子や女の子が好むテレビゲームついて正しいのは次のうちどれか。

①「男の子は空想系のゲームよりも冒険もののゲームを好む。」

②「男の子は身体の動きに結び付いたゲームを好む。」(l.11)

③「女の子は伝統的なゲームよりも空想系のゲームを好む。」

④「女の子は知識や戦略を必要とするゲームを好む。」

問 2　among ~ be S「～の中には S がある」(ll.6 ~ 7) 文頭に副詞句が置かれたことによる倒置が起きている。主語は increases in ~ behavior の名詞句。

問 3　①「暴力的なテレビゲームにさらされることで受ける影響は長く研究されてきた。」(ll.1 ~ 2)

②「暴力的なゲームを行うことは，生理的な興奮や身体的に攻撃性のある行動を増加させる。」(ll.6 ~ 7)

③「グリーンバーグ教授は，電子ゲームをすることは給与の高い科学技術関係の仕事への機会を広げると言っている。」(ll.15 ~ 16)

Let's try　「～ (O) を… (C の状態) にさせる」get O (名詞) C (形容詞)
「～と関わる」be involved in〔with〕~

概要を整理しよう

・テレビゲームが与える影響
→全般的に見ると，テレビ・映画の暴力シーンの影響の調査結果と同じ
→生理的な興奮や攻撃的な行動の増加，人を助ける行動が減少

・ミシガン州の調査結果によると，男性が好むゲームと女性が好むゲームは異なる

・グリーンバーグ教授の意見
→若者は電子ゲームで科学技術と関わり，高所得の科学技術関係の仕事の機会が広がる

42 テレビゲームの影響力（2）［社会］

1 "It is believed [that these opportunities accrue to boys / because they spend more time working with electronic games and computers]," / says Greenberg.// "If girls become more involved with technology / at an early age, / it is likely [that the interest in technology will continue into the work world]."// If females do become more involved / in technology fields, **including** game development, / they may create less-violent games [that promote cooperation rather than aggression].//

2 Video games are in 80% of U.S. homes with children; / they generated $6 billion in 2000 and $11 billion by 2003.// "All indications are [that the industry will continue to grow / at a healthy clip]," / says Greenberg.// "The emerging market is for games <designed more with girls in mind>/ [that engage them for longer periods of time / and force them <to investigate more the technology / behind the games>].// The next frontier involves transferring video game technology to educational settings and using the young people's fascination with the games <to involve them more with innovative teaching technologies>."// Until that day comes, / **however**, / more awareness is needed / of the impact of violent games on young people's behavior, / Anderson and his colleagues conclude.//

解答

問 1 (1) ③　(2) ③　**問 2** 仮に女性がゲームの開発も含めて，科学技術分野に実際にもっと従事するようになるなら，彼女たちはあまり暴力的ではないゲームを作り出すかもしれない

問 3 ① ×　② ×　③ ○

Let's try I was so engaged in video games that I lost track of time.

解説

問 1(1)　グリーンバーグによると，正しいのは次のうちどれか。

①「女の子は幼い年齢で科学技術分野により関わるようになった。」

②「新しいテレビゲームのために，男の子はより攻撃的でなくなるだろう。」

③「女の子は将来，協力を促進するゲームを作り出すかもしれない。」(ll.5 ~ 7)

④「男の子と女の子どちらも電子ゲームをするのにより多くの時間を費やすだろう。」

(2)　テレビゲームについて正しくないのは次のうちどれか。

①「テレビゲームは 2000 年と比べて 2003 年にほぼ 2 倍の利益を生み出した。」(ll.8 ~ 9)

②「グリーンバーグはゲーム産業が成長し続けると考えている。」(ll.9 ~ 10)

③「将来のゲームは女の子よりも男の子のために設計されるだろう。」

④「テレビゲームの科学技術は教育分野に使われるだろう。」(ll.13 ~ 15)

問 2　強調の do「実際に〔本当に〕…する」(l.5) ／ including ～「～を含めて」

問 3　①「女性がもっとゲームの開発に従事するようになるなら，彼女たちは新しいゲームを作り出すもっと効率的な方法を見つけるかもしれない。」(ll.5 ~ 6)

②「すべてのことは，まもなくテレビゲーム産業が衰退することを示している。」(ll.9 ~ 10)

③「アンダーソンは，私たちは暴力的なゲームが若者の行動に与える影響をより注意深く観察すべきだと結論づけている。」(ll.17 ~ 19)

Let's try　「～に没頭する」be engaged in ～
「とても～なので…」so ～ that ...
「時間が過ぎるのを忘れる」lose track of time

概要を整理しよう

主張　女性がゲーム開発に従事すれば，暴力的ではない，協力を促進するゲームを作るかもしれない

・グリーンバーグ教授の意見
→新興市場は女性を念頭に置いてゲームを開発し，背後の科学技術の研究を促す
→テレビゲームの科学技術を教育環境に応用する

・アンダーソンらの意見：暴力的なゲームが若者に与える影響にもっと配慮すべきだ

43 真実を使ったうそ（1）[人間]

1 Beware of those / [who deliberately use aspects of the truth / <to deceive you and others>].// When someone tells you something / [that is true], but intentionally leaves out important information / [that should be included / <for full comprehension on your part to take place>], they can create a false impression.//

2 **For example**, / an acquaintance might tell you, "I just won a hundred dollars in the state lottery / and it was fantastic / when I took that one dollar ticket back to the store / and turned it in / for one hundred bucks!" // This woman's a winner, right?// Maybe, maybe not.// **In fact**, / you later learn [that she had purchased not one ticket but instead two hundred / for this specific lottery — and only one of these ∧a winner]!// Eventually, / you realize [∧this woman, [who / you thought / was 'lucky' or 'fortunate'] is, / **in fact**, / a huge loser].// Although she didn't say anything false, / she clearly left out important information / and likely did so / on purpose.// That's called a half-truth / [which is not technically a lie], / but it's just as dishonest∧.//

解答

問 1　(1)　④　　(2)　③

問 2　彼女は何も事実に反することは言わなかったとはいえ，明らかに重要な情報を省き，そしておそらく故意にそうしたのだろう。

問 3　①　○　　②　×　　③　×

Let's try　What she needs is not money but sympathy〔compassion：kindness〕.

解説

問 1(1)　本文によると，人はあなたや他の人たちをどのようにだますのか。
①「無意識に誰かに誤った情報を与えることによって。」
②「真実であるように思えるうそをつくことによって。」
③「誤った情報を明らかにするために故意に真実の側面を使うことによって。」
④「真実を伝えながら故意に重要な情報を省くことによって。」(ll. 2 ~ 5)

(2)　ある女性は 1 ドルの宝くじ券を 200 枚買って，そのうちの 1 つが当たりだと判明した。彼女はその当たりくじと引き換えに 100 ドルを得た。彼女は 100 ドルを得て気分が最高だとだけ言ったが，実は彼女は損をしていたのだ。(ll. 6 ~ 12)

問 2　did so (l. 15) = left out important information 代動詞 did は，文の前半の left out ~の内容を指す。on purpose「わざと」

問 3　①「話から重要な情報を省くことであなたをだます人もいる。」(ll. 1 ~ 5)
②「その女性は州の宝くじに費やした金額以上が当たった。」(ll. 10 ~ 12)
③「その女性は筆者に何枚宝くじを買ったかを伝えた。」(ll. 13 ~ 15)

Let's try　「A ではなくて B」not A but B
「彼女に必要なもの」what she needs（関係代名詞 what を使う）

概要を整理しよう

主題　真実から重要情報を故意に省くと，誤った印象を作り出せる

具体例　◆ **For example「例えば：例示」**(l. 6)
「1 枚の宝くじが 100 ドルの当たりだった」と言う女性。
◆ **In fact「実際には：主張」**(l. 10)
この女性が買った宝くじは 1 枚ではなく 200 枚だった。
→購入した宝くじの枚数を話から故意に省き，「幸運な話」に変えた

結論　これを half-truth と呼ぶ。厳密にはうそではないが，不誠実である。

背景知識　情報操作

事実であっても，伝える部分と省略する部分の操作によって，人をだます行為は「情報操作」と呼ばれる。近年メディアリテラシーに関して，メディアによる情報操作に焦点が当てられる傾向にあるが，この情報操作は直接的に個人レベルでも行われることがある。「だます」という意図は情報の送り手によるものであり，送り手はそれに応じた情報の構成を行う。一方，そのような情報の受け手は送り手の意図どおり「だまされる」か，意図に反して「だまされない」かのどちらかとなる。

44 真実を使ったうそ (2) [人間]

1 Untrustworthy candidates in political campaigns often use such deceptive communication strategies / <to trick voters into supporting them>.// **Let's say [that** / during Governor Smith's last term, / her state lost one million jobs but gained three million new ones].// Then she seeks another term in office / and enters the election race.// One of her opponents in that race subsequently begins a multimedia advertising campaign / <saying, / "During Governor Smith's term, / the state lost one million jobs!">// That is **indeed** true / **but**, / at the same time, / it is intentionally deceptive.// A more honest statement from her opponent would have been, / "During Governor Smith's term, / the state had a net gain of two million jobs." //

2 Advertisers sometimes use half-truths as well.// Because it's illegal / in many countries / <to openly make false claims about a product or service>, / some advertisers try to mislead you with the truth.// An ad might **consequently** boast, / "Nine out of ten doctors recommend Yucky Pills <to cure nose pimples>."// This is **also** a factual statement **but** one [which deliberately fails to mention [that only ten doctors were asked about Yucky Pills / and nine of these actually work for the Yucky Corporation]].//

解答

問 1 (1) ③ (2) ③ **問 2** (スミス州知事の前任期中に,) この州が 100 万の職を失ったのは確かに真実であるが, 同時にそれはわざと人をだますような内容である。

問 3 ① × ② × ③ ○

Let's try A word from her would have helped solve the problem.

解説

問1(1)　信頼できない政治戦略の例は次のうちどれか。

①「ある州知事が，彼女の州は100万の職を失ったが300万の新たな職を得たと言った。」

②「ある州知事が，彼女の州は100万の職を犠牲にして300万の新たな職を得たと言った。」

③「州知事の対立候補者が，300万の新しく得た職に言及することなくその州は100万の職を失ったと言った。」(ll.3～8)

④「州知事の対立候補者が，州知事の不十分な政治的手段にもかかわらずその州は300万の新しい職を得たと言った。」

(2)　広告主はどのように人をだますコミュニケーション戦略を用いるのか。

①「製品やサービスについて虚偽の主張をすることによって。」

②「会社の業績を自慢しすぎることによって。」

③「否定的な側面に言及することなく肯定的なデータを強調することによって。」(ll.14～19)

④「研究結果を公開することによって。」

問2　主語のThatは，前文の対立候補者が述べている内容(ll.7～8)を指す。
indeed ～ but …「なるほど〔確かに〕～だが…」(l.8)

問3　①「スミス州知事の前任期中に雇用は減少した。」(ll.3～4)

②「ヤッキー・ピルズの広告では，ヤッキー・ピルズについて質問された10人の医者全員に偏りがないと認められる。」(ll.17～19)

③「製品やサービスについて一部だけが真実である主張をすることは違法ではない。」(ll.12～14)

Let's try　「Sなら…だっただろうに」仮定を含むS＋would have＋過去分詞
「彼女からの一言」A word from herを主語にするとよい。

概要を整理しよう

具体例2　信頼できない政治家の情報操作
300万の職を得たことにふれず，100万の職を失ったと州知事を批判。
→真実だが人をだますような内容。「正味200万の職が増えた」が正直。

具体例3　広告主の情報操作
ある広告は「10人中9人の医者がヤッキー・ピルズを推薦」と自慢
→事実だが，質問したのは10人だけで，9人がヤッキー株式会社の社員

45 個人主義と協調主義［人間］

1 Have you ever noticed the different approaches / [∧people use <to deal with problems>]?// **Some** people, / "individualists", / generally try to work through problems on their own.// **Other** people, / "cooperators", / tend to approach problem-solving as a group matter.// Each approach has positive and negative points.//

2 Individualists may often be the quickest <to find an answer to a problem>, / and they tend to be willing to take responsibility.// **However**, / this approach is not perfect.// They may be too committed to a particular position / to be able to change their opinions.// In this way, / the individualists' approach may result in difficulties later.//

3 Cooperators are valued as team members / — in sports or school or work.// They tend to be flexible enough / to recognize the importance of other points of view / when problems arise.// This approach, / **however**, / can take a long time/, [which may lead to delays in solving problems].// Such difficulties sometimes cannot be avoided with the cooperators' approach.//

4 We should learn to recognize the different approaches to dealing with problems.// This knowledge can help us <build smoother relations / between people with different approaches to problem-solving>.//

解答

問1 (1) ②　(2) ①　**問2** 彼らは，十分融通がきく傾向にあるので，問題が発生すると他の視点の重要性を認識する。

問3 ① ○　② ×　③ ○

Let's try These letters may be too small to read.

解説

問 1(1)　個人主義者について正しいのは次のうちどれか。

①「時間をかけて問題に対する最高の解答を見つける。」

②「自分の意見を変えるのが難しいと思うことがある。」(*ll*. 8 ~ 9)

③「自分の立場がどうであるか気にしない。」

④「自分の決定が引き起こすかもしれない困難を申し訳なく思う。」

(2)　協力者について正しいのは次のうちどれか。

①「他の人の意見を重んじる。」(*ll*. 12 ~ 13)

②「さまざまな視点を気にしすぎて融通がきかない。」

③「責任を負いたがらない。」

④「長い時間がかかり，最高の解答を見つけられないことがよくある。」

問 2　tend to *do*「…する傾向にある」

形容詞＋ enough to *do*「…できるほど十分～」(*l*. 12)

points of view「視点」

問 3　①「個人主義者は協力者よりも速く問題への解答を見つけることが多いかもしれない。」(*ll*. 6 ~ 7)

②「個人主義者は自分の意見を変えるのをいとわない傾向がある。」(*ll*. 8 ~ 9)

③「問題に対処するための協力者の取り組み方は時間がかかる可能性がある。」(*ll*. 13 ~ 14)

Let's try　「～すぎて…できない」too ～ to *do*

「この文字」these letters を主語にするとよい。(文字なので，通常複数形)

概要を整理しよう

主題	「個人主義者」⇔「協力者」の長所と欠点
個人主義者	・長所：対処が速く，自分で責任を負う
	・欠点：自分の立場に傾倒し過ぎて意見を変えられない
協力者	・長所：チームの一員として重んじられ，柔軟性がある
	・欠点：対処に時間がかかり，解決の遅れにつながる場合がある
結論	問題に対処する異なる取り組み方を認めれば，より円滑な関係を築ける

46 テクノロジーは人間の職を奪うか（1）［科学］

In 1983, / the Nobel Prize-winning economist Wassily Leontief highlighted the debate / through a clever comparison of humans and horses.// For many decades, / horse labor appeared unaffected by technological change.// Even as railroads replaced the stagecoach and the Conestoga wagon, / the U.S. horse population grew / seemingly without end.// The animals were vital / not only on farms / but also in the country's rapidly growing urban centers.// **But** then, / with the introduction and spread of the powerful and efficient engine, / the trend was rapidly reversed.// As engines found their way into automobiles in the city and tractors in the countryside, / horses became largely irrelevant.// **Then**, / the question is [whether a similar outcome is possible for human labor].// Are autonomous machines and supercomputers indicating a coming wave of technological progress / [that will finally sweep humans out of the economy]?// For Leontief, / the answer was yes.// **However**, / he missed a number of important points.// Humans, / fortunately, / are not horses / and remain an important part of the economy.//

- the Nobel Prize-winning economist ＝ Wassily Leontief：同格
- The animals = horses
- not only A but also B「AだけでなくB」
- the country = the U.S.
- But：逆接
- find one's way into ～「～に入り込む」
- Then：主張
- a similar outcome：S' = 前文の内容
- that：関係代名詞
- However：逆接
- a number of ～「多数の～」

解答

問1 (1) ④　(2) ②

問2 鉄道が駅馬車や大型ほろ馬車に取って代わった時でさえ，アメリカにおける馬の固体数は果てしなく増え続けるように思われた。

問3 ① ×　② ○　③ ○

Let's try The question is whether (or not) Ryota told us a lie.

解説

問1(1)　(2) the trend was rapidly reversedの意味に最も近いのは次のうちどれか。

①「鉄道はすぐに時代の流行となった。」

②「19 世紀初頭，他の動物が急速にエンジンに取って代わった。」

③「初めは，馬の労働はそれほど急速には技術の変化の影響を受けなかった。」

④「馬の労働は農場と都市部の両方で急激に減少した。」(*ll*. 9 ~ 11)

(2)　本文で筆者が言及している問いは何か。

①「技術の進歩が来たるべき波なのかどうか」

②「人間の労働は将来不要になるのかどうか」(*ll*. 11 ~ 14)

③「機械とスーパーコンピューターは自律的になるのかどうか」

④「機械でできた馬が生きている馬に取って代わるのかどうか」

問2　接続詞 as「…時」(*l*. 4)

他にも文脈によって‘理由’,‘比例’などいろいろな意味になる。

without end「果てしなく」

問3　①「ワシリー・レオンチェフは人間と馬の比較で表彰された。」(*ll*. 1 ~ 3)

②「馬の労働は強力で効率的なエンジンの影響を急速に受けた。」(*ll*. 9 ~ 11)

③「レオンチェフは自律機械とスーパーコンピューターが人間を経済活動から一掃することに同意しただろう。」(*ll*. 12 ~ 15)

Let's try　「問題は…かどうかだ」the question is whether …（or not）
whether 節の内容が長い場合，or not は whether の直後に続くこともある。
「うそをつく」lie〔tell a lie〕

概要を整理しよう

導入	ワシリー・レオンチェフによる人間と馬の例 →エンジンの導入で，馬は役に立たなくなった
問題提起	問題は，人間の労働にも同じことが起きるのかどうか →レオンチェフは，自律機械やスーパーコンピューターが人間を経済活動から一掃すると考えた
主張	◆ **However「しかし：逆接」**(*l*. 15) レオンチェフは重要な点を見落としていた。 →人間は経済の重要な一部であり続ける

47 テクノロジーは人間の職を奪うか（2）［科学］

Alfred Marshall, / a British economist, / in his foundational 1890 book, / Principles of Economics, / said, / "Human wants and desires are countless in number / and very various in kind."// Ever since Marshall, / people have linked unlimited wants to full employment.// **After all**, / who else but workers will be able <to fulfill all those wants and desires>?// We humans are a deeply social species, / and the desire for human connections carries over to our economic lives.// We come together <to appreciate human expression or ability> / when we attend plays and sporting events.// Regular customers often visit particular restaurants, / not only because of the food and drink, / but because of the hospitality offered.// In these cases, / human interaction is central to the economic transaction, / not incidental to it.// Humans have economic wants / [that can be satisfied only by other humans], / and that makes us <deny / [that we will go the way of the horse]>.//

解答

問1 (1) ④　(2) ②

問2 人間は他の人間によってしか満たされることのない経済的欲望を持っていることが，我々が馬と同じ道をたどるであろうという考えを否定させる。

問3 ① ○　② ×　③ ○

Let's try He succeeded in business not only through〔because of〕his own efforts but also thanks to〔because of〕the support of his family.

解説

問 1(1)　アルフレッド・マーシャルの考えは次のうちどれか。

①「人間の欲求や願望はあまりにも多くてそのすべてを処理することはできない。」

②「人間は限りない欲求を結び付けられないので，機械が必要である。」

③「人間は独力ですべての雇用を確保しようとしてきた。」

④「人間だけが数えきれない量の人間の欲求や願望を満たすことができる。」

(ll. 5 ～ 6)

(2)　本文の主な結論は次のうちどれか。

①「アルフレッド・マーシャルは人間の欲求や願望について正しく想定した。」

②「将来の経済取引も引き続き人的交流を中核とするだろう。」(ll. 11 ～ 14)

③「人間だけが他の人間の経済的欲求を満足させられることに私たち全員が気づいている。」

④「私たちは今後，人間の表現や能力を賞賛するために集まる必要がある。」

問 2　that は前文の Humans ～ other humans を指す。economic wants「経済的欲望」の wants は名詞。

S make O *do*「S が O に…させる」／ deny that ...「…ということを否定する」

問 3　①「アルフレッド・マーシャルは自著に人間の欲求や願望に終わりはないと書いた。」(ll. 1 ～ 3)

②「演劇やスポーツのイベントですら，将来人的交流が必要でなくなるかもしれない。」(ll. 7 ～ 9)

③「もし特定のレストランが人間の従業員をロボットに取り替えたら，常連客ですらそのレストランに行くのをやめるかもしれない。」(ll. 9 ～ 11)

Let's try　「A だけでなく B」not only A but (also) B

「～のおかげで」は because of としてもよいが，文脈をふまえて through ／ thanks to などを用いるとより自然。

概要を整理しよう

・数えきれない人間の欲求は，労働者こそが満たしてくれる

・人とのつながりへの願望は，経済生活にも及ぶ

→人的交流は経済取引の中心である

結論　人間には他の人間だけが満たせる経済的欲望があるので，馬のようにはならない

1 You are on your way / to a concert.// At an intersection, / you encounter a group of people, / <all∧staring at the sky>.// Without even thinking about it, / you look upwards, / too.// Why∧?// *Social proof*∧.// In the middle of the concert, / when the soloist is giving an excellent performance, / someone begins to clap / and suddenly the whole room joins in.// You do, / too.// Why∧?// *Social proof*∧.// After the concert / you go to the coat check / <to pick up your coat>.// You watch / [how the people in front of you place a coin / on a plate], / even though, / officially, / the service is included in the ticket price.// What do you do?// You probably leave a coin / as well.// Why∧?// *Social proof*∧.//

2 Social proof, / <sometimes roughly termed the *herd instinct*>, / dictates / [that individuals feel / [they are behaving correctly] / when they act the same / as other people].// **In other words**, / if a large number of people follow a certain idea, / others will find this idea truer or better.// And the more people / [who display a certain behavior]∧, / the more appropriate others will judge it.// This is, / of course, / ridiculous.// Social proof is the evil / behind economic bubbles and stock market panic.// It exists / in fashion, management techniques, hobbies, religion and diets.// In some cases, / it can even negatively affect whole cultures.//

解答

問1　(1)　②　　(2)　②　　問2　ある振る舞いを示す人の数が多ければ多いほど，他の人たちはそれがいっそう適切だと判断するだろう

問3　①　○　　②　×　　③　×

Let's try　Let's see how people behave in case of emergency.

解説

問1(1)　いわゆる「社会的証明」の例でないのは次のうちどれか。

①「コンサートで誰かが拍手を始めたらそれに加わる。」(ll.4〜6)

②「車の往来がないとき，赤信号を渡る。」

③「他の人がチップを置いていく場合，レストランでチップを置いていく。」(ll.7〜10)

④「人々が同じ方向を向いている場合，彼らの視線の先を追う。」(ll.1〜3)

(2)　いわゆる「群居本能」の背後にある害悪の例は次のうちどれか。

①「他のクラスメイトが友達を責める場合，彼の無実を主張する。」

②「群居本能は，株式市場の混乱を引き起こすものである。」(ll.17〜18)

③「パーティーに招待されると，私たちは何を着るべきか悩む傾向にある。」

④「群居本能は，選挙活動中に人々をだます可能性がある。」

問2　the＋比較級〜，the＋比較級…「〜すればするほど，…」(ll.15〜16)
others judge it appropriate「他の人々はそれ（より多くの人々の振る舞い）を適切だと判断する」の appropriate が前に出て the more appropriate …の語順になっている。

問3　①「周囲の人々がみな上を見たら上を向くだろう。」(ll.1〜3)

②「音楽家の演奏を本当に評価している時のみ，コンサートで拍手をするだろう。」(ll.4〜6)

③「社会的証明は群居本能と不当に呼称されることがある。」(l.11)

Let's try　「S がどう…するかを見る」see how S *do* ...
本文では watch how ... が用いられているが，watch の場合は「注意深く見る」というニュアンスが含まれる。
「緊急事態に」in case of emergency

概要を整理しよう

導入　空を見ること／コンサートでの拍手／クロークへのチップ
→すべて社会的証明が基盤にある行動

本論　社会的証明（群居本能）とは
→他の人と同じように行動する時，正しく振る舞っていると感じること
社会的証明は悪にもなり得る。
→場合によっては，文化全体にまで悪影響を与えかねない

49 群集心理（2）［人間］

A simple experiment <carried out / in the 1950s / by legendary psychologist Solomon Asch> / shows / [how common sense is influenced by peer pressure, / the tendency <to want to act the same / as the members of one's social group>].// In Asch's experiment, / a research participant is shown a line / <drawn on paper>, / and next to it / three lines / — numbered 1, 2 and 3 — / one∧ shorter∧, one∧ longer∧ and one∧ / of the same length / as the original one.// The participant must indicate / [which of the three lines corresponds to the original one].// If that participant is alone / in the room, / he gives correct answers / — unsurprising, / because the task is really quite simple.// Now / five other people enter the room; / they are all actors, / a fact / [that the participant does not know].// One after another, / they give wrong answers, / saying "number 1," / although it's very clear / [that number 3 is the correct answer].// Then / it is the participant's turn again.// In one third of cases, / he will answer incorrectly / <to match the other people's responses>.// Why do we act / like this?//

解答

問 1 (1) （ア）⑤　（イ）②　（ウ）④　（エ）⑥　(2) ③

問 2 部屋に入ってくる他の５人はみな演技をしているのだが，これは被験者の知らない事実である

問 3 ① ×　② ○　③ ○

Let's try Students must tell the teacher which of the optional subjects they are going to take.

解説

問1(1)　ある実験で，被験者は部屋に1人でいる時は（　ア　）答えを出せる。しかし，部屋で（　イ　）人と一緒にいると，それらの人たちが間違った答えを選択する時（　ウ　）に1回は（　エ　）答えを出した。

①「別の」②「他の」→（イ）(ll.10～11) ③「2回」④「3回」→（ウ）(ll.14～15)
⑤「正しい」→（ア）(ll.8～9) ⑥「間違った」→（エ）(ll.14～15)

(2)　アッシュの実験について正しいのは次のうちどれか。

①「研究の被験者は異なる長さの4本の線を見せられる。」
②「5人の他の被験者はプロの俳優なのでみな演技が得意である。」
③「他人が誤った答えを示すと間違えて答える被験者もいる。」(ll.12～15)
④「アッシュは研究の被験者にする質問を注意深く選ぶ。」

問2　ここでは，they are all actorsという節をa fact以降が修飾している。theyは前のfive other people enter the roomのfive other peopleを指す。

問3　①「ソロモン・アッシュによる実験は，人々の仲間の圧力から逃れたい欲望を明らかにしている。」(ll.2～4)

②「アッシュの実験で他の5人はわざと間違えるように言われる。」(ll.11～13)
③「アッシュの実験では，研究の被験者は間違える可能性はまったくないほど単純な質問をされる。」(ll.9～10)

Let's try　「～のどれが…か」which of ～ …　tell the teacherの後に，which of ～を続ける。「とる」はtakeやchooseを用いると自然。

概要を整理しよう

実験　常識がいかにピア・プレッシャーに影響されるかを示す実験
→被験者1人の時は，正しい答えを出すが，他に人がいて，その全員が誤った答えを出すと，3分の1のケースで被験者も誤った答えを出す

問題提起　なぜこのように行動するのか

背景知識　インターネット上での群集心理

群集心理はインターネットが普及した現代において，より強まった形で表れる可能性が高まっている。例えば，SNS上におけるいわゆる「炎上」も，群集心理の現れといえる。ある投稿やコメントを批判するという方向性に場が傾くと，その方向性の大量のレスポンスで場が埋め尽くされる。世界中から一瞬でおびただしい数の人間を動員することができるインターネットにおいて，群集心理は常に切実な問題である。

50 群集心理（3）［人間］

1 In the past, / <following others> was a good survival strategy.// Suppose / [that 50,000 years ago, / you were travelling in the wild / with your hunter-gatherer friends, / and suddenly they all fled / at the sight of an animal].// What would you have done?// Would you have remained still, / <wondering about / [what you were looking at]>?// Was it a lion, / or something / [that just looked like a lion but was in fact a harmless animal]?// No, / you would have followed your friends.// Later on, / when you were safe, / you could have reflected on / [what the "lion" had actually been].// Those / [who acted differently from the group] / did not pass their genes on to the later generations.// We are directly descended from those / [who copied the others' behavior].// This pattern is so deeply rooted in us / that we still use it today, / even when it offers no survival advantage, / [which is most of the time].// Only a few cases come to mind / [where social proof is of value].// **For example**, / if you find yourself hungry / in a foreign city / and don't know a good restaurant, / it makes sense <to pick the one / [that's full of local people]>.// **In other words**, / you copy the local people's behavior.//

- following others: S / was: V / a good survival strategy: C
- they = your hunter-gatherer friends
- at (the) sight of ～「～を見て」
- would have done: 仮定法過去完了
- Would you have remained: S V 仮定法過去完了 / still: C
- wondering about: 分詞構文 '付帯状況' / wonder about ～「～について思い巡らす」
- that: 関係代名詞 / look like ～「～のように見える」 / in fact「実際は」
- would have followed: 仮定法過去完了
- later on「後で」
- reflect on ～「～を熟考する」
- those who…「…する人々」
- pass A on to B「A を B に伝える」
- This = copying the others' behavior
- so ～ that ...「あまりに～なので…」
- it = this pattern
- it = this pattern / which: 関係代名詞の非制限用法
- come to mind「頭に浮かぶ」 / where: 関係副詞
- example: 例
- it: 形式主語 / to pick: 真主語 / the one = the restaurant / that: 関係代名詞 / full of ～「～でいっぱいの」
- In other words: 言い換え / you: S / copy: V / the local people's behavior: O

2 Comedy and talk shows make use of social proof / by inserting sounds of people / laughing / at key moments, / <encouraging the audience to laugh along>.//

- laughing: 現在分詞の修飾
- encouraging: 分詞構文 '動作の連続'
- encourage O to *do*「O を…する気にさせる」

解答

問 1　(1) ①　(2) ②

問 2　社会的証明が有用な事例として思い浮かぶものは数少ない。

問 3　① ○　② ×　③ ○

Let's try　It makes sense for you to choose this book for Eri's present.

解説

問 1 (1)　なぜ昔の人は他人に従ったのか。

①「それがよい生存戦略であった。」(ℓ. 1)

②「彼らは集団のリーダーに従わなければならなかった。」

③「彼らは自分の遺伝子を後世に伝えなければならなかった。」

④「彼らの大部分は何をすべきか自分で決められなかった。」

(2)　社会的証明について正しいのは次のうちどれか。

①「社会的証明に従った後はそれについて熟考しなければならない。」

②「社会的証明は私たちの遺伝子に深く根付いていて，いまだにそれに従う傾向にある。」(ℓℓ. 11 ～ 12)

③「私たちは社会的証明が生存上の優位を与えてくれることを知っているので，いまだにそれを用いる。」

④「社会的証明は今やトークショーの観客にとってよい戦略である。」

問 2　come to mind「～が思い浮かぶ」

of value「価値がある（= valuable)」(ℓ. 14)

関係副詞 where 以降の節は，Only a few cases を修飾しているが，動詞が come to mind と短いため，このように離れた位置から修飾している。

問 3　①「昔は，社会的証明は必要不可欠な生存戦略だった。」(ℓ. 1)

②「古代の人々が，他人に従う必要はなかったとのちにわかった時，がっかりすることがあった。」(ℓℓ. 8 ～ 10)

③「現在社会的証明が生き残るのに必要とされるケースはほとんどない。」(ℓ. 14)

Let's try　「…するのは賢明だ」it makes sense to *do*

It is wise of you to *do* も可。

概要を整理しよう

昔の社会的証明	昔は他人に従うことがよい生存戦略だった →集団と違う行動をする者は後の世代に遺伝子を伝えなかった
今の社会的証明	今，そのような社会的証明に価値があるケースはわずかである

◆ **For example「例えば：例示」**(ℓℓ. 14 ～ 15)

・海外の街で地元の人でいっぱいのレストランを選ぶ

・コメディやトークショーで笑いを促すために人々の笑い声を挿入する

51 ゴミ0への挑戦（1）［環境］

1 Can we create a waste-free society?// It would seem like an ideal goal <to realize>,/ **since** mass production has forced a shift in our way of living.// Clothes have become 'fast fashion,' / <worn once and then thrown away < like a finished bag of potato chips>>.// **Sure,**/ most people will recycle their cans and bottles,/ **but** that doesn't alter the fact / [that we are still throwing away pounds and pounds of waste every day].// That will never change / in a world [where convenience is appreciated over all else].// Or will it∧?//

2 Kamikatsu, a small town in Tokushima Prefecture,/ had been working <for years> <to reduce waste>.// **However,**/ when they learned about zero-waste philosophy, / an idea popped into the residents' minds:/ to become the first zero-waste town in Japan.// The town doesn't collect domestic waste;/ **instead** the residents bring their waste to the waste collection site.// There,/ they sort it into 45 very specific and detailed categories.// **Although** some common stuff cannot be recycled,/ Kamikatsu has been able to recycle more than 80% of its waste.// Kamikatsu is **also** encouraging residents to reuse goods.// An area of its waste collection site offers used stuff < for free>.//

解答

問1 (1) ①　(2) ④

問2 衣類は「ファストファッション」となり，一度着るとそのあとは食べ終わったポテトチップスの袋のように捨てられてしまうのだ。

問3 ① ○　② ×　③ ×

Let's try Good ideas often pop into my mind while I am taking a bath.

解説

問1(1)　(　2　) を埋めるのに最も適当な答えを下記から選べ。

①「それとも」

※ That will never change と対照するように Or will it (change)? となっている。

②「だから」

③「なお」

④「それから」

(2)　上勝町がゴミ0の町になることに決めたのはなぜか。

①「当時，別のゴミ0の町が魅力的に思えたから。」

②「そこではゴミの削減に成功していたから。」

③「そこでは多すぎるゴミに悩まされていたから。」

④「住人がゴミ0の考え方に触発されたから。」(ll. 10 ~ 11)

問2　worn 以下は分詞構文で，and (then) によって worn と thrown が並列されている。finished は bag を修飾する過去分詞で，ここでは「(食べることを) 終えられた (ポテトチップスの袋)」という意味。「食べ終わった」のように訳せばよい。

問3　①「私たちは便利さを追求して多くのゴミを捨てている。」(ll. 5 ~ 7)

②「上勝町では，町に代わって住民が順番に家庭ゴミを収集している。」(ll. 12~14)

③「上勝町は，ゴミ収集所で中古品を販売している。」(ll. 17 ~ 18)

Let's try　「〜にふと浮かぶ」pop into 〜 (l. 11)／「入浴中に」は during bathing でも可。

概要を整理しよう

問題提起　私たちはゴミのない社会を創れるだろうか

現状　大量生産によって私たちは大量にゴミを出す生活様式へと変化している
→この事実は今後変わるのだろうか

具体例　日本初のゴミ0の町を目指す上勝町
・町の代わりに住民が自らゴミを収集所に持っていき，そこで細かく分別している
・中古品を無料で提供するなど，住民に物の再利用を奨励している

52 ゴミ0への挑戦（2）［環境］

1 Recycling and reusing, / **however**,/ are not enough <to keep our world from becoming swallowed up in waste>.// Kamikatsu **also** makes an effort /<to get people to brush up their understanding of the environment / and make society <as a whole> think 'why?' // Why are you buying or selling the product?// Is it good for the environment?// Will it become a favorite possession / or will it be thrown away /<after one use>?// **Whereas** <before> some believed / [they had a sacred right <to buy or produce [whatever they desired]>], /<now> they realize /[that their actions affect the world <around them>].//

2 <In recent years>, / Kamikatsu built a complex facility <called the Zero Waste Center>.// A hotel <located <in the grounds of this facility>>/ is run <on the understanding / [that creating a waste-free society applies not only to individuals,/ but also to businesses]>.// **For example**,/ <instead of offering an individual soap bar to each guest>,/ it encourages them to cut off the amount of soap [they need] /<at the front desk>.// Fitting into a new strategy is not easy,/ **but** <through its actions>,/ Kamikatsu is leading the nation / <in finding ways <to gain the prize of a truly waste-free society>>.//

解答

問1 (1) ①　(2) ②

問2 しかし，リサイクルと再利用は，私たちの世界がゴミに飲み込まれるのを防ぐのに十分ではない。

問3 ① ○　② ○　③ ○

Let's try Jane always makes an effort to explain difficult topics clearly.

解説

問1(1)　下線部 (2) の質問の目的は何か。

① 「後者のような商品を買うのを避けるよう消費者を促すため。」

※下線部後半の「一度の使用のあとに捨てる」という内容は，「ゴミ0」という本文の主旨を考えると避けるべきこととして言及されているとわかる。

② 「最も有用な製品を買うよう消費者を促すため。」

③ 「自分のお気に入りは何かを消費者に決めさせるため。」

④ 「物をほとんど持たずに暮らすことを検討するよう消費者に強く勧めるため。」

(2)　(　3　) を埋めるのに最も適当な答えを下記から選べ。

① 「要するに」

② 「例えば」

※空所以降は，ゴミのない社会を目指すホテルの取り組みの具体例になっている。

③ 「加えて」

④ 「対照的に」

問2　keep O from …ing「O が…するのを防ぐ」(ℓℓ.1～2) ／ swallow up ～「～を飲み込む」(ℓ.2) ／ここでは，「私たちの世界」が「ゴミに飲み込まれる」状態になるのを防ぐ，ということ。

問3　① 「購買と生産についての意見を変えた人もいる。」(ℓℓ.7～9)

② 「ゼロ・ウェイストセンターには宿泊することができる。」(ℓℓ.10～11)

③ 「上勝町はゴミのない社会を達成する上でのロールモデルとなりつつある。」(ℓℓ.16～17)

Let's try　「…するよう努める」make an effort to *do* (ℓ.3) ／「わかりやすく」clearly

概要を整理しよう

主張　環境に関する社会の理解を促進させようとする上勝町の取り組み
→購買や生産といった行動が環境に与える影響を人々が理解するようになっている

具体例　上勝町のゼロ・ウェイストセンター内のホテル
→ゴミのない社会を創ることは個人だけでなく企業の課題でもあるという考えに基づく

結論　ゴミのない社会を実現する上で，上勝町は日本で先頭に立っている

53 クローン技術の是非（1）［科学］

1 A basic rule of medical science / is [that no human life should be used for the benefit of another].// **Some people** are against human cloning and related techniques / for this reason.// In cloning, / an egg cell is used <to develop ordinary cells>.// The opponents of cloning insist [that this is killing], / because it destroys the potential of the egg <to develop into a human being>.//

2 **Other people** oppose cloning / because / at this stage / it is unreliable.// In animal experiments, / **for example**, / success rates are very low.// **Still others** are concerned about the future [that cloning might bring about].// They are afraid [that cloning will lead to the production of human beings for body parts].// They **also** fear [that cloning might lead to attempts <to create "superior" humans>].//

解答

問 1　(1)　③　　(2)　③

問 2　彼らは，クローニングが，身体の一部を得るためにヒトを生産することにつながることを恐れている。

問 3　①　×　　②　×　　③　○

Let's try　Are you for the project〔plan〕or against it?

解説

問 1(1)　クローニングについて正しくないのは次のうちどれか。

①「いかなるヒトの命も他人の利益のために使われるべきではない。」(*ll*. 1～2)

②「現段階ではヒトのクローニングを認めていない人もいる。」(*ll*. 2～3)

③「ヒトの卵細胞は今，普通の細胞を作り出すのに利用されている。」

④「クローニングは卵がヒトに成長するのをさまたげる。」(*ll*. 5～6)

(2)　クローニングに反対する人々の懸念は次のうちどれか。

①「実用的なクローン技術をうみだすことは高額の費用がかかるだろう。」

②「クローニングで動物実験が果たす役割の価値には疑問の余地がある。」

③「クローニングを通じてヒトの身体の一部を生産するためにヒトがつくられるかもしれない。」(ll.10～11)

④「クローン技術は身体改造を促進するかもしれない。」

問2　be afraid that ...「…ということを恐れている」

S lead to ～「Sが～の結果をもたらす〔～を引き起こす〕」(l.10)

問3　①「医学は基本的に，ヒトの命が他人の利益のために使われなければならないことを認めている。」(ll.1～2)

②「クローニングを通じて，卵細胞がヒトになる可能性をもつ。」(ll.5～6)

③「実験における成功率がとても低いので，クローニングの信頼性を疑う人もいる。」(ll.8～9)

Let's try　「～に賛成である」be for ～⇔「～に反対である」be against ～

概要を整理しよう

主題　クローニングに反対する理由

理由1　◆　**Some people ～「ある人は～：列挙」**(l.2)

ヒトの命は他人の利益のために使われるべきではない。

理由2　◆　**Other people ～「～という人もいる：列挙」**(l.7)

信頼できない。←動物実験での成功率の低さ。

理由3　◆　**also「また：列挙」**(l.11)

クローニングがもたらす将来への懸念。

→身体の一部を得るためのヒトの生産／「優れた」ヒトを作り出す試みへの危惧

背景知識　クローン技術をめぐる論争

現代の最新技術ではすでに，霊長類であるサルの体細胞クローンを誕生させるまでに至っており，近い将来，技術的にはクローン人間をつくることが可能になると言われている。クローンの反対論では，「人間の尊厳」という観念が最も大きな根拠となる。他人を道具扱いしてはならないという考えのもと，クローン胚を「人間」という範疇に含めるならば，クローン胚の利用はまさに人間の「道具扱い」となり，人間の尊厳を損なう行為とみなされるのである。この問題については研究者たちだけではなく，社会全体で正しい選択を探らなければならない。

54 クローン技術の是非（2）[科学]

1 Not everyone is against human cloning, / **however**.// **Some people** support cloning / if it is for the purpose of medical treatment, / **although** they oppose the cloning of babies.// The medical benefits of cloning and related techniques, / they argue, / could be huge.// **For example**, / if a heart can be developed from a patient's own cell, / the body will not reject it.// **Furthermore**, / he or she will not have to wait for someone to die <to get a new heart>.//

2 Supporters claim [that the use of such techniques is not killing].// **Just as** ordinary store-bought eggs do not develop into chickens, / the eggs <used for cloning> do not develop into human beings by themselves.// They **also** argue [that it is already practically impossible / <to stop a patient from receiving medical treatment / [that / in some way / depends on cloning and related techniques]>].// Even if **one** country bans cloning, / there will always be **another** country [that promotes it].// The supporters, / **therefore**, / maintain [that scientists should have the freedom <to experiment>] and [that people should have the freedom <to seek lifesaving treatments>].// **In other words**, / they feel [that cloning should be continued / unless it is clearly shown to be harmful].// The debate over this issue is likely to go on for some time.//

解答

問 1 (1) ② (2) ② **問 2** 患者は新しい心臓を手に入れるために，誰かが死ぬのを待つ必要はないだろう

問 3 ① ○ ② × ③ ○

Let's try Not everyone in the class agrees to the plan.

解説

問 1(1)　クローニングの医学的な恩恵でないのは次のうちどれか。

①「患者自身の細胞から臓器を作り出せる。」(ll. 4 ~ 5)

②「クローニングによってほとんどすべての種類の臓器を作り出せる。」

③「患者自身の細胞から作られた臓器は, 移植後に拒絶されないだろう。」(l. 5)

④「臓器を手に入れるのに患者は誰かが死ぬのを待つ必要がない。」(ll. 6 ~ 7)

(2)　臓器のクローニングを支持する人々の主張ではないのは次のうちどれか。

①「患者自身の細胞から臓器を作り出す技術の利用は殺人ではない。」(l. 8)

②「ヒトの卵細胞は決してヒトに成長しない。」

③「科学者がクローン技術を使うのをやめさせることは望ましいものではない。」(ll. 15 ~ 17)

④「クローニングは誰にとっても有害でない限り続けられるべきだ。」(ll. 17 ~ 18)

問 2　will not have to *do*「…する必要はないだろう」／ wait for ~ to *do*「~が…するのを待つ」(l. 6) he or she は前文の a patient を指す。

問 3　①「ヒトのクローニングを支持する人がいる。」(l. 1)

②「人がクローニングに使うかもしれない卵は, やがて自動的にヒトになる。」(ll. 9 ~ 10)

③「臓器のクローニングを支持する人々は科学者が自由に実験できるべきだと主張する。」(ll. 14 ~ 16)

Let's try　「全部の~が…というわけではない」not every ~
「~に賛成する」agree to ~〔be for ~〕

概要を整理しよう

主題	誰もがクローニングに反対というわけではない
理由 1	◆ **Some people ~「ある人は~：列挙」**(l. 1) クローニングの医学的な恩恵。
理由 2	治療用のクローニングは殺人ではない
理由 3	◆ **also「また：列挙」**(l. 11) 科学者には実験の自由が, 患者には救命治療利用の自由があるべきだ。 ◆ **In other words「言い換えれば：言い換え」**(l. 17) 有害と明らかに示せないなら, クローニングを続けるべきだ。
結論	クローニングについての議論はまだ続きそうだ

55 ビタミンAの重要性とサツマイモ（1）［科学］

1 HarvestPlus, / an agricultural research organization, / is teaching people around the world / <how to grow [what it calls “smart” crops]>.// Its project in Mozambique is having surprising effects.// In 2006, / HarvestPlus workers provided orange sweet potato plants / to people in 24 villages in Mozambique.// The workers taught these people / <how to grow the vegetables>.// They **also** explained the importance of Vitamin A / to staying healthy.//

HarvestPlus（S）／an agricultural research organization（同格）／is teaching（V）／people around the world（O）／how to…「…する方法」O／what it calls ～「いわゆる～」／Its＝HarvestPlus's（S）／is having（V）／surprising effects（O）／provide A to B「BにAを提供する」／The workers（S）＝HarvestPlus workers／taught（V）／these people（O）＝people in 24 villages in Mozambique／how to grow the vegetables（O）＝orange sweet potato plants／They＝HarvestPlus workers／also：追加

2 Farmers in Mozambique had been planting white and yellow sweet potatoes, / not the orange-colored ones.// The white and yellow potatoes have very little Vitamin A.// **However**, / one small, orange sweet potato has a full day's supply of Vitamin A.// A lack of Vitamin A is dangerous.// Without enough Vitamin A, / you face an increased risk / of getting a serious disease / or dying from infections.//

Farmers in Mozambique（S）／had been planting（V）／white and yellow sweet potatoes（O）／ones＝sweet potatoes／The white and yellow potatoes（S）／have（V）／very little Vitamin A（O）／However：逆接／one small, orange sweet potato（S）／has（V）／a full day's supply of Vitamin A（O）／A lack of Vitamin A（S）／is（V）／dangerous（C）／you（S）／face（V）／an increased risk（O）／die from ～「～で死ぬ」

3 The World Health Organization (WHO) reports / [that around the world, / 190 million young children are not getting / enough of this important vitamin / in the foods [∧they eat]].//

The World Health Organization (WHO)（S）／reports（V）／that …（O）／190 million young children（S'）／are not getting（V'）／enough of this important vitamin（O'）／this important vitamin＝Vitamin A／∧：関係代名詞（which）

4 Economist Alan de Brauw is with the International Food Policy Research Institute / and was involved with the project.// He says / [about 70 percent of children there were Vitamin A deficient].// They were not getting enough Vitamin A.//

Economist／Alan de Brauw（同格）／be involved with ～「～に関わる」／the project＝第1，第2パラグラフの内容／He＝Alan de Brauw／about 70 percent of children（S'）／there＝in Mozambique／were（V'）／Vitamin A deficient（C'）／They＝about 70 percent of children there

5 “About 70% of kids under the age of five were Vitamin A deficient.// So, / you have this huge need / for new solutions.// If you can do something / through agriculture / <to increase the amount of vitamin in the diet ...> / you're in much better shape / because that's much more sustainable” / than using vitamin supplements.//

About 70% of kids under the age of five（S）／were（V）／Vitamin A deficient（C）／in good shape「うまくいって」／that＝something ～ in the diet

解答

問 1　④

問 2　ハーベストプラスという農業研究組織は，世界中の人々にいわゆる「賢い」作物の栽培方法を教えている。

問 3　①　×　　②　○　　③　○

Let's try　We provided warm soup to children〔provided children with warm soup〕at the festival.

解説

問 1　アラン・デ・ブロウが関わった事業について正しいのは次のうちどれか。

①「彼の事業はビタミン A が欠乏している子供たちの 70%を救えた。」

②「彼の事業はより持続可能にするために再考する必要がある。」

③「彼の事業は，農民の収入を増やし，病気のリスクを減らす助けになった。」

④「彼の事業はモザンビークの深刻な病気や感染症のリスクを減らすのに大きな助けになるだろう。」(ll. 11 ～ 13)

問 2　how to *do*「…する方法」／ what it calls ～「いわゆる～ (= what is called ～)」(l. 2) 関係代名詞 what 以降が grow の目的語になっている。

問 3　①「2006 年より前，モザンビークの農民はオレンジ色のサツマイモよりも白色や黄色のサツマイモの味を好んでいた。」(ll. 8 ～ 9)

②「アラン・デ・ブロウは国際食糧政策研究所のスタッフである。」(ll. 17 ～ 18)

③「モザンビークでは約 70%の子供たちがビタミン A 不足に苦しんでいた。」(l. 19)

Let's try　「A に B を提供する」provide B to〔for〕A；provide A with B

概要を整理しよう

主題　ハーベストプラスのプロジェクトの驚くべき効果

→ 2006 年，モザンビークの村にオレンジ色のサツマイモを提供した

背景　オレンジ色のサツマイモはビタミン A が豊富

→モザンビークの子供の約 70%はビタミン A の欠乏に苦しんでいる

→農業を通じて食事に含まれるビタミンの量を増やすことはより継続しやすい方法である

56 ビタミンAの重要性とサツマイモ（2）［科学］

1 Anne Herforth, / an expert on global food security and nutrition, / calls supplements a short-term "solution / to a more fundamental problem, / [which is <people not having access to high-quality diets>]." //

2 Mr. de Brauw says / [the potatoes had a surprising effect / on the health of children].// At the end of the three-year study, / the researchers compared the health of children / in villages <growing orange sweet potatoes> / with those <not growing them>.//

3 Children <living in the sweet potato villages> had 40% fewer cases of diarrhea / than other boys and girls.// Among children under the age of three, / the difference was 50% .// According to Mr. de Brauw / showing the effect of a food-growing project on health / is very important, / or as he says, / "a big deal." //

4 "This is a big deal / because nobody has shown / in the past / [that an agricultural production intervention can have big health impacts ... / *any* health impacts]." //

5 Experts say / [that teaching farmers / <how to grow healthier food> / is one of the best ways <to improve health>].// Ms. Herfoth says [the findings do a good job / <making the link / between food production and health>].// It's important / to show [that / if "you produce a food / and it's available to people <to eat> / and they like it, / then it does good things for health]." //

6 HarvestPlus is now helping farmers in other countries.// In India, / the group is helping farmers grow iron-rich millet.// And in Bangladesh, / it is helping farmers grow high-zinc rice.//

解答

問 1　③

問 2　より健康的な食料の栽培方法を農業従事者に教えることは健康を改善するための最良の方法の 1 つだという研究結果が，食料生産と健康とを関連づけるうえで役に立つ

問 3　①　×　　②　○　　③　×

Let's try　We compared the environments of the schools in the city with those in the countryside.

解説

問 1　アン・ハーフォースによると，根本的な問題は次のうちどれか。

①「やり方を知らないので，多くの農民がより健康的な食料を育てたくない。」

②「多くの人々が食料の栄養について十分な知識をもたない。」

③「人々は日々健康的で質の高い食料を手に入れるのに苦労する。」(ℓ.3)

④「ビタミンのサプリメントは健康問題の短期的な解決策にすぎない。」

問 2　the finding は，第 3 段落以降の研究結果をまとめた前文の内容，食料栽培プロジェクトが健康改善に効果的であることを示すといえる。

do a good job *doing* ～「…に役立つ」

問 3　①「ほとんどすべての種類のジャガイモが子供の健康に驚くべき影響を及ぼした。」(ℓℓ.4 ～ 7) ②「オレンジ色のサツマイモを育てた村では，3 歳未満の子供はある健康上の問題に悩まされることが 50%減った。」(ℓℓ.8 ～ 10) ③「今はいくつかのアジアの国のすべての農民が健康的な食料を生産することの重要性に気づいている。」(ℓℓ.19 ～ 23)

Let's try　「A と B を比較する」compare A with B schools in the city と those（the environments ～の重複を避ける）in the countryside を比較する。

概要を整理しよう

問題提起	根本的な問題は人々が高品質な食事を得られないこと
解決策	オレンジ色のサツマイモは，子供たちの病気に対する抵抗力を高めた
結論	健康的な食料の育て方を教えるのは，健康改善の最良の方法の 1 つ
展開	ハーベストプラスは，他の国でも支援をしている

57 ダイエットに関する意外な論文（1）［人間］

1 No more TV dinners, / no more snacking / with Paul McCartney on the kitchen stereo / and certainly no listening / to the more intellectual bits of Radio 4 / over breakfast.// [If you want <to lose weight>, / the best accompaniment to a meal / is the sound of your own chewing], / a study suggests.// Psychologists in the US have found [that people consume less food / when they can hear themselves eating].// They believe the effect <to be so powerful / that even simply telling somebody / [that they are eating a crunchy snack] / makes them eat less>.// In a considerable benefit / to those [who cannot get through a packet of crisps / without making the noise of a small gunfight], / experiments show [that the more people concentrate / on the noise of their meal, / the less they eat / and they think [the flavours are more intense]].//

2 Gina Mohr, / assistant professor of marketing at Colorado State University, / said [the findings suggested [that people [who wanted <to diet>] / could cut down on distracting sounds]].// In one experiment, / Dr Mohr and a colleague asked 71 students <to sit in a room with a bowl of ten pretzels / while wearing a pair of headphones>.// Half of the participants had their ears flooded with white noise, / <drowning out the sound of their chewing>.// They ate an average of four pretzels each.// The other half, / [who were able to hear themselves eat much more distinctly], / took 2.8 ∧ each.//

解答

問 1　④
問 2　参加者の半分は，耳をホワイトノイズでいっぱいにされて，自分の咀嚼音はかき消されていた。
問 3　①　×　　②　×　　③　○
Let's try　The more time children spend playing video games, the less time they spend playing with friends.

解説

問 1　自分自身の咀嚼音について正しいのは次のうちどれか。
①「食事を楽しみたい場合，食事の最も適当なお供である。」
②「とても強力な効果があるので誰かに何かを食べていると伝えたくなる。」
③「楽しみたい食べ物に集中できなくなるので，食欲をなくさせる。」
④「食べる量を減らし，より食べ物の味を強く感じさせるのに役立つ。」
(*ll*. 10 ～ 12)

問 2　have O 過去分詞「O を…される」(*l*. 18)
drowning out ～以降は‘付帯状況’を表す分詞構文になっている。

問 3　①「体重を減らしたいなら，朝食中に Radio 4 を聞くのが役に立つ。」(*ll*. 1 ～ 5)
②「アメリカの心理学者は，自分の咀嚼音を聞ける人は，聞けない人よりも食べる量が多いことを発見した。」(*ll*. 5 ～ 6)
③「誰かにその人が音のする何かを食べていると伝えると，その人の食べる量は減るだろう。」(*ll*. 7 ～ 8)

Let's try　「～すればするほど，…」the 比較級～，the 比較級 ...
「…して時間を過ごす」spend time *doing*

概要を整理しよう

主題　体重を減らしたいなら，自分の咀嚼音を聞くのがよい
本論　自分が食べている音を聞けると食べる量が減ることを発見した
→味をより濃く感じさせる効果もある
ダイエットをしたいなら気が散るような騒音を減らせばよい。
実験　⇔咀嚼音が聞こえにくくなると，食べる量が減る効果は弱くなる

58 ダイエットに関する意外な論文（2）［人間］

1 The marketing psychologists **also** sat 156 undergraduates down in a room / with eight baked crackers / <made from pitta bread>.// One group read a piece of paper [that said: [“Our pitta crackers / deliver the crunch [∧you crave].// You'll love the crispy sound of each bite].”// They each ate an average of one fewer / than the other group, / [who were shown an instruction / [that emphasised the taste / instead]].//

also 追加／過去分詞の修飾／make A from B「BからAを作る」／関係代名詞／関係代名詞（which）／They = one group／関係代名詞の非制限用法／関係代名詞／the taste = the taste of pitta crackers

2 The researchers believe [that food manufacturers have long understood this phenomenon].// When the company behind the Magnum brand of ice creams / changed their chocolate coating / to stop it slipping off the bar, / they were inundated with complaints.// It eventually emerged [that people had largely been buying the bars / precisely because they liked / the brittleness of the chocolate / and crackling noise [∧it made / when they ate it]].//

O' ＝前文の内容／their = ice creams'／不定詞の副詞用法／stop O (from) *doing*「Oが…するのを防ぐ」／they = the company／it emerges that ...「…ということが明らかになる」／they = people／関係代名詞（which）／it = the chocolate

3 “To our knowledge, / this relationship had not been examined / in existing research / despite the importance [that food sound has / in the consumer environment],” / the authors wrote / in the journal / Food Quality and Preference.//

to one's knowledge「〜の知る限りでは」／this relationship ＝第2パラグラフ最終文の内容／despite 〜「〜にもかかわらず」／関係代名詞／the journal / Food Quality and Preference 同格

解答

問1 (1) ③　(2) ③

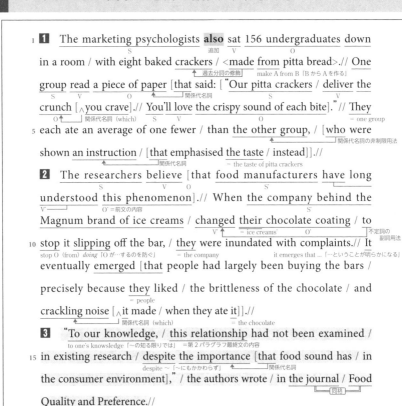

問2 結局明らかになったのは，人々が大量にそのアイスバーを買っていたのは，まさにそのチョコレートの砕けやすさとそれを食べる時に聞こえるパリパリとした音を気に入っていたからだったのだ。

問3 ① ×　② ×　③ ○

Let's try Lisa seems to have enjoyed her day off〔holiday(s)〕despite the bad weather.

解説

問 1(1)　本文で言及された研究が示唆したのは次のうちどれか。

①「消費者はサクサクした音がするからピタクラッカーを好む。」

②「消費者はピタクラッカーがサクサクした音がすると言われた時に，ますますサクサクした音が大好きになった。」

③「ピタクラッカーがサクサクした音を立てると言われた消費者は，言われなかった消費者よりも食べる量が少なかった。」(*ll*. 4 ～ 6)

④「消費者は食べ物が立てる音よりも味を重視する。」

(2)　なぜマグナムのアイスクリームを作る会社は多くの苦情を受けたのか。

①「チョコレートコーティングがもっとアイスバーにくっつくように改良が必要だった。」

②「消費者はパリパリした音を立てずにアイスクリームを食べることが難しかった。」

③「改良されたチョコレートコーティングが，改良前より砕けやすくパリパリしなかった。」(*ll*. 12 ～ 13)

④「消費者は，アイスバーから簡単に滑り落ちてしまうチョコレートコーティングが気に入らなかった。」

問 2　it emerges that ...「…ということが明らかになる」

precisely because 「まさに…だからこそ」

they liked の目的語は the brittleness ～と crackling noise ～の 2 つ。

問 3　①「学部生はサクサクしたクラッカーよりおいしいクラッカーを好んだ。」(*ll*. 1 ～ 6) ②「アイスクリームのマグナムブランドを製造する会社は，消費者の声を参考にして商品を改良した。」(*ll*. 10 ～ 13) ③「食べ物の音が消費者の選択にどのように影響を与えるかはこれまで十分に調べられてこなかった。」(*ll*. 14 ～ 16)

Let's try　「～にもかかわらず」despite ～／「S は…したようだ」S seemed to have 過去分詞〔It seems that S 過去形〕

概要を整理しよう

具体例 1	クラッカーの音を強調した説明書を読んだ学生は，味を強調した説明書を読んだ学生よりも食べる量が少なかった
具体例 2	アイスバーの立てる音が変わることで，消費者からクレームが殺到
まとめ	食べ物の音と消費者の好みの関係は，これまで調べられてこなかった

59 家族で食事をすることの重要性（1）[社会]

1 When it comes to eating, / the United States has a lesson <to learn from France>.// I'm not talking / about the kind of elaborate dinners [∧ Americans often associate with the French].// Many of the meals [∧ the French eat] are quick and simple.// The difference is [that the French eat together].// They have managed to preserve a tradition / [that is good for everyone's health] — the family meal.//

2 According to the French government's Committee for Health Education, / 75 percent of the French eat dinner together / as a family / and many French schoolchildren still go home / for lunch.//

3 These figures haven't changed much in decades.// In the United States, / **on the other hand**, / national studies show [that on average, / only one family in three sits down for dinner together / on a daily basis].// Over the last two decades, / there has been a steady decline / in the number of American families [that eat together regularly].// It looks like / the family meal is disappearing.//

解答

問1 (1) ①　(2) (ア) ④　(イ) ⑥　(ウ) ③

問2 フランス人は，皆の健康によい慣習，すなわち家族そろっての食事を何とか維持してきたのだ。

問3 ① ○　② ×　③ ×

Let's try It looks like it's going to rain at any moment.

解説

問 1(1)　アメリカ合衆国がフランスから学べる教訓でないのは次のうちどれか。

①「フランス人は家族のために手の込んだ食事を作る。」(ll. 2 ~ 3)

②「フランス人はさっと済ませる簡単な食事を食べるが，一緒に食べる。」

③「フランス人はいまだに家族そろっての食事という慣習を維持している。」

④「多くのフランス人の親は学校に通う子供を昼食のために家に帰らせる。」

(2)　アメリカ合衆国では，家族の（　ア　）だけしか一緒に食事の席に着いていない。過去（　イ　）年間にわたって，いつも一緒に食事をするアメリカ人家族の数の着実な（　ウ　）が起こっている。

①「増加」②「24」③「減少」→（ウ）(l. 13)

④「3 分の 1」→（ア）(ll. 11 ~ 12) ⑤「不足」⑥「20」→（イ）(l. 13)

問 2　manage to *do*「何とか…する」(l. 5)

They は前文の「フランス人」を指す。a tradition ~ health と the family meal は同格の関係なので，「すなわち」などで結ぶとよい。

問 3　①「アメリカ合衆国がフランスから学ぶべき 1 つの教訓は，一緒に食事を取ることの利点である。」(ll. 4 ~ 5)

②「統計によると，すべてのフランスの家族のうち半分しか一緒に食事を取っていない。」(l. 8)

③「いつも一緒に食事をするアメリカ人家族数は過去 20 年にわたって着実に増加してきた。」(ll. 13 ~ 14)

Let's try　「…のようだ」it looks like S + V ...
「今にも」at any moment

概要を整理しよう

主題　食事について，アメリカはフランスに学ぶべき教訓がある
→フランス人は家族で食事をする

本論　フランス人の 75%が家族で食事をしている　／生徒の多くが昼食を食べに家に帰る

◆　**on the other hand「他方：対比」**(l. 11)

アメリカの家族で日常的に食事をするのは 3 分の 1 のみ。
→過去 20 年で家族で食事をとる家は減り続けている

60 家族で食事をすることの重要性 (2) [社会]

1 How and why did the family meal start to disappear in the United States?// My friends in the United States have various explanations / ∧ (as to) [why meals together aren't an option for their families].// Parents and children lead hectic lives / and there just isn't time for a sit-down meal.// Kids' sports schedules run on into dinner hour.// After a long day at work, / parents are too tired to cook.// Teenagers are off on their own after school.// "Everyone likes different foods," / they say, / "**so** what is the point of eating together?"//

2 **Yet** study after study shows [that having meals together as a family is good / for both adults and children].// A University of Michigan study found [that mealtime at home was the single strongest factor / <predicting better achievement scores and fewer behavioral problems for children>].// Mealtime was far more powerful / than time <spent in school, studying, worshiping, playing sports or doing arts activities>.//

3 Other studies show [that children like family meals].// In one report, / nearly four-fifths of adolescents cited eating dinner at home / as one of their top-rated family activities.// In a national YMCA poll in 2000, / when teenagers were asked about their worries, / 21 percent rated "not having enough time with parents" / as their top concern.//

解答

問1 (1) ① (2) ③ **問2** 青年のほぼ5分の4が，重要な家族の活動の1つとして，家で食事を取ることを挙げた

問3 ① ○ ② × ③ ○

Let's try I don't have enough time to talk with my parents about what course I should take after graduation.

解説

問 1(1)　(　　) ので，家族そろっての食事がアメリカ合衆国では消滅し始めた。

① 「親も子供も忙しすぎて家で食事を取る時間を作れない」(*ll.* 3 ～ 4)

② 「学童が放課後スポーツに参加しなければならない」

③ 「親が夕食を作るのにうんざりしている」

④ 「10 代の若者は家族よりも友達と時間を過ごすのを好む」

(2)　(　　) ので家族で一緒に食事を取ることは誰のためにもなることが，研究により明らかになっている。

① 「子供が問題を起こすのを防ぐ」

② 「誰にとっても最も人気のある家族で達成することである」

③ 「学校の成績や素行を向上させる強い要因である」(*ll.* 11 ～ 13)

④ 「スポーツをしたり芸術活動をしたりするよりも楽しい」

問 2　four-fifths「5 分の 4」

cite A as B「A を B として挙げる」この文では A に当たるのが eating dinner at home の動名詞句。

問 3　① 「合衆国では親や子供が腰を下ろして食事をするには忙しすぎると言っている。」(*ll.* 3 ～ 4)

② 「学校で過ごす時間は家庭での食事時間よりも強力な学力得点向上の要因である。」(*ll.* 11 ～ 13)

③ 「80％近くの若者が家で食事を取ることを好む。」(*ll.* 17 ～ 18)

Let's try　「十分な時間がもてていない」don't have enough time

「進路について」→「どんな進路をとるべきか」と言い換えて what course I should take〔what course to take〕と間接疑問を使う。

概要を整理しよう

問題提起　アメリカ人は家族そろっての食事をしなくなり始めている

本論　◆ **Yet「しかし：逆接」**(*l.* 9)

家族での一緒の食事は大人にも子供にもよいことだ。

→子供の成績がよくなり，問題行動が減る

→子供は家族そろっての食事を好む

61 スーパーの便利さと運搬燃料（1）［環境］

1 A modern supermarket is a thing of wonder.// Even if it's snowing outside / and summer is a distant memory, / you can buy strawberries, peaches or grapes.// If you want root vegetables / in the middle of a heatwave, / you can have them.// Ex-pat Americans can have their Oreo cookies, / while homesick New Zealanders can console themselves / with wine and kiwi fruit.// Within days of being picked off the vines, / the fruit is in your trolley, / <tasting of spring / as the leaves are falling outside>.//

2 It's all great / until you start contemplating the vast mileage <sitting in your shopping basket>.// Those kiwi fruits have travelled nearly 20,000 kilometers — **or** 12,000 miles.// They've flown in a plane / and travelled by road.// By the time they reach the supermarket, / they're responsible for five times their own weight in greenhouse gases <being pumped into the atmosphere>.// Increasingly, / our food is coming from further and further away, / and we're becoming more and more dependent on the fuel [∧ it takes to get them to us].//

解答

問1 (1) ①　(2) ④

問2 スーパーマーケットに到着するまでには，それら〔そのキーウィフルーツ〕は，それ自体の重量の５倍の重さの，大気中に排出される温室効果ガスに対して責任がある。

問3 ① ×　② ×　③ ○

Let's try We need to get the gas〔fuel〕it takes to go to Hiroshima from here.

解説

問 1(1)　なぜ筆者は現代のスーパーマーケットを不思議なものと表現するのか。

①「住む場所や季節にかかわらず食べ物が買える。」(*ll*. 1 ~ 6)

②「どんな天気であっても，あらゆる種類の食べ物が手に入る。」

③「アメリカ人は地元のスーパーマーケットであってもオレオクッキーを買える。」

④「ニュージーランド人は同じ棚にワインとキーウィフルーツを見つけられる。」

(2)　(1) the vast mileage は何の問題を引き起こすか。

①「ますます多くの人がどこに住んでいても熱帯の果物を欲しがる。」

②「飛行機で，あるいは道路を通って輸送しなければならない果物がある。」

③「温室で育てて長距離を輸送しなければならない野菜がある。」

④「果物や野菜を長距離にわたって輸送するのに大量の燃料を必要とする。」

(*ll*. 13 ~ 15)

問 2　By the time S V ...「S が…するまでには」／ be responsible for ～「～に対して責任がある」／being pumped ～は greenhouse gases を修飾している。

問 3　①「故郷が恋しいニュージーランド人はキーウィフルーツを蔓から摘み取ることで自分自身を励ます。」(*ll*. 5 ~ 7)

②「その食品が遠くから輸送されてくればくるほど，多くの農薬が含まれる。」

(記述なし)

③「たくさんの燃料を消費するので，さまざまな食物を輸送することによって，私たちは温室効果ガスを排出している。」(*l*. 11 ~ 13)

Let's try　「…するには～がかかる」it takes ～ to *do* ／「ガソリン」gas〔fuel〕／「～から…へ行く」go to ... from ～

概要を整理しよう

具体例　現代のスーパーマーケットの便利さ
→どんな季節にも，欲しい野菜や果物が手に入る
→世界のどこにいても，自分の欲しいものが手に入る

問題提起　便利さの裏に隠れている環境負荷
→食物が運ばれる過程で，膨大な温室効果ガスが排出されている
→私たちはますます食物輸送のための燃料に頼るようになってきている

62 スーパーの便利さと運搬燃料（2）［環境］

1 This dependence was illustrated very clearly / during the September 2000 fuel price protests / in Britain.// <Inspired by similar actions in France>, / a group of farmers and lorry drivers decided to blockade the Stanlow oil refinery / in Cheshire.// The protest quickly snowballed, / and petrol tankers were unable to leave refineries.// Panic buying saw more than 90 per cent of petrol stations run dry.// And with supplies unable to get through, / supermarket shelves quickly emptied.//

This dependence ＝燃料への依存 / Inspired 過去分詞の分詞構文 / a group of farmers and lorry drivers S / decided V / to blockade the Stanlow oil refinery O / were unable to ＝ could not / Panic buying S / saw V / more than 90 per cent of petrol stations O / run C（動詞の原形） / with 付帯状況の with / supermarket shelves S / emptied V

2 It's estimated [that food now accounts for as much as 40 per cent of all UK road freight], / and the international food trade is increasing faster / than the world's population and food production.// **In other words**, / food is moving around more than ever, / and the environmental impact could be huge.//

It 形式主語 / [that … freight] 真主語 / account for ～「～の割合を占める」 / In other words 言い換え

3 Despite the UK's cool climate being perfectly suited / for growing apples, / nearly three-quarters of the apples <eaten in the UK> are imported, / and more than 60 per cent of Britain's apple orchards have been destroyed / in the past 30 years.// We're now putting more energy into transporting some crops / than we get out of eating them.// For every calorie of lettuce <imported to the UK from America's west coast>, 127 calories of fuel are used.// **Put it another way**: flying over a kilogram of Californian lettuce uses enough energy <to keep a 100-watt light bulb glowing for eight days>.//

the UK's cool climate 動名詞の意味上の主語 / being 動名詞 / nearly three-quarters of the apples S_1 / eaten in the UK 過去分詞の修飾 / are imported V_1 / more than 60 per cent of Britain's apple orchards S_2 / have been destroyed V_2 / imported to the UK 過去分詞の修飾 / Put it another way ≒ in other words / flying over a kilogram of Californian lettuce S / uses V / enough energy O / to keep … 不定詞の副詞用法

解答

問 1　(1)　(ウ) → (ア) → (イ)　　(2)　③　　**問 2**　パニック買いにより，90 パーセントを超えるガソリンスタンドが干上がった。
問 3　①　○　　②　○　　③　×
Let's try　Inspired by the writer he respected, my elder brother decided to write a novel.

解説

問 1(1)　(ア)「パニック買いで，ほとんどのガソリンスタンドが在庫切れとなった。」
(イ)「スーパーマーケットの棚から消費財が消えた。」
(ウ)「燃料価格抗議のために石油精製所が燃料を供給できなくなった。」
(2)　①「今，食物はイギリスのすべての道路運送貨物のうちあまりにも大部分を占めている。」②「60 パーセントを超えるイギリスのリンゴ果樹園が過去 30 年間に破壊されている。」③「**食物の輸送は環境への大きな影響がある。**」(ℓℓ. 11 ～ 12) ④「私たちは農産物から摂取するのと同量のエネルギーをその輸送につぎ込んでいる。」

問 2　直訳は「パニック買いは～干上がるのを見た」だが，主語は「パニック買いにより～」と‘原因’を表す副詞のように訳せるとよい。／ run dry「干上がる」

問 3　①「人々がパニックになってガソリンを買ったので，抗議の間，90% を超えるガソリンスタンドが干上がった。」(ℓℓ. 5 ～ 6) ②「国際的な食物貿易は環境に大きな影響を与えそうである。」(ℓℓ. 9 ～ 12) ③「イギリスのリンゴ果樹園の大部分が破壊され，イギリスはリンゴ不足に苦しんでいる。」(ℓℓ. 13 ～ 16)

Let's try　「～に触発されて」inspired by ～ (ℓℓ. 2 ～ 4) 分詞構文を用いる。「…することにした」→「…することを決心した」decide to *do* を用いる。

概要を整理しよう

具体例	燃料価格に対する抗議行動で石油精製所が封鎖 →パニック買いでガソリンがなくなり，スーパーマーケットの棚が空に
現状 1	◆ **in other words「言い換えれば：言い換え」**(ℓ. 10) 輸送による環境への影響は巨大なはず。
現状 2	農産物を食べることで得られるエネルギー以上のエネルギーを輸送で消費

63 熱湯の方がより速く氷になる？（1）［科学］

1 One of the most popular ways <to demonstrate this year's severe US winter> / appeared <to be <tossing out a glass of boiling water> and <watching it freeze instantly in mid-air>>.// Of course, / the reason [∧the fun experiment impressed viewers] is / [because nobody expects boiling water <to turn to ice that quickly>].// It turns out [that / contrary to intuitive thinking, / it actually freezes faster than cold water]!// Why?// That's a mystery <still waiting <to be solved>>.//

（注：ways ← to demonstrate … 不定詞の形容詞用法／to be 不定詞の名詞用法／watch O do「O が…するのを注意して見る」／the reason：S ← 関係副詞（why）／the fun experiment：S'　impressed：V'　viewers：O'　is：V　C／nobody：S"　expects：V"　boiling water：O"／it turns out that ...「…であることがわかる」／contrary to ～「～に反して」／it = boiling water／a mystery ← still waiting 現在分詞の後置修飾）

2 While this phenomenon has been observed for thousands of years, / it was brought to the world's attention in 1963 by Tanzanian high school student, Erasto Mpemba.//

（注：this phenomenon =第 1 パラグラフ第 3 文の that 節の内容／thousands of ～「数千の～」／it = this phenomenon／Tanzanian high school student, Erasto Mpemba：同格）

3 It all began / when the young boy was learning to make ice cream in cooking class.// After dissolving the sugar in boiling milk, / the students were instructed to allow the mixture to cool down, / before putting it in the ice cream churner.// <∧Too impatient to wait>, / Mpemba put his mixture in / while it was still hot.// To his and everyone's surprise, / his ice cream was the first to freeze!// His explanation appeared so unbelievable that even his teacher thought [Mpemba must be mistaken].//

（注：the young boy = Erasto Mpemba／it = the mixture／（Being）分詞構文 '理由'／it = his mixture／be the first to *do*「最初に…する」／so ～ that ...「あまりに～なので…」）

解答

問 1　(1)　③　　(2)　④

問 2　その面白い実験が見る人に感銘を与えた理由は，熱湯がそんなにも速く氷に変わるだろうとは誰も思わないからである

問 3　①　○　　②　×　　③　○

Let's try　Tom was the first to come to the classroom and the last to leave.

解説

問1(1)　コップの水を空中に放つ結果についての直感的な考えは何か。

①「コップの水は空中に放つだけでは氷になれない。」②「冷水と熱湯は同時に氷になる。」③「冷水は熱湯よりも速く氷になる。」(*ll*. 4 ～ 5) ④「熱湯は冷水よりも速く氷になる。」

(2)　1963年にエラスト・ムペンバがしたことについて正しいのは次のうちどれか。

①「手順を間違えたので，彼は攪拌機に熱い混合物を入れた。」②「混合物に何が起きるのかを知りたかったので，彼は攪拌機に熱い混合物を入れた。」③「クラスメイトに言われて，彼は攪拌機に熱い混合物を入れた。」④「混合物が冷めるのを待てなかったので，彼は攪拌機に熱い混合物を入れた。」(*ll*. 14 ～ 15)

問2　the reason ... is because ～「…理由は～からだ」／ expect ～ to *do*「～が…すると思う」(*ll*. 3 ～ 4)／ that quickly の that は「そんなにも」の意味の副詞。

問3　①「コップの熱湯を空中に放つことで今年のアメリカの冬の厳しさを実証できる。」(*ll*. 1 ～ 3)

②「熱湯は冷水よりも速く氷になるかもしれないと予想した人もいた。」(*ll*. 4 ～ 5)

③「先生は，ムペンバの混合物が熱いままアイスクリーム攪拌機に入れられたとは信じることができなかった。」(*ll*. 17 ～ 18)

Let's try　「最初に…する」be the first to *do*
「教室に来る」come to the classroom

概要を整理しよう

主題　空中にコップの水を放つ時，冷水より熱湯の方が速く凍る
→数千年前から観察されていた現象だが，謎はまだ解けていない

経緯　エラスト・ムペンバによってこの現象が注目された
→熱いうちに混合物を入れたら，誰よりも速くアイスクリームが凍った

背景知識　ムペンバ効果の検証の難しさ

冷水よりも熱水を冷やした方が速く氷になるという現象を指すムペンバ効果は，再現性があまり高くない現象としても知られている。例えば，水に不純物がどれだけ混じっているかどうかで，水の氷点は変わってくる。また，どのような環境で凍結させるかも，水の凍結の仕方に大きな影響を及ぼす。さまざまな条件上の留保と調整が必要である。

64 熱湯の方がより速く氷になる？（2）［科学］

1 <Convinced [that he had discovered something]>, / Mpemba told a visiting physics professor about his accidental experiment.// Like his teacher, / the professor was a little doubtful, / but invited him <to test the theory>.//

分詞構文 '理由'　S　V　O　= Mpemba's　不定詞の副詞用法

2 The two began / by filling 100 mL beakers with 70 mL samples of water of varying temperatures / and placing them in the ice box of a normal refrigerator.// [What they noticed] / was [that it took longer for the water to freeze / when the temperature was at 25° C / than when it was at a much hotter 90° C].// **Since then**, / the phenomenon has been known as the Mpemba effect.// **However**, / while the two were able to demonstrate it, / neither ∧ could find a scientific explanation for [why it occurred].// Over the years, / researchers have come up with several theories.//

= Mpemba and the professor　fill A with B「A を B で満たす」　= 100mL beakers　S　= the two　V　C　it takes ～ for A to *do*「A が…するのに～かかる」　= the temperature　時間的順序　be known as ～「～として知られる」　逆接　= the Mpemba effect　(of the two)　= the Mpemba effect　come up with ～「～を思いつく」

3 The theory [that most believe] is fairly straightforward.// It is a known fact that hot water evaporates faster than cold.// **Hence**, / when boiling water is tossed into cold air, / some of it turns into steam and disappears, / <leaving behind less ∧ <to turn to ice!>> ∧Sounds plausible, right?// **In fact**, / Mpemba had thought of this possibility / and even tested it.// Unfortunately, / he found no difference in the volumes of the ice / <formed at different temperatures>.//

S　関係代名詞　V　C　形式主語　真主語　因果関係　(boiling water)　= boiling water　分詞構文 '付帯状況'　不定詞の形容詞用法　(It)　主張　= 2 つ前の文の内容　= this possibility　S　V　O　= Mpemba　過去分詞の後置修飾

解答

問 1　(1)　①　　(2)　②

問 2　彼らが気づいたのは，水は温度が 25℃の時の方が，はるかに高温の 90℃の時より凍るのに時間がかかるという点だった。

問 3　①　○　　②　×　　③　○

Let's try　It is a known fact that smoking is bad for your health.

解説

問 1 (1)　(1) something は何を意味するか。

①「物質が冷たい時より熱い時により速く凍る現象」(ll.7～9) ②「なぜ熱湯がそれほど速く氷になるのかの示し方」③「これまで誰も知らなかった現象」④「熱湯がそれほど速く氷になるある種の超自然現象」

(2)　ムペンバと教授が行った実験について正しいのは次のうちどれか。

①「彼らは 100ml のビーカーをさまざまな温度の水のサンプルで満たした。」②「温度が 90℃のビーカーの水は，より冷たいビーカーの水よりも速く氷になった。」(ll.7～9) ③「彼らは熱湯が冷水よりも速く蒸発する理論を実験に応用できると考えた。」④「最終的に教授は 1 人で実験結果の科学的説明を見つけることができた。」

問 2　文の主語は関係代名詞 what の節，補語に that 節が続く。

it takes ～ for A to *do*「A が…するのに～かかる」

問 3　①「初めは，ムペンバの先生も物理学の客員教授もムペンバが発見したと言ったことについて疑った。」(ll.2～3) ②「ムペンバと教授は彼らの実験結果を『ムペンバ効果』と名付けた。」(ll.9～10) ③「ムペンバは，熱湯は冷水よりも速く蒸発するという既知の事実は実験結果の科学的説明になり得ないことを発見した。」(ll.19～20)

Let's try　「…は既知の事実である」it is a known fact that ...

概要を整理しよう

導入	ムペンバは物理学の客員教授と実験することに
実験	90℃の水より 25℃の水の方が凍るのに時間がかかった
仮説	熱湯の方が速く蒸発することで水の量が減り，速く凍るのではないか
結果	ムペンバもこのことについて実験をしたが，生じる氷の量は変わらなかった

65 熱湯の方がより速く氷になる？(3) [科学]

1 A more recent scientific study / <conducted by Xi Zhang at the Nanyang Technological University in Singapore> / attributes the phenomenon to the chemistry / between the hydrogen and oxygen molecules [that make up water].// The researcher believes [that / as the temperature rises, / it provides the molecules with a lot of pent-up energy].// When this water is tossed into a cold environment, / the energy 'jumps' out <in a way> [∧similar to [how a highly compressed spring would∧, / when ∧ released]].// This results in the hot water cooling down much more rapidly than cold water, / [which does not contain as much energy∧].//

S / 過去分詞の後置修飾 / V / O　attribute A to B「AをBのせいにする」 / 関係代名詞　make up ～「～を構成する」　S = Xi Zhang　V　O / = the temperature　provide A with B「AにBを供給する」 / S　V　(which is)　S' / ('jump' out)　(it is)　=前文の内容　result in ～「～をもたらす」 / 関係代名詞の非制限用法 / (as hot water)

2 While all these theories are plausible / and explain the phenomenon under certain conditions, / none seems to provide a satisfactory universal solution to this strange physical property [that has confused scientists / since Aristotle observed it in 380 BCE].//

S'　V'1　C'1　V'2 / O'2　provide A to B「AをBに与える」 / 関係代名詞 / = this strange physical property

解答

問1　(1)　③　　(2)　①

問2　強く押しつけられたバネが解放されたと時に飛び出すのと同じように，そのエネルギーが「飛び」出す

問3　①　○　　②　○　　③　×

Let's try　The carelessness of the driver resulted in this accident.

解説

問 1(1)　シー・チャンの最近の科学的研究について正しいのは次のうちどれか。

①「シー・チャンは，温度が上がると分子は多量の抑圧されたエネルギーを失うと考えている。」

②「シー・チャンは，強く押しつけられたバネは飛び出す時エネルギーを放出することを発見した。」

③「シー・チャンは水を構成する水素と酸素の化学反応によってこの現象を説明しようとした。」(ll. 1 ～ 4)

④「特定の条件下では結果が安定しないため，シー・チャンは彼の研究がこの現象を完全に説明しているか疑わしいと思っている。」

(2)　この現象について現在の私たちの理解を説明しているのは次のうちどれか。

①「あらゆる条件下で正しい，この現象に対するもっともらしい説明はいまだにない。」(ll. 12 ～ 14)

②「シー・チャンの説明は，寒い環境で熱湯のみを使った時特に，正しい。」

③「シー・チャンは，この現象の説明で多くの理論を参考にした。」

④「シー・チャンのこの現象の説明は紀元前 380 年のアリストテレスの説明と似ている。」

問 2　in a way (which is) similar to ～「～と似た方法で」と考える。そのあとに how が導く名詞節が続く。would のあとには jump out が省略されている。

問 3　①「シー・チャンは現象を説明するために南洋理工大学で科学的研究を行った。」(ll. 1 ～ 4)

②「冷水は熱湯ほどのエネルギーを放出できない。」(ll. 8 ～ 10)

③「アリストテレスは紀元前 380 年にこの奇妙な現象を説明しようとした。」

(ll. 11 ～ 14)

Let's try　「～の結果として…が起きる」～ result in ... ／「運転者の不注意」the carelessness of the driver を主語にして result in ～や cause を用いる。

概要を整理しよう

仮説　シー・チャンは水素と酸素の化学反応が現象の原因であると考えた
→温度が上がると，分子に多量の抑圧されたエネルギーが供給される
→それが寒い環境で放出されるので，熱湯が速く冷める原因となる

結論　どんな条件下でも説明できる理論はいまだにない

66 読書の重要性（1）［文化］

1 **Even with** the hard work and caring of many dedicated teachers and concerned parents, / the U.S. continues to have a reading problem.// According to the National Center for Educational Information, / 38 percent of fourth grade students cannot read and understand a short paragraph of the type <found in a simple children's book>.// Results from a 1998 study showed [that 60 percent of U.S. teenagers could comprehend specific facts, / **but** fewer than 5 percent ∧ could elaborate / on the meanings of the material <read>].//

2 No wonder many parents are discouraged, / **but** they needn't be∧.// By doing simple things / **like** reading to their child, / sharing their thinking about [what they read], / and telling their child stories, / they can help <∧develop the foundation <needed for children / <to become good readers and learn [that reading is not a chore but a lifetime adventure]>>>.//

解答

問 1 (1) ② (2) ③

問 2 子供が読むことが得意になるために必要な基礎を発達させる手助けをすることが，親にはできる

問 3 ① ○ ② ○ ③ ×

Let's try No wonder Japanese people have the highest life expectancy (in the world). ／ No wonder the Japanese have the longest average life-span (in the world).

解説

問 1 (1)　アメリカの読むことに関する問題について正しいものは次のうちどれか。

①「教師が彼らに対して無関心なので，子供は読むことに苦労している。」

②「簡単な子供向けの本の短い段落を理解できない学童がいる。」(ll. 3 ~ 5)

③「アメリカのティーンエイジャーのうち 60 パーセントしか読んだ資料の意味を詳しく理解できない。」

④「多くの 4 年生の生徒は特定の事実と資料の意味との区別ができない。」

(2)　どのように親は子供を読むことが得意にする手助けができるか。

①「読むことを子供の日課にすることによって。」

②「難しい本を子供に読み聞かせることによって。」

③「読んだことについて子供と話すことによって。」(ll. 10 ~ 11)

④「読むことが得意になるように子供を促すことによって。」

問 2　they は ℓ. 9 の主語 many parents を指す。／ help + (to) *do*「…する助けになる」(ℓ. 12) ／ needed for children ～は the foundation を修飾している。

問 3　①「アメリカは読むことに関する問題を抱えていたし，今も抱えている。」(ll. 1 ~ 2)

②「研究結果は，多くのアメリカのティーンエイジャーは読んだ資料の正確な意味を説明できないことを示した。」(ll. 5 ~ 8)

③「読む技術を子供が発達させる手助けをするために親ができることは何もない。」(ll. 11 ~ 13)

Let's try　「…は当然だ」no wonder ... ／「寿命」life-span〔life expectancy〕life-span であれば long，life expectancy であれば high を形容詞として用いる。

概要を整理しよう

問題提起	アメリカでは依然，子供の読解力に問題がある
裏づけ	1. 国立教育情報センター：4 年生の 38%が，子供向けの本にあるような短い段落を理解できない 2. 1998 年の研究：ティーンエイジャーのうち，読んだ資料の意味を詳述できたのは 5%未満
解決策	親の手助けによって，子供は読むことが得意になる →読書が一生の冒険であると学ぶために必要な基礎が身に付く

67 読書の重要性（2）[文化]

1 Good readers follow a number of key strategies, / whether they're reading a magazine or a textbook.// **Firstly**, / they create a wide range of mental and visual images / as they read, / <to feel involved with [what they are reading]>.// **Then**, / they use their background and relevant prior knowledge / before, during and after reading / <to enhance their understanding of [what they are reading]>.// They **also** make and ask questions / before, during, and after reading / <to clarify meaning, / ∧ make predictions, / and ∧ focus their attention on [what's important]>.//

2 Good readers infer and determine the most important ideas or themes, / and distinguish between these and unimportant information.// **Next**, / they track their thinking / while reading, / <to get the overall meaning>.// **Finally**, / if they have trouble understanding specific words, / phrases, / or longer passages, / they use a wide range of problem-solving strategies **including** skipping ahead, / re-reading, / asking questions, / using a dictionary, and reading the passage aloud to "fix-up" their understanding.//

3 Reading is fundamental to success in life.// It's that simple.// Reading opens the door to virtually all other learning.// You have to be able to read <to learn mathematics, science, history, engineering, mechanics, political science>, / **not to mention** / <to surf the web / or figure out <how to operate that new DVD player>>.// Basically, / you have to be able to read <to succeed>.//

解答

問1　(1)　(イ) → (ア) → (ウ)　　(2)　②

問2　もし優れた読者が特定の言葉，句，あるいはより長い文章を理解するのが困難である場合，幅広い問題解決の戦略を利用する

問3　①　×　　②　○　　③　○

Let's try　You should follow the coach's advice whether you like it or not.

解説

問1(1)　(ア)「彼らは最も重要な考えあるいは主題を特定し，全体の意味を把握しようとする。」(イ)「彼らは観念的かつ視覚的なさまざまなイメージを作り上げて，知識を利用して，質問をする。」(ウ)「彼らが何かを理解するのが困難な時，問題解決の戦略を利用する。」(ℓℓ. 2 ～ 14)

(2)　本文の主な結論は次のうちどれか。

①「読むことは非常に単純で根本的な技術だ。」②「読むことは人生で成功するためにできるようにならなければならないことだ。」(ℓ. 17) ③「読むことなしには何も操作できないから，読むことは重要だ。」④「読むことはウェブを見て回るのに不可欠な技術だ。」

問2　have trouble (in) *doing*「…するのが困難である」(ℓ. 12) ／
a wide range of ～「幅広い～」

問3　①「優れた読者は雑誌を読んでいる時理解するために何の戦略も利用しない。」(ℓℓ. 1 ～ 2) ②「優れた読者は最も重要な考えあるいは主題と重要ではない情報とを区別できる。」(ℓℓ. 9 ～ 10) ③「さまざまなことを学ぶために読めなければならない。」(ℓℓ. 18 ～ 21)

Let's try　「A であれ B であれ」whether A or B
「アドバイスを聞く」は単に listen to ～を用いてもよい。

概要を整理しよう

主題	優れた読者は，読むものに関わらず，いくつもの重要な戦略に従う
列挙	優れた読者の読み方
結論	読書は人生の成功の基盤となるものだ

68 AIについて（1）［科学］

1 How would you feel / if a robot looked after your child?// ∧ Worried?//
仮定法過去　look after ～「～の世話をする」　(Would you feel)
∧ Anxious?// What if that robot was as intelligent as yourself, / if ∧ not
(Would you feel)　What if ...?「…だとしたらどうだろう。」　(that robot was)
more so, / and was able to react to every problem and whim / without
= intelligent than yourself　without *doing*「…することなく」
ever tiring or wanting to scream?// For those [∧ studying and working
(who are)
in artificial intelligence (AI)], / <creating this kind of situation> could so
S
easily become a reality.//
V　C

2 "AI is embedded in many educational applications," / explains Janet
V　S
Read, a professor in child computer interaction at the University
同格
of Central Lancashire, / <pointing to new gesture recognition and
分詞構文 '付帯状況'
interpretation technologies>.// "Brain computer interfaces are
S_1
detecting mood and emotion / and in the near future / robotic
V_1　O_1
and virtual systems might be able to partially take on the care of
S_2　V_2　C_2　take on ～「～を引き受ける」
children."//

解答

問１　(1) ④　(2) ④

問２　もしそのボットが，あなたに勝るほどではないにしても，あなたと同じくらい知能があるとしら，そしてあらゆる問題や気まぐれに対応できるとしたらどうだろう

問３　① ○　② ×　③ ×

Let's try　For those (who are) learning English, AI may〔might〕be useful for practicing speaking.

解説

問1 (1)　近い将来ロボットがすると期待されることについて正しくないのは次のうちどれか。

①「ロボットは何の不満もなく多くの問題に対処できるだろう。」

②「ロボットは子供の世話ができるだろう。」

③「ロボットは人間と同じくらい知能が高くなるだろう。」

④「ロボットは人間の気まぐれに叫びすらするだろう。」(ℓℓ.3～4)

(2)　現在の脳とコンピューターをつなぐシステムについて正しくないのは次のうちどれか。

①「その時私たちがどのように感じているか検知できる。」(ℓℓ.10～11)

②「多くの教育アプリに埋め込まれている。」(ℓ.7)

③「私たちのさまざまなジェスチャーを認識して解釈できる。」(ℓℓ.9～10)

④「ロボットがちょうど親のように子供たちの世話をするようにできる。」

※ AIが子供の世話を引き受けるのは「部分的」とある。

問2　What if ...?「…だとしたらどうだろう。」(ℓ.2) ／ if not more soは，略さず書くとif that robot was not more intelligent than yourselfとなる。

問3　①「ロボットが子供の世話をするとしたら，あなたは不安に感じるかもしれない。」(ℓ.1)

②「AIについて研究し，取り組んでいる人たちは，人間の代わりに多くの問題に対処できるロボットを作るのには長い時間がかかるだろうと予想している。」(ℓℓ.4～6)

③「子供の世話を担うロボットを作ることは現在ジャネット・リードが目指している目標である。」(記述なし)

Let's try　「…する人たちにとって」for those (who are) *doing*
「～に役立つ」be useful for ～　help O *do*を使った組み立ても可。

概要を整理しよう

主題　あらゆる問題に対応できるロボットを生み出すことは簡単に現実になる

具体例　ジャネット・リード教授の説明

ジェスチャーの認識・気分や感情の検知ができる技術

→近い将来仮想ロボットシステムは子供の世話を部分的に担えるかもしれない

69 AIについて (2) [科学]

1 AI is one of the most exciting fields of technological study, / <giving computers the ability <to 'think', 'learn' and adapt> / when faced with a host of data>.// **But** it is not a technology of the future.// It is all around us today, / <pervading our everyday lives and / allowing us to take advantage of image and voice recognition software, intelligent web searching and medical advances, / <the latter made possible / thanks to robot scientists <formulating hypotheses and interpreting data>>>.// Modern video games use AI / <to generate intelligent behaviour in non-player characters>.// NASA's Mars Rover was designed to make its own decisions, <stopping / and analysing only the rocks [(it felt) would be useful]>.// **And** more is to come, / with driverless cars and intelligent home systems on their way.//

2 **As a result**, / many universities have been promoting AI courses and modules / for both undergraduate and postgraduate students. // Each of them requires a solid background in computing, maths and physics / and explores knowledge representation, planning and learning.// "Studying AI is perfect for students [who can solve problems in abstract ways and devise new angles]," / says Dr Richard Watson, senior lecturer in electronics and computer science at the University of Southampton.// "**But** AI is **also** about learning techniques of advanced computer science, / **so** students should have a broad education in computer science / before they tackle it."// **For that reason**, / very few undergraduate degrees will concentrate entirely on AI.// **Instead**, / it tends to be offered as modules within an overall computer science degree.//

解答

問1　(1)　②　　(2)　④　　問2　①　×　　②　○　　③　×

Let's try　The Internet is all around us today, giving 〔offering〕 us both useful information and false information.

解説

問1(1)　AIについて正しいのは次のうちどれか。

①「AIは将来，考え，学び，順応する能力をコンピューターに与えるために使われるだろう。」

②「AIは今日，画像音声認識ソフトを私たちに利用させてくれる。」(ll.4～5)

③「AIはロボット科学者が仮説を形成しデータを解釈することを可能にした。」

④「現代のテレビゲームはすべてのキャラクターについて知能を持った行動を生み出すためにAIを利用する。」

(2)　多くの大学はどのようにAIの課程や履修単位を推進しているのか。

①「大学生にまずコンピューター操作のしっかりした背景を習得することを要求することによって。」②「問題を抽象的な方法で解決でき，新しい観点を考案できる学生を招くことによって。」③「発展的なコンピューターサイエンスの技術を学生に教えることによって。」④「AIの履修単位を含む，全般的なコンピューターサイエンスの学位を与えることによって。」(ll.24～25)

問2　①「ロボット科学者のおかげで高度なウェブ検索と医学の進歩がともに可能になった。」(ll.4～6) ②「NASAのマーズ・ローバーは自分で判断ができ，有用な岩のみを分析できた。」(ll.9～11) ③「多くの大学で，多くの学士の学位が完全にAIに集中している。」(ll.23～24)

Let's try　「～の周りの至るところにある」be all around ～／本文を参考に分詞構文で続けるか，単純にandでつないでand it gives us ～としても可。

概要を整理しよう

導入　AIの発展・浸透

展開　多くの大学がAIの課程や履修単位を推進

→全般的なコンピューター科学の学位の中の履修単位として与えられている

70 ヒトの自然治癒力［医療］

1 Neglect of the mind-body link by technological medicine is actually a brief aberration / when ∧ viewed against the whole history of the healing art.// In traditional tribal medicine / and in Western practice from its beginning in the work of Hippocrates, / the need <to operate through the patient's mind> has always been recognized.// Until the nineteenth century, / medical writers rarely failed to note the influence of grief, despair, or discouragement on the onset and outcome of illness, / nor did they ignore the healing effects of faith, confidence, and peace of mind.// Contentment used to be considered a prerequisite for health.//

2 The modern medicine man has gained so much power over certain diseases through drugs, / **however**, / [that he has forgotten about the potential strength within the patient].// One elderly physician friend recently told me / of reading the diary of his uncle, also a doctor.// In the early years, / the diarist always recorded [what happened to the individual or the community / prior to an illness or epidemic], / **but** / as medicine became more technological, / this part of the history grew less and less important to him / and finally was omitted altogether.// Awareness of the mind's powers was lost / as medicine cast out all "soft" data, / the information [that's not easily quantified or scientific].//

解答

問 1　(1) ①　　(2) ④
問 2　心の安らぎは，健康の必要条件であるとかつては考えられていた。
問 3　① ○　　② ×　　③ ×
Let's try　The conclusion is the most important thing〔part〕, but I failed to hear it.

解説

問 1 (1)　(1) medical writers rarely failed to note の意味に最も近いのは次のうちどれか。
① 「医学に関して記した人たちはほとんどいつも書いた」(ℓℓ. 6 ～ 9)
② 「医学に関して記した人たちはめったに書かなかった」③「医学に関して記した人たちは書き留めるのに失敗した」④「医学に関して記した人たちは決して書き留めなかった」
(2)　医学に携わる現代の人間について正しいのは次のうちどれか。
①「患者の心を通じて処置をする必要性を認識している。」②「患者の中にある潜在的な力に気づいている。」③「科学的でなくともすべての情報を考慮しようとする。」④「心身の関連性を軽視する傾向があり，科学技術的な医学だけに頼っている。」(ℓ. 1, ℓℓ. 16 ～ 18)

問 2　used to *do*「かつては…したものだ」(ℓ. 9)

問 3　①「昔は，人々は治療の過程での患者の心の重要性を認識していた。」(ℓℓ. 3 ～ 5)
②「19 世紀まで，医学に関して記した人たちは肯定的な感情の効果を無視した。」(ℓℓ. 5 ～ 9) ③「現代の医学は容易に数量化できない情報を利用する。」(ℓℓ. 19 ～ 20)

Let's try　「…しそびれる」fail to *do* ／ I missed that. などの表現も自然。

概要を整理しよう

主題　現代医学では心身の関連性が軽視されている
⇔かつては，感情が病気に与える影響，治療効果を考慮した

問題提起　◆ **however「しかし：逆接」**(ℓ. 12)
現代の医師は，患者の中にある潜在的な力を忘れている。

具体例　(かつて) 病気の発生前に個人や社会に起こったことを記録
(現在) 数量化できない情報や非科学的な情報が失われた

英文出典

1～10 センター試験
11～14 獨協大学　外国語，経済，国際教養，法
15 センター試験
16 京都女子大学　文，発達教育，家政，現代社会，法
From THINK YOU KNOW ALL ABOUT THE COMMON COLD? THINK AGAIN (April 17, 2011 Voice of America) (posted on http://www.voanews.com/content/think-you-know-all-about-the-common-cold--think-again-120059924/138207.html) by Ayesha Khalid. Copyright©2011 by Voice of America. Used by permission of Voice of America.
17～20 獨協大学　外国語，経済，国際教養，法
21 22 センター試験
23 24 明海大学　ホスピタリティ・ツーリズム，外国語，経済，不動産　改
25 26 大阪大学　医，基礎工，経済，法，理
27 28 センター試験
29 30 東海大学　海洋，開発工，教養，健康科学，情報理工，政治経済，法
31～33 南山大学　外国語
From BOTTOM LINE DROVE DISNEY ANIMATORS TO SWAP PENCILS FOR COMPUTERS (September 19, 2005 The New York Times) (posted on https://www.nytimes.com/2005/09/19/technology/bottom-line-drove-disney-animators-to-swappencils-for-computers.html) by Laura M. Holson. Copyright©2005 by Laura M.Holson. Used by permission of The New York Times Company.
34 センター試験
35 36 東洋大学　経営１部，国際地域，法１部，文１部
From TEACHERS EDITION: SPEECH COMMUNICATION MATTERS 2ND REVISED by Randall McCutheon, James Schaffer, Joseph R. Wycoff. Copyright©2001 by Randall McCutheon, James Schaffer, Joseph R. Wycoff. Used by permission of McGraw-Hill LLC.
37 38 神奈川大学
From PRACTICAL HOMESCHOOLING #27 WHY THE INTERNET WILL NEVER REPLACE BOOKS (Practical Homeschooling #27, 1999) (posted on http://www.home-school.com/Articles/why-the-internet-will-never-replace-books.php) by Sam Blumenfeld. Copyright© by Sam Blumenfeld. Used by permission of Home Life, Inc.
39 40 センター試験
41 42 法政大学　人間環境
From AGGRESSION AND VIOLENT MEDIA (THE FUTURIST, July 2004 Vol.38, No.4) (posted on https://www.wfs.org/trend3ja04.htm) by Cynthia G Wager. Copyright©2004 by the World Future Society. Originally published in THE FUTURIST.
43 44 明海大学　ホスピタリティ・ツーリズム，外国語，経済，不動産　改
45 センター試験
46 47 関西学院大学　文，法，商，人間福祉，国際，教育，総合政策，理工

From WILL HUMANS GO THE WAY OF HORSES? Labor in the Second Machine Age (Foreign Affairs, July/August 2015 Issue)(posted on https://www.foreignaffairs.com/articles/2015-06-16/will-humans-go-way-horses) by Erik Brynjolfsson and Andrew McAfee. ©2015 Council on Foreign Relations, publisher of Foreign Affairs. All rights reserved. Distributed by Tribune Content Agency.

48～**50** 関西大学　文，経済，社会，政策創造，総合情報
"If Fifty Million People Say Something Foolish, It Is Still Foolish" from THE ART OF THINKING CLEARLY by ROLF DOBELLI. Copyright©2013 by Rolf Dobelli. Translation copyright©2013 by Nicky Griffin. Used by permission of HarperCollins Publishers.

51 **52** Z会オリジナル

53 **54** センター試験

55 **56** 東北福祉大学　総合福祉，総合マネジメント，教育，健康科
From SWEET POTATOES AS MEDICINE (June 30, 2015 Voice of America) (posted on https://learningenglish.voanews.com/a/sweaet-potatoes-as-medicine/2841957.html) by Anna Matteo and Steve Baragona. Copyright©2015 by Voice of America. Used by permission of Voice of America.

57 **58** 早稲田大学　商
From TOASTED PITA, MAGNUM ICE-CREAM, PRETZELS & SECRET OF DIETING (posted on https://www.theaustralian.com.au/life/health-wellbeing/toasted-pitamagnum-icecream-pretzels-and-the-secret-of-dieting/news-story/4d67831c527375d43111c1bc7a7956d3) by Oliver Moody. Copyright©2016 by Oliver Moody. Used by permission of News UK & Ireland Ltd.

59 **60** 学習院大学　経済
From MEANWHILE: THE FRENCH KNOW HOW TO MAKE A MEAL OF IT (The New York Times, March 6, 2004) (posted on https://www.nytimes.com/2004/03/06/opinion/meanwhile-the-french-know-how-to-make-a-meal-of-it.html) by Marianne Jacobbi. Copyright©2004 by The New York Times Company.

61 **62** 明治薬科大学　薬
50 FACTS THAT SHOULD CHANGE THE WORLD by Jessica Williams. Copyright©2007 by Jessica Williams. Permission from Icon Books Ltd. arranged through The English Agency(Japan) Ltd.

63～**65** 福島県立医科大学　医
From THE UNEXPLAINED MYSTERY OF WHY HOT WATER FREEZES FASTER THAN COLD (posted on https://www.dogonews.com/2014/5/18/theunexplained-mystery-of-why-hot-water-freezes-faster-than-cold) by Meera Dolasia. Copyright© by DOGOnews Com

66 **67** 京都産業大学　法，経済
Excerpts from 7 KEYS TO COMPREHENSION: HOW TO HELP YOUR KIDS READ IT AND GET IT! by Susan Zimmermann and Chryse Hutchins, copyright ©2002 by Susan Zimmermann and Chryse Hutchins. Used by permission of Three Rivers Press, an imprint of Random House, a division of Penguin Random House LLC. All rights reserved.

68 **69** 三重大学　人文，教育，医
From CAREERS IN TECH: ARTIFICIAL INTELLIGENCE (The Independent, 18 November 2014) (posted on https://www.independent.co.uk/student/career-planning/careers-in-tech-artificial-

70 兵庫医科大学　医

Z-KAI